Writing the Motherline

Mothers, Daughters, and Education

Edited by
Leigh M. O'Brien and
Beth Blue Swadener

D0874770

UNIVERSITY PRESS OF AMERICA,® INC.
Lanham • Boulder • New York • Toronto • Oxford

Copyright © 2006 by
University Press of America,® Inc.
4501 Forbes Boulevard
Suite 200
Lanham, Maryland 20706
UPA Acquisitions Department (301) 459-3366

PO Box 317
Oxford
OX2 9RU, UK

All rights reserved
Printed in the United States of America
British Library Cataloging in Publication Information Available

Library of Congress Control Number: 2006924497
ISBN-13: 978-0-7618-3506-6 (clothbound : alk. paper)
ISBN-10: 0-7618-3506-7 (clothbound : alk. paper)
ISBN-13: 978-0-7618-3507-3 (paperback : alk. paper)
ISBN-10: 0-7618-3507-5 (paperback : alk. paper)

$\circledcirc^{TM}$ The paper used in this publication meets the minimum
requirements of American National Standard for Information
Sciences—Permanence of Paper for Printed Library
Materials, ANSI/NISO Z39.48-1992.

DEDICATION

This book is dedicated to our mothers, Nancy Anderson O'Brien and Maxine Hudlow Blue, and our daughters, Lydia O'Brien-Lynn and Rachel Blue Swadener, of course. We would not be who we are without them.

Contents

Preface

As we have worked with others on this book over the past several years, we have frequently been reminded that making meaning is not a straightforward process; any reading of a text is partial and dependent on the interpretation of the reader. We have found George Marcus's notion of "messy texts" to be useful as we engaged with issues of positionality and questions of how to complete a text. Marcus writes, "In messy texts, there is a sense of whole, without an evocation of totality, that emerges from the research itself . . . Messy texts are messy because they insist on their own open-endedness, incompleteness, and uncertainty about how to draw a text/analysis to a close" (1998, pp. 188–189). We hope there will be a sense of wholeness to our text, but resist the assumption that we must come to closed, complete, and certain conclusions.

This stance is especially important for us as this text foregrounds personal narratives and tries to avoid meta-narratives or "master scripts." Settled, transcendent meanings (that is, meta-narratives), have not historically served women well. In fact, they have often sought our erasure, enforced our silence, endangered us, and sometimes killed us. Because of this, what bell hooks calls "feminist movement" has been about, first and foremost, meaning making. "[W]e have had to make our meanings, relying on ourselves and each other, intellect and intuition, experience and theory, inheritance and imagination" (Griffin, 2000, p. 104). Nothing is more radical than meaning making; ultimately it is what we are about here as we write our messy text of mothers, daughters, and education.

The tapestry represented in this volume has been under construction for a number of years as we tell of our intersecting personal and professional lives as women educators—and of the implications of the intersections for our work and life projects, foregrounding ways in which they relate to our various positionings on the "Motherline." We are fortunate in that emerging feminist theory informs and strengthens the mother-daughter bond as mothers, daughters, and granddaughters together continue to nourish a vision of education informed by personal experience and social justice perspectives. For, we believe, "therein lies the healing of ourselves, each other, and the world" (Baker, 2000, p. 210).

REFERENCES

Baker, C. (2000). Telling our stories: Feminist mothers and daughters. In A. O'Reilly & S. Abbey (Eds.), *Mothers and daughters: Connection, empowerment, and transformation* (pp. 203–212). Lanham, MD: Rowman & Littlefield.

Griffin, G. B. (2000). Unsettled weather. In P. R. Freeman & J. Z. Schmidt (Eds.), *Wise women: Reflections of teachers at midlife* (pp. 95–106). New York: Routledge.

Marcus, G. E. (1998). *Ethnography through thick and thin*. Princeton, NJ: Princeton University Press.

Leigh M. O'Brien
Montclair, NJ
February, 2006

Beth Blue Swadener
Tempe, AZ
February, 2006

Acknowledgments

We first want to acknowledge the publisher, *University Press of America*, and our helpful editor, Michael Marino. We also thank our many chapter authors for their contributions, and commend their patience as this book was coming together over several years. Daniel Swadener prepared the photographs for publication and that work is much appreciated.

Next, we must acknowledge our intellectual debt to our foremothers and forefathers who have written about women and education, and all the infinite complexities of the intersections between them. For this book, Andrea O'Reilly and Sharon Abbey, authors of *Mothers and daughters: Connection, empowerment, and transformation*, deserve special acknowledgment.

Among others who have influenced her, Leigh acknowledges Nel Noddings for her argument that caring must be the top priority of schools; Beth Swadener and Sally Lubeck for their notion of children of promise; Deborah Reed-Danahay for putting a name to auto-ethnography; Becky New and Bruce Mallory for their theoretical work on the inclusion of young children; and always, Maxine Greene for her insistence that we have and work toward a vision of the possible.

Beth acknowledges Mimi Bloch, Lourdes Diaz Soto, Mary Smith Arnold, Valerie Polakow, and Mara Sapon-Shevin, all of whom have been mentors and sister-friends, and who have greatly influenced her work and ways of being a scholar, ally, feminist, mother, and activist. She also acknowledges the influence of bell hooks' scholarship on feminism and a range of contemporary issues.

Last, but never least, we want to acknowledge our families for their encouragement, support, and understanding. Leigh gives special thanks to her daughter, Lydia, who makes her professional life worthwhile and her personal life a joy. Beth acknowledges the influence of her late father, Merle Blue, her life partner Daniel, and her daughter, Blue, who gave birth to Liam Merle Russ as we completed this book.

PERMISSIONS

The stories included in Chapter Two appeared in Novinger, S. & Compton-Lilly, C. (2005). Telling our stories: Speaking truth to power. *Language Arts*, *82* (3), 195–203. Copyright 2005 by the National Council of Teachers of English. Reprinted with permission.

Introduction:
Women Educators in the Red Tent

Leigh M. O'Brien & Beth Blue Swadener

> Motherline stories evoke a worldview in which all beings and times are in-
> terconnected, and in which the feminine mysteries are honored. They are
> as common as the repetitive loops made in weaving, crocheting, and knit-
> ting. They are as powerful as the memory of touching a grandmother's
> face or seeing a daughter suckle her newborn child.

—Lowinsky, 2000, p. 234

MATERNAL NARRATIVE AND THE MOTHERLINE

In this volume, written by women educators with or about daughters (and
granddaughters), we utilize the critical, often explicitly feminist, narrative
and the politicized personal, framing the project in the idea that it is through
the telling of stories that we make sense of our worlds. According to Jean
Clandinin and Michael Connelly (1996), stories are the closest we can come
to experience. We can make sense of what we do "both as living our stories
in an ongoing experiential text and as telling our stories in word as we reflect
on life and explain ourselves to others" (Clandinin, 1993, p. 1). We are "constantly telling and retelling stories . . . that both refigure the past and create
purpose in the future" (Connelly & Clandinin, 1990, p. 4). The act of story-
ing seems "inextricably linked with the act of making meaning, an inevitable
part of life in a . . . postmodern world" and only becomes problematic ". . .
when its influence on thinking and perception goes unnoticed" or is ignored
(Goldstein, 1997, p. 147).

Jonathan Kozol writes that when trying to understand an individual's ideas,
we must first listen to the voice, the ways in which ideas are expressed. For

him, voice reveals "some sense of character and value—lived experience—within the person who is telling us what he or she believes" (cited in Campbell, 2001, p. 770). Similarly, Maxine Greene contends that storytelling is a mode of understanding, of knowing. Ayers and Ford (1996) go even farther, contending that self-identity and meaning making are *causal* for humans—more important in shaping action and behavior than any conceivable cause and effect research design.

Thus, through the telling and reading of our own and other women educators' stories, we may discover our selves, gain self-knowledge, and be empowered. In this book, women educators are figuratively gathering in "the red tent" (Diamant, 1997) to share our stories of the inseparability of what we do as mothers of daughters (and grandmothers of granddaughters) from our work as educators and social activists. While we do not want to essentialize, idealize, or romanticize the mother-daughter relationship, we do believe there are unique aspects of mothering a daughter that occur in no other relationship.

Much has been written in recent years about the social and cultural construction of modernist notions of "motherhood" and the nuclear family, including notions of "the good mother" and often punitive models of governing mothers through public policy (e.g., Bloch & Popkewitz, 2000; Burman, 1994; Cannella, 1997; Cannella & Viruru, 2004; Hultqvist & Dahlberg, 2001; Polakow, 1993, 2000). To quote Gaile Cannella,

> We 'talk' as if the nuclear, heterosexual family has always existed and that we have evidence as to its superiority; that the best place for children to thrive is in the arms of mother within this idealized family unit. Yet critical examination reveals that ideas of motherhood and family have varied in different historical periods, from generation to generation, in different cultural contexts, and have tended to be controlled by those in power. (1997, p. 78)

We share with Cannella and others concerns about constructions of motherhood based on normalizing discourses that assume "natural" biological imperatives of motherhood, or dominant culture discourses that exclude or implicitly critique diverse household organizations, nontraditional families, gay and lesbian families, and intercultural families. Contributing authors to this text resist such over-determined signs or restrictive definitions of motherhood and family and have, in varying ways, problematized these assumptions, in some cases *with* their daughters, as part of interrogating patriarchy, power relations, and the dynamics of oppression. Authors draw from diverse parenting or family contexts and cultures. It is our intention as editors and feminists, to heed Audre Lorde's warning about using the "master's tools to dismantle the master's house," as we attempt to erode paternalistic power relations in higher education and other contexts. It is also our intention to be evocative rather than didactic, to continue a conversation rather than to discover "truth."

CRITICAL NARRATIVE AND AUTO/ETHNOGRAPHY

We acknowledge the trend toward self-reflexivity in many realms of writing and invited contributing authors to view their task in the context of critical auto/ethnography (Mutua & Swadener, 2004; Reed-Danahay, 1997). By using auto/ethnography and critical narrative, we are self-consciously examining our own lives and practices, not those of a colonized "Other." Our deliberate use of very personal—in fact, embodied—approaches still not widely accepted in the academy is intended to foreground "women's ways of knowing" (Belenky, Clinchy, Goldberger, & Tarule, 1986) and thereby push for changes not only in terms of whose voices are heard, but how these voices are heard. This term combines work within one's own identity or affinity group(s) and autobiographical writing that has ethnographic interest. We join with Deborah Reed-Danahay (1997) and Pat Burdell and Beth Blue Swadener (1999) in finding this a useful construct for questioning the often binary conventions of a self/ßsociety or, in this case, a maternal-personal/professional dichotomy. We subscribe to the belief that a critical appraisal of action is best taken from within it, and expect that as we describe and reflect on our own situations, people from other contexts will be able to understand and reflect on theirs.

Women have relatively recently begun the writing of their stories; although women have had a long history of oral tradition—telling the family stories, of child birth, marriage, death, and so forth—these stories have rarely been made permanent. Writing our stories allows them to become a part of the permanent record of women's lives, gives them a sense of longevity and worth that an oral rendition may not have. Whereas oral tradition has been the hallmark of many indigenous/colonized cultures, "hard copy" is powerful; it's observable; it's concrete. Perhaps we are now writing our stories because we finally feel strong enough to make them visible. Or, perhaps we are writing because this rather Eurocentric convention is still a requirement in the academy, where many of us have made our careers.

Although women's stories are all around us, often we don't hear them, for our perceptions are shaped by a culture that trivializes "women's talk" and devalues women's experiences and ideas. Tillie Olsen contends, "Most of what has been, or is, between mothers, daughters, and in motherhood, in daughterhood, has never been recorded, nor written with comprehension in our own voices, out of our lives and truths" (cited in Baker, 2000, p. 203; see also Lowinsky, 2000). With this text we attempt to address this lack of voice by writing with passion and power, in multiple voices, of our lives and truths as grand/mother-educators and grand/daughters.

FEMINISMS AND THE MOTHERLINE

For us, a feminist perspective is important because "[b]y fusing women's emotional and concrete lives through feminist critique, it is possible to make problematic the conditions under which women learn, and perhaps to make a feminist political agenda viable in women's own lives wherein they can transcend the split between personal experience and social form" (Lewis, 1990, p. 485). Most feminists assume the oppression of women and have as one of their major goals the correction of both the invisibility of women and the distortion of women's experiences that lead to ending women's subordinate social position. There are multiple feminist perspectives (i.e., many feminisms) and many ways to be a feminist. However, several essentials are at the core of feminist thinking.

> Feminist theory is based on the observation that women have been oppressed and devalued by the patriarchal bias in our society. Feminists believe that women must be empowered, and advocate the acknowledgment, affirmation, and celebration of women, women's experiences, and women's perspectives. Women have traditionally been marginalized in our culture, but feminists place women and women's ways of knowing at the center of their worldview. Finally, feminist theory is transformative: it provides the groundwork for our collective effort to recast and make the world. (Goldstein, 1997, p. 9)

When we speak of feminism(s) in this text, we are referring to a critical perspective that values women's ideas, words, and ways of being and thinking. We also refer to a politics that is dedicated to transforming those social and domestic arrangements that penalize or marginalize women because of their sex, and see ourselves as partisans of women, fighting *for* a space for all to speak, and *against* anything that threatens their/our full capacity to work and to love. Feminism shifts the balance within maternal practice from denial to knowledge, from parochialism to awareness of others' suffering, and from compliance to decisive capacities to act (Ruddick, 1994). This work situates women educators' voices within the larger framework of feminist theory about voice, narrative, collaboration, and action (Belenky et al., 1986; Brown & Gilligan, 1992; Gilligan, 1982; Hollingsworth, 1992; Noddings, 1992).

One of the most important perspectives to our thinking is that of feminist standpoint theory. This approach, based on Marxian theory, provides an epistemological tool for understanding and opposing all forms of domination. Despite the difficulties feminists have correctly pointed to in Marxian theory, there are several good reasons to adapt Karl Marx's approach. First, Marx's method and the method developed by the contemporary women's movement share a belief that the socially mediated interaction with nature in the process of production shapes both human beings and theories of knowledge (Fraser, 1997; Hartsock, 1974). Nancy Hartsock argues that Marx is most helpful to feminists in his claim that society is viewed from differing power positions, and that women's lives differ structurally from those of men. From that position, women can provide a particular vantage point on male supremacy that can then be used to ground a critique of phallo-centric institutions and ideologies that constitute the capitalist form of patriarchy. A feminist standpoint allows ". . . us to understand patriarchal institutions and ideologies as perverse inversions of more humane social relations" (1974, p. 107). From that standpoint, we are then able to better differentiate between what Sara Ruddick identified as "invariant and *nearly* unchangeable" features of human life (e.g., bearing children) and those that despite being *nearly* universal are certainly changeable (e.g., caring for children).

Using feminist standpoint theories, the experiential dimension stresses the problematizing of everyday experience as the focal point in dialogue. The female experience of bearing and rearing children represents the ultimate in grounding understandings in everyday experience as well as a unity with nature and of mind with body that is unparalleled. A new life changes the world and the consciousness of the woman; in the process of producing human beings, relations with others may take a variety of forms—forms which range from a deep unity with others to the many-leveled and changing connections mothers experience with growing children.

THE POWER OF STORY

It is also important to understand that to be human is to be interpretive. Searching meanings from inside out captures the hermeneutic or interpretive understanding of people's life experiences, viewing reality through the lens of the participants and generating ideas and information through their own voices. Thus the linkages of objectivity and lived experience, intersubjective construction of meaning, and identity formation are articulated and illuminated (Chow, 2000).

Carolyn Heilbrun, in *Writing a Woman's Life*, speaks of the twin issues of power and control as being central to women's writing about their lives. As she notes, "[w]omen of accomplishment . . . have had to confront power and control. Because this has been declared unwomanly, and because many women would prefer (or think they would prefer) a world without evident power or control, women have been deprived of the narratives, or the texts, plots, or examples, by which they might assume power over—take control of—their own lives" (1988, pp. 16–17).

In *Composing a life*, Mary Catherine Bateson (1989) talks about the necessity for women, in times when there is no clear-cut vision for the future, to reinvent themselves again and again over a lifetime. She writes, "When the choices and rhythms of lives change, as they have in our time, the study of lives becomes an increasing preoccupation" (p. 4). This is especially true for women who "today read and write biographies to gain perspective on their own lives" (p. 5). Through the telling and reading of our own and other women educator's changing stories, we may discover our selves, gain self-knowledge, and be empowered. After all, if Jerome Bruner's (1990) theory is correct, we are by nature narrative beings.

We will also consider how being a mother affects almost everything we do and are; we acknowledge the centrality of motherhood in most women's lives for we are all daughters and most of us are also mothers in some way. No one says it more eloquently than the writer Tillie Olsen, who was in her mid-eighties when the following was recorded:

> Motherhood remains central to my life—more than illuminator, instructor of my feminism—touchstone for sustenance, hope, connectedness, self knowledge; human understanding, beauty, and anguish; yes, and well-spring, passionate source for all I am, do, write. (Baker, 2000, p. 205)

A number of renowned women educators have addressed the integral nature of mothering to their teaching (see, e.g., Neumann & Peterson, 1997; Witherell & Noddings, 1991). For instance, Greene (1997) writes about the dishes and the guilt and the balancing of her personal and professional lives as she continues to "compose" her life. Nel Noddings (1997) says reflection on the personal dimension of her life has, perhaps, been more important than any philosophical argument to her perspective on the aims and equality of education. For a mother, coming to know the truth includes looking at the real feelings and conflicts of mothering. It is a feminist project to describe the angers and ambivalences of maternal love, and to acknowledge the social status of women and resultant sacrifices mothers are often required to make. We believe that by acting and speaking jointly and publicly about our varying "projects" of mothering and educating, we can celebrate mothers' strengths and maybe even effect small transformations.

We further contend that mothering daughters and feminism are—or can be—inextricably linked. Recent Anglo-American feminist work has argued that a strong mother-daughter connection is what makes possible a strong female self in daughters. Two primary and intersecting ways attention to strengthening the mother-daughter bond has been considered are through maternal storytelling or narrative, and through the Motherline. We are concerned here with how "daughters and mothers may unravel the patriarchal script to write their own stories of motherhood and daughterhood" (O'Reilly, 2000, p. 145). Attention to maternal narrative links hearing of one's mother's voice as she attempts to challenge patriarchal norms (e.g., mother blame, separation vs. connection) to forging a strong female bond and establishing self-identity. Similarly, the Motherline allows daughters to gain strength from their identities as girls or women as they strengthen the mother-daughter bond through connection.

Naomi Lowinsky puts it like this:

> When a woman comes to understand her life story as a story from the Motherline, she gains female authority in a number of ways. First, her Motherline grounds her in her feminine nature as she struggles with the many possibilities now open to women. Second, she reclaims . . . knowledge of her own body. . . . Third, as she makes the journey back to her female roots, she will encounter ancestors who struggled with similar difficulties in different . . . times. This provides her with a life-cycle perspective . . . [F]ourth, she uncovers her connection to the archetypal mother and to the wisdom of the ancient worldview, which holds that body and soul are one and all life is interconnected. And finally, she reclaims her female perspective, from which to consider how men are similar and how they are different. (cited in O'Reilly & Abbey, 2000, p. 146)

Lowinsky also sees the Motherline as living knowledge of our selves as life vessels. That is, every woman is born of woman and every woman alive is connected to all the women before her through the roots of her family and culture. "The Motherline is body knowledge and birth story and family story and myth" (Lowinsky, 2000, p. 230). Hope Edelman expands on Lowinsky's definition, adding that, "Motherline stories ground a daughter in a gender, a family, and a feminine history" (cited in O'Reilly & Abbey, 2000, p. 146). They provide a map, guidance from her foremothers, as she makes her way in the world. Every woman, contends Lowinsky (2000), who wishes to be her full, female self needs to know the stories of her Motherline. She asks us to

> envision the word *line* as a cord, a thread, as the yarn emerging from the fingers of a woman at the spinning wheel. Imagine cords of connection tied over generations. Like weaving or knitting, each thread is tied to others to create a complex, richly textured cloth connecting the past to the future. (p. 231)

The mother-daughter connection, however, only empowers the daughters if the mothers with whom the daughters are identifying are themselves living lives of authority, agency, and autonomy. As Adrienne Rich writes, ". . . the quality of the mother's life . . . is her primary bequest to her daughter, because a woman who can believe in herself, who is a fighter, and who continues to create livable space around her, is demonstrating to her daughter that these possibilities exist" (cited in O'Reilly & Abbey, 2000, p. 146). Anita Diamant, in her 1997 book *The Red Tent*, explains it like this: "If you want to understand any woman you must first ask about her mother and then listen carefully. . . . The more a daughter knows the details of her mother's life—without flinching or whining—the stronger the daughter" (p. 2). She also suggests that one of the reasons women in Biblical times wanted daughters was to keep their memories, their stories, alive. Perhaps things have not changed all that much from that time to this.

We are sharing, then, stories of "courageous mothering;" stories which link daughters' tenacity, self-respect, determination, and autonomy to their mothers' actions. In the words of Judith Arcana, "If we want girls to grow into free women, brave and strong, we must be those women ourselves" (cited in O'Reilly & Abbey, 2000, p. 147). Rich, who maintains mothers must try to expand the limits of their lives, calls for the sharing of

> a kind of strength, which can only be one woman's gift to another, the bloodstream of our inheritance. Until a strong line of love, confirmation, and example stretches from mother to daughter, from woman to woman across generations, women will still be wandering in the wilderness. (1976, p. 246)

Although this connection-empowerment emphasis is relatively new to Anglo-American feminist theory, it has long been foregrounded in African-American feminist theory as motherhood is valued in, and central to, Black culture (O'Reilly, 2000). The narratives here will also foreground this theory, and seek to link it with practice, as grand/mother-educators and their grand/daughters weave their personal and professional lives into an ever-evolving tapestry.

We also want to emphasize the role of praxis and the interrogation of power relations embodied in the stories in this volume. We share several of the arguments of Teresa Ebert's (1999) critique that much of postmodern feminist theory, or ludic feminism, has "largely abandoned the problems of labor and exploitation and ignored their relation to gender, sexuality, difference, desire, and subjectivity" (p. ix). She further argues that ludic feminism has "displaced economics, labor, and class struggle. The cost of this displacement has been enormous for feminist politics, especially for socialist feminism" (ibid). While much of this volume implicitly engages post-structuralist feminist theory with the everyday lives of mothers in various education endeavors, an underlying theme of this book is resistance and struggle to support our daughters in a revolution that has lost much ground in the growing neo-liberal, globalized economy. Thus, many of the chapters emphasize social justice work, direct action, and an on-going interrogation of privilege and power.

Janet Miller (1998) suggests the only valid reason to use autobiography as a form of educational inquiry is if it assumes the potential "to disrupt rather than reinforce static versions of our 'selves' and our work as educators" (p. 151). Miller urges us to recognize constructions of our "selves" as mediated by social and cultural (and, we would add, economic and political) forces and contexts to move us beyond the telling of teacher stories as an end in and of itself. Instead, autobiography can call into question both the notion of one true, stable and coherent self and the cultural scripts for that self. The goal of utilizing autobiography to challenge the normative, the ordinary, and the taken-for-granted is to assist us in inventing "visions of what should be and what might be in our deficient society . . . in our schools" (Greene, cited in Miller, p. 152). And only an understanding of the daily realities of mothering and teaching will lead us to beneficial social and political changes. We are all "embedded and embodied" (Benhabib, 1992, p. 6); we can only come closer to understanding and gaining knowledge as we expand our conversations and encourage others to join in the dialogue. Rather than "wandering in the wilderness" as it were, we hope other women educators will come into the red tent to hear our stories, and to tell their own.

ORGANIZATION OF THE BOOK

Our stories are shared this way: The first section of the book comprises four chapters that set the stage for what is to follow. These chapters look critically at the interwoven lives of teacher educators and their daughters and granddaughters. The first chapter tells the story of a mother and teacher educator whose life was profoundly changed by her daughter's "special needs." In Chapter Two, the author explores and critiques her experience of negotiating the complex intersections between being a grandmother of a granddaughter and being an early childhood/critical literacy teacher educator. Chapter Three examines the development of moral feminism by exploring three overlapping data sources (from a mother and her two daughters), while the fourth chapter investigates the use of family stories to provide a sense of a connection and heritage between an adoptive mother and an East Indian girl's developing sense of self.

The second section contains four stories detailing the impacts of academe on two generations of women. In Chapter Five a mother and daughter provide a reflective analysis of cross-cultural experiences over more than 20 years.

The second chapter in this section (Chapter Six) addresses the frustrations and pleasures of doing research and teaching experienced by professional colleagues and co-researchers who are also mother and daughter. In Chapter Seven, a mother-daughter narrative exposes and interrogates the experiences that have shaped lives lived within communities dominated by the Mormon culture. The section concludes with a chapter (Eight) that looks at what it was like to grow up with a mother who was consumed by a challenging career in academe.

The final section links women's work as educators with social activism, raising numerous difficult questions. Chapter Nine poses the question: What does social justice have to do with care in schools? In Chapter 10 the authors ask, who could be against social justice?, and share reflections on a mother and daughter's "first twenty years together in activism." The questions addressed in chapter 11 are: What does it mean to "mother" when you are a social justice activist? And what is it like being the daughters of a mother whose life revolves around struggle and protest?

We invite readers to engage with these critical personal narratives, as they relate to women in education and their daughters and granddaughters—as well as to broader struggles for social justice. Drawing from a range of feminist theories in action, contributors to this volume offer stories of their Motherlines that illuminate some of the complexities of these powerful relationships. Using counter-narratives to patriarchal framings of family, this collection affirms the power of women telling and reading their/our stories as a means of self-discovery, empowerment, and ultimately, cultural transformation.

REFERENCES

Ayers, W. & Ford, P. (Eds.). (1996). *City kids, city teachers: Reports from the front row*. New York: The New Press.

Baker, C. (2000). Telling our stories: Feminist mothers and daughters. In A. O'Reilly & S. Abbey (Eds.), *Mothers and daughters: Connection, empowerment, and transformation* (pp. 203–212). Lanham, MD: Rowman & Littlefield.

Bateson, M. C. (1989). *Composing a life*. New York: Penguin Press.

Belenky, M. F., Clinchy, B. M., Goldberger, N. R., & Tarule, J. M. (1986). *Women's ways of knowing: The development of self, voice, and mind*. USA: Basic Books.

Benhabib, S. (1992). *Situating the self: Gender, community, and postmodernism in contemporary ethics*. New York: Routledge.

Bloch, M. N. & Popkewitz, T. (2000). Constructing the teacher, parent, and child: Discourses of development. In L. D. Soto (Ed.), *The politics of early childhood education* (pp. 7–32). New York: Peter Lang.

Brown, L. M. & Gilligan, C. (1992). *Meeting at the crossroads: Women's psychology and girls' development.* Cambridge, MA: Harvard University Press.

Burdell, P. & Swadener, B. B. (1999). Critical personal narrative and auto/ethnography in education: An emerging genre. *Educational Researcher, 28* (6), 21–26.

Burman, E. (1994). *Deconstructing developmental psychology.* New York: Routledge.

Campbell, P. (2001). Books for summer reading. *Phi Delta Kappan, 82* (10), 769–772.

Cannella, G. S. (1997). *Deconstructing early childhood education: Social justice and revolution.* New York: Peter Lang.

Cannella, G. S. & Viruru, R. (2004). *Childhood and postcolonization.* New York: RoutledgeFalmer.

Caplan, P. (2000). Don't blame mother: Then and now. In A. O'Reilly & S. Abbey (Eds.), *Mothers and daughters: Connection, empowerment, and transformation* (pp. 237–245). Lanham, MD: Rowman & Littlefield.

Chow, E. N. (2000). Exploring critical feminist pedagogy. In P. R. Freeman & J. Z. Schmidt (Eds.), *Wise women: Reflections of teachers at midlife* (pp. 197–210). New York: Routledge.

Diamant, A. (1997). *The red tent.* New York: Picador USA.

Ebert, T. L. (1999). *Ludic feminism and after: Postmodernism, desire, and labor in late capitalism.* Ann Arbor, MI: The University of Michigan Press.

Felman, J. L. (2001). *Never a dull moment: Teaching and the art of performance—Feminism takes center stage.* New York: Routledge.

Fisher, B. M. (2001). *No angel in the classroom: Teaching through feminist discourse.* Lanham, MD: Rowman & Littlefield.

Frasier, N. (1997). *Justice interruptus: Critical reflections on the "postsocialist" condition.* New York: Routledge.

Freeman, P. R. & Schmidt, J. Z. (Eds.). (2000). *Wise women: Reflections of teachers at midlife.* New York: Routledge.

Greene, M. (1997). Exclusions and awakenings. In A. Neumann & P. Peterson (Eds.), *Learning from our lives: Women, research, and autobiography in education* (pp. 166–182). New York: Teachers College Press.

Hartsock, N. C. M. (1974). *The feminist standpoint revisited and other essays.* Boulder, CO: Westview Press.

Heilbrun, C. G. (1988). *Writing a woman's life.* New York: Ballantine Books.

Hultqvist, K. & Dahlberg, G. (Eds.). (2001). *Governing the child in the new millennium.* London: Routledge/Falmer.

Johnson, E. B. (2000). Mothers at work: Representations of maternal practice in literature. In A. O'Reilly & S. Abbey (Eds.), *Mothers and daughters: Connection, empowerment, and transformation* (pp. 21–35). Lanham, MD: Rowman & Littlefield.

Lowinsky, N. (2000). Mothers of mothers, daughters of daughters: Reflections on the Motherline. In A. O'Reilly & S. Abbey (Eds.).*Mothers and daughters: Connection, empowerment, and transformation* (pp. 227–235). Lanham, MD: Rowman & Littlefield.

Miller, J. L. (1998). Autobiography and the necessary incompleteness of teachers' stories. In W. C. Ayers & J. L. Miller (Eds.), *A light in dark times: Maxine Greene and the unfinished conversation* (pp. 145–154). New York: Teachers College Press.

Mutua, K. & Swadener, B. B. (Eds.). (2004). *Decolonizing research in cross-cultural contexts: Critical personal narratives*. Albany: State University of New York.

Neumann, A. & Peterson, P. (Eds.). (1997). *Learning from our lives: Women, research, and autobiography in education*. New York: Teachers College Press.

Noddings, N. (1997). Accident, awareness, and actualization. In A. Neumann & P. Peterson (Eds.), *Learning from our lives: Women, research, and autobiography in education* (pp. 166–182). New York: Teachers College Press.

O'Reilly, A. (2000). "I come from a long line of uppity irate black women": African-American feminist thought on motherhood, the Motherline, and the mother-daughter relationship. In A. O'Reilly & S. Abbey (Eds.), *Mothers and daughters: Connection, empowerment, and transformation* (pp. 227–235). Lanham, MD: Rowman & Littlefield.

O'Reilly, A. & Abbey, S. (2000). Introduction. In A. O'Reilly & S. Abbey (Eds.), *Mothers and daughters: Connection, empowerment, and transformation* (pp. 1–18). Lanham, MD: Rowman & Littlefield.

Polakow, V. (1993). *Lives on the edge: Single mothers and their children in the other America*. Chicago: University of Chicago Press.

Polakow, V. (Ed.). (2000). *The public assault on America's children: Poverty, violence, and juvenile injustice*. New York: Teachers College Press.

Reed-Danahay, D. (Ed.). (1997). *Auto/ethnography: Rewriting the self and the social*. New York: Berg Publishers.

Rich, A. (1976). *Of woman born: Motherhood as experience and institution*. New York: W.W. Norton & Company, Inc.

Ruddick, S. (1989). *Maternal thinking: Toward a politics of peace*. New York: Ballantine.

Ruddick, S. (1994). Maternal thinking, maternal practice. In M. B. Mahowald (Ed.), *Philosophy of woman: An anthology of classic to current concepts* (pp. 442–451). Indianapolis, IN: Hackett.

Witherell, C. & Noddings, N. (Eds.). (1991). *Stories lives tell: Narrative and dialogue in education*. New York: Teachers College Press.

CRITICAL EXPERIENCES OF TEACHER EDUCATORS MOTHERING AND GRANDMOTHERING GIRLS

Leigh and Lydia

Chapter One

My Daughter, My Self: On Being a Teacher Educator and the Mother of a Daughter with "Special Needs"

Leigh M. O'Brien

Having a child with special needs is motherhood magnified

—Marsh, 1994

My daughter, Lydia Lacey, was named after her maternal great, great grandmother. In fact, the name Lydia has been used in my grandmother's family since at least the 1600s, when this part of my family came to North America. This certainly represents a long and strong Motherline (e.g., Lowinsky, 2000)! However, to the best of my knowledge, none of Lydia's foremothers had developmental delays as she does. This is the story of how being Lydia's mother has impacted my work in teacher education; as I compose and re-compose this narrative, I am "edging toward speech," always mother and teacher becoming (Ruddick, 1989).

INTRODUCTION

"Lydia is a happy, well-adjusted, beautiful and loving three-year-old girl." These are the words I wrote to take to my daughter's first Committee on Preschool Special Education (CPSE) meeting, words which started me on the path to rethinking and clarifying my beliefs about the purposes and practices of early childhood special education (ECSE), my primary area of focus in teacher education. I wrote these words in response to the negative and jargon-filled report I received on her initial evaluation. I was determined not to have her viewed in a reductionist, deficit-focused manner, and my ongoing efforts to make sure her care and education reflect my beliefs have colored my entire perception of the field of ECSE. While I acknowledge that she has "special needs" that should be addressed in school, I want her to be seen as a child first, a "real little girl" with a full, real life (Soriano-Nagurski, 1998).

I wrote this sentence near the end of my description of Lydia: "Put simply, Lydia enjoys life and is (most of the time) a pleasure to be around because of her cheerful demeanor and loving nature." The words I used to describe Lydia—"enjoys life," "a pleasure to be around," "loving"—are increasingly reflective of the characteristics I would like early childhood educators to encourage. Though Lilian Katz speaks of a distinct separation between the roles and feelings of mothers and teachers as being natural and appropriate (1984); frankly, I'd like a little more irrationality, intensity of affect, and strength of attachment in the early educators who spend time with my daughter. Hence, as an early childhood teacher educator, I utilize my parental lens here to suggest practices which are consistent with what I've learned in order to make ECSE a little more loving and a lot more responsive to individual differences and needs (e.g., Goldstein, 1997; Noddings, 1992). Instead of so often focusing on what she *can't* do, I want the educators who work with my daughter to view her as strong, capable, and competent.

The title of this chapter reflects my growing belief that being Lydia's mom colors *everything* I do as a teacher educator, not just my work in ECSE. No matter what class I am teaching, I introduce myself as the mother of a daughter with special needs, and I utilize my understandings from being her mother in my research and writing as well (e.g., O'Brien, 1999, 2001). Based on my experiences with her education, I now argue for a conception of learning that is far broader than the traditional academic model. For instance, I encourage students to become familiar with Gardner's theory of multiple intelligences (e.g., 1983); I more strongly advocate for inclusive models of education; I offer a look at many "alternative" schools which practice something like the model I suggest above; I introduce students from day one to the idea of children "of promise" (Swadener, 1990; Swadener & Lubeck, 1995), and so forth. To sum up, many of the things I've learned about ECSE through being a parent of a child with special needs apply to education for children of *all* ages with and without disabilities.

I think of this chapter as being based on "humble knowledge" (Kincheloe, 1998), created by the ultimate "indigenous-insider" (Banks, 1998): the mother of a daughter with special needs. This work, then, falls into the category of auto-ethnography as I utilize my story vis-à-vis early education to make inferences about the field as a whole. As have others (e.g., Kellor, 1999), I used stories in my academic work before a name was given to this way of making sense, before there were complex theories to describe this approach. As Kellor notes,

> Bringing my life experiences into educational settings seemed commonsensical. How could I avoid doing so? I had entered academe with a storied body. Hence it seemed self-evident that I would also bring embodied life experiences to the theories I studied. (p. 40)

Here, I use my/our story to give "testimony" or "bear witness" (Burdell & Swadener, 1999) to our ongoing struggles with the education system. Through narration, I, like other mothers, ". . . may name, claim, and transform . . . lived realities; and bequeath to daughters—and other mothers—a vision of emancipatory connectedness and care" (O'Reilly & Abbey, 2000, p. 5) that serves to empower. I hope that one day my daughter will view this work as a gift to her, my primary bequest, a work that captures the strategies I've used for living and surviving—and for nurturing her.

It has been to my advantage that, because of my insider status as an educator, in many ways I am a "native in a native land" (see Reed-Danahay, 1997). But however much a native, I am also a traveler in a new, strange, and unexpected land as well. I prepared for travel to the land of typically developing children, but when I disembarked, I found I had not packed the right clothes, knew the language only marginally, and didn't have a clear map of where to go or how to get there. I felt, and I *still* feel, what Johnson (2000) calls a cross-cultural dislocation. I am only gradually, with many wrong turns and detours, finding my way in this fascinating and beautiful, but at times perplexing, frustrating, exhausting, and scary new place.

And as a traveler to this new place, I find I cannot separate my personal and professional lives. For many educators, who we are and what we do are inextricably linked and interdependent. Thus my background in education impacts my parenting, and my parenting impacts my teaching and scholarship. In fact, I find that my philosophy of parenting and education are inseparable. As I alluded to earlier, I believe in a holistic, positive, integrated approach to education, seeing each child as inherently worthy, with something special to offer. This world view, I've found, is often in conflict with the rather Calvinistic, negative, efficiency model which pervades far too much of our schooling. I now argue with my students for a new vision: a model of education that calls for our collectively imagining what *ought to be*, rather than what is; a model that attends to happiness (Noddings, 2003) and supporting the "irrepressible possibility of humans" (Booth, 2001). Transmuting this vision into reality has taken on a new impetus since my daughter has entered the system. It is this vision of the possible and the desirable that now drives my teacher education.

THE EARLY YEARS

It was when Lydia was six months old that her father and I first began to sus-
pect something might be "wrong." Although she had showed early promise,
she seemed a bit slow reaching physical milestones and was rather passive in
her demeanor. She sat up barely on time, she never crawled, and she walked
on time but shakily. We noticed especially that her verbal skills were limited.
When she turned two, I remember lying in bed reviewing the 50 words she
was supposed to be using according to one of the parenting books I was reading. It was at her two-year check up that the nurse practitioner suggested we
should consider getting an evaluation of her language proficiency. She was
found to have some delays (using a rather questionable testing procedure, the
education professional in me noted), so we began speech therapy.

By her three-year check up, it was becoming clear that she was not developing at the same rate as her peers. But when the physician described her
as "iffy", and recommended we get a formal evaluation done, we were dev-
astated. Not so incidentally, and apparently not so atypically when children
have special needs, it was at about this time that my (now ex-) husband
moved out, so I was pretty much left on my own to do and deal with all this.
(I am sure that feeling alone and overwhelmed had much to do with the anxiety and depression I was treated for during this time period.) I also, finally,
began talking with others about Lydia's special needs. While most attempted to be reassuring, the comments made often devalued my knowledge of my daughter. As another mother of a child with special needs puts
it, "It's really too bad that a mother's knowledge about her child is mini-
mized and invalidated, even by her family, unless supported by the 'experts'" (Marsh, 1995, p. 10).

I also experienced, and continue to experience, what has been identified as
"mother blame." That is, no matter what was wrong, I was, and am often assumed to be responsible for the problem (Caplan, 2000). Further, feeling
guilty about Lydia's special needs—Did I have her too late in life? Should I
have insisted on a Caesarian? What if she ingested some of the old lead-based
paint on the windowsills somehow?—and being a single parent, I often
owned the blame alone. Because Lydia's special needs had no clear etiology,
perhaps somehow *I* had caused her delays.

At any rate, I got the recommended evaluation done after much calling
around to colleagues in education for support and suggestions. To my an-
guish, it came back full of technical language and enough heartbreak to last
a lifetime. There it was in black and white: Lydia had significant delays in
a number of areas and was eligible for special education services. I became
aware of how strongly I resented this disembodied, narrowly focused cri-

tique when I, all alone in my home, read the written evaluation and sat sobbing on my bed, saying over and over, "But you don't know her! You don't *know* her!"

THE PRESCHOOL YEARS

Although I have long been an advocate for inclusive models of ECSE, my belief in inclusion was strengthened when I went to investigate local early childhood programs for children with special needs and found none on our side of the city, and few elsewhere that I would consider truly inclusive. After a number of observations, multiple phone calls, and much gnashing of teeth, I finally settled on a brand new preschool program. It had a lot going for it: The teachers seemed well-trained, pleasant, and competent; the location was good; transportation would be provided to and from school; the teacher-child ratio was low, especially to start; and it was the closest thing to inclusion I could find in our area. However, although the Committee on Preschool Special Education (CPSE) chair told me the program was "inclusive," being in a self-contained classroom in the basement of a child care center (albeit with *carpeting*, as the chair pointed out) and "visiting" the "regular" preschool classroom doesn't constitute is not what I call inclusion.

This is an area where we need to do more work. While progress has been made, there is still much to be done in terms of teacher education, classroom teaching, and public perception and support. I now advocate for inclusion more categorically because of its emphasis: a recognition that all have a right to belong and participate in education, employment, social and leisure activities, and so on. [Note: Mine is a *moral/philosophical* rationale for inclusion, although there are also legal, educational, rational, and empirical foundations that can be and are invoked]. The major goal of inclusion, one I would think all parents and most educators would support, is building acceptance and community, not just skills or academic development. "Rather than face an eternity of trying to measure up, students with disabilities and their parents want schools to enable students to find meaningful participation in democratic communities now" (Ferguson & Ferguson, 1998, p. 305). Why segregate children with special needs, or even congregate them? Why not integrate them into all "regular" settings such as the school classroom? To me, it seems *immoral* not to include children with special needs in the community.

In fact, I think "disability" should be thought of as an addition to the concept of diversity; that is, a difference in degree, not type. In this view, difference and diversity are viewed as opportunities for enriching and supporting each and every student's learning. By definition, if all are included, then there will be diversity of many kinds, and the school community will learn to appreciate and celebrate such diversity.

But when you have so-called special needs, apparently it's okay to exclude you, to label you, to try to fix your "problems," to behavior modify you. I disagreed with this stance on a theoretical level before having Lydia. Now, coming from a parent's more personal perspective, I do all I can to counter this orientation. In my teacher education classes, I argue for an expanded world view: one which includes, which does not label, which treats each individual as just that—a person with potentialities, strengths, talents, and yes, weaknesses; a person who has the same rights to self determination the more "typically developing" child does.

I am reminded here of Swadener's (1990) critique of the "at-risk" label and her call for a conception of each child as "of promise." As she and others (e.g., Ayers, 1993; Sapon-Shevin, 1994; Swadener & Lubeck, 1995) remind us, we miss so much when we focus primarily on deficits. With a deficit model our conception of education becomes one of narrow, technical rationality, instead of one which says life ought to feel infinitely open, happiness is crucial, caring and connection are central, exploration and curiosity are learning tools, and growth is variable but integral to each person's life. We must ask ourselves, what happens when we primarily view children as needy rather than capable?

I'm also reminded of critiques (e.g., Jipson, 1991; Lubeck, 1998; O'Brien, 1991 & 1993) of Developmentally Appropriate Practice (DAP), the current mainstream guide to ECE (Bredekamp, 1987; Bredekamp & Copple, 1997). DAP comes from and supports a white, middle-class perspective and works best for typically developing children from relatively "advantaged," Anglo home environments. Children from non-mainstream and "disadvantaged" backgrounds may not have the requisite knowledge, skills, learning styles, and dispositions allowing them to benefit from this approach. Thus, these guidelines for practice provide a necessary but not sufficient base for the early care and education of children with disabilities.

This was forcibly brought home to me when I saw how Lydia reacted to the unstructured, incidental learning model of early care and education she first experienced. It has become clear to me that she, and other young children with special needs, require more than what is outlined in the guidelines for DAP. Lydia needs teachers who look at her as an individual, who recognize her strengths as well as her weaknesses, and who provide the supports and instruction necessary for her continued growth. She needs teachers who will ask, "*Who is this child, and what can she do?*" This perspective would be enhanced by teacher preparation in both early childhood and special education, preferably in the form of a unified program (e.g., Kemple, Hartle, Correa & Fox, 1994; NAEYC, 1998).

Because of Lydia's learning difficulties, I've moved away from a strict reliance on constructivism as a basis for practice, and now advocate with my students for what Mallory calls "inclusive policy, theory, and practice." This approach draws on multiple theoretical perspectives and ". . . allows teachers . . . to plan programs that can meet the needs of a diverse population" (1994, p. 59). In order to implement such an approach, special and general early childhood educators need to work together to find the intersections between their respective fields.

My students often asked me what I thought about an application of constructivism to children with special needs and whether Piaget or others had addressed this (he has; he stated that his theories applied only to children who experience typical development), and I was at a loss. Although I had been part of the critique of DAP, I must admit that the question about its applicability to young children with special needs did not trouble me overly much—until Lydia entered the world of early care and education. Now I am deeply concerned that we in ECE often act as if all children benefit equally from the same approach to teaching and learning when my experiences with my daughter tell me they do not.

Also largely absent from DAP is attention to caring, interconnectedness, and mutual responsibility (Jipson, 1991; Noddings, 1992). It is interesting to note that how parents define success is often very different than how professionals define it. Parents want their children to be happy, safe, and fulfilled, a rather Emersonian conception of success, whereas education professionals tend to see success as achieving clearly identified, usually academic, outcomes. I hope that parents and educators, working on the edges can help push our societal paradigm in a different direction, a more humanistic one. As we focus more on so-called quality of life issues—feelings and beliefs and dreams, for instance—the purposes and practices of education also need to change.

One of the changes we might work for is attention to self-determination. Self-determined individuals know what they want and how to get it and advocate for their own interests. Why is this so important? According to Abery, "A sense of self determination is necessary for the development of individual identity, and it is a crucial catalyst of independence and autonomy" (1994, p. 345). Now we certainly might argue whether independence and autonomy ought to be goals for our children. But we do at least give lip service to these goals for "typically developing" children, so why should things be any different for those children who have special needs?

Throughout the 1960s and '70s, U.S. special education programs stressed a didactic, adult-directed and controlled approach; compliance with teacher directive was central and is still a notable tendency. This pedagogical model certainly would seem to interfere with student development of self-regulation.

Fortunately, these practices have (slowly) begun to change as early childhood special education moves to reconcile with traditional ECE in support of inclusion models for young children. If we are to raise children with the capacity to care for self and others, to think critically and to make healthy choices, we must nurture their initiative.

I concur with a newspaper article titled, "Lighten up on special education kids" (Rosen, 1992, p. 3C). While fault certainly could be found with the wording of this headline, it's hard to argue with the study's findings. Deci and his colleagues found that traditional ways of "managing" children with learning disabilities and emotional handicaps actually may be undermining their academic achievements. They suggest children in special education classes are best motivated much like other children. Imagine that!

A piece by Joan Goodman (1992) notes much the same thing. Based on a field study of 20 early intervention programs for preschoolers, she notes ". . . there are risks involved in pushing children to make rapid gains in the hope of a 'catch-up' effect. Such efforts may conflict with their natural developmental pace and allow them inadequate time to make sense of the world through their own actions." She goes on to say, "Children comply with the daily routine and obey their teachers . . . The calm, however, is purchased through subtle and repressive control devices; the child compliance too often masks low levels of learning and genuine participation" (p. 40). Her conclusion jibes with mine: The evidence of cognitive improvement is insufficient to justify the heavy control of children so often seen in early intervention programs. I agree with Goodman who puts the blame for this situation not on classroom teachers (although often they do play a role), but on a society that values success in very narrow terms and hence supports such programming. As one of my graduate students wrote in response to the language of the Individualized Education Plans (IEPs) for her students, "Where's the wonder?"

I love Maxine Greene's suggestion that it all begins in wonder, in a sense of awe about the world. She writes, "The individual must be moved to ask questions about the universe, to engage in dialogue with him [or her] self about the world as it impinges on him [or her] and about the explanations others provide" (1973, p.21). Why would I want any less for my daughter, or for that matter, anyone else's child?

Rachel Carson put it like this:

> If I had influence with the good fairy who is supposed to preside over the christening of all children I should ask that her gift to each child in the world be a sense of wonder so indestructible that it would last throughout life, as an unfailing antidote against the boredom and disenchantments of later years, the sterile preoccupation with things that are artificial, the alienation from the sources of our strength. (1956, p. 43)

Perhaps early childhood educators should play the role of 'good fairies' for young children to guard against the boredom and disenchantments I fear pervade far too many school experiences. Again, we should want this for all children, but for children with disabilities, this role may be crucial as they are often subjected to the most artificial experiences imaginable in the name of addressing purported deficits—and are likewise often alienated from their strengths. When we work with children with special needs, "it becomes . . . especially important for us to love a little more, accept a little more, encourage and guide a little more . . ." (Bakley, 1997, p. 21).

It was our good fortune that the preschool experiences Lydia had, while not exactly what I might wish, did provide individualized attention, did support the development of self-determination, did allow for creativity and choices, and did, I think, keep intact Lydia's sense of wonder. Teacher directives were not central, classrooms were not quiet and passive, and learning and growing and questioning were not secondary to "management" or "control". Lydia benefited cognitively, socially, physically, emotionally, aesthetically, and morally from her time in preschool, and I was, if not a full partner, at least involved. Then came the transition to the school-age years.

KINDERGARTEN

"Mommy, am I going to go to school on the bus with Lainie?" "No, honey; you're going to go to a different school." "Why, mommy?" "Well, because the teachers at Rosselot* didn't think they could do a good job teaching you." "Why, mommy?" "I don't know, honey." This is the gist of a conversation Lydia and I had the spring before she was to start kindergarten while walking around the block as school buses were picking up neighborhood children. Her questions shook me, although I had expected them at some time, for it was just one week after the meeting regarding her transition from her preschool to a school-age setting. Lydia's innocent queries brought to the fore all my concerns about teaching, education, and school "readiness."

Perhaps naively, I had started from the premise that Lydia would go to her "home school" in the "regular" kindergarten class. After all, we lived in what was named, in 1995, an *Excelsior* school district (an annual New York State governor's award), a district people had always said was "good." Surely the teachers and other school people there could and would include my daughter! From my first phone call to the principal in December to set up an initial observation, however, I knew it was not going to be easy. First, the prin-

---

*This is a pseudonym.

cipal did not want me to observe before the parent orientation night, to be held the end of January, and second, she suggested a range of options including a self-contained special education classroom, although I had been quite clear about my wish for an inclusion setting. And at the kindergarten parent orientation meeting, it became all too clear what is meant by the term, "push-down curriculum." I was shocked, although I probably shouldn't have been, knowing what I do about primary education these days and this school district in particular. It also became clear that there was no way Lydia would meet the school's expectations of kindergartners, so I began to consider the so-called Young Kindergarten.

Young Kindergarten, according to the school brochure, "is an option for children who are chronologically, but not developmentally, ready for kindergarten. The major goals of the Young Kindergarten are to relieve undue stress and frustration, provide an appropriate program, and give the children an additional year of time in which to develop." As someone with an early childhood background, I wanted to ask, What was all this about readiness? What about starting where each child was and moving him or her forward? What about the school's responsibility not to create stressful or frustrating situations? Was the regular kindergarten, then, **not** "appropriate"? And where was this outdated "gift of time" model coming from?

However, despite my reservations, I went to visit the Young Kindergarten teacher and classroom. The teacher shared some of my concerns about the Young K model, but said she had learned that this is what parents in this school district want: a strong emphasis on academics starting early on. I described Lydia a bit and she agreed that Young K might work well for her.

Meanwhile, I was looking into other local options and talking with colleagues in education and friends who had young children with special needs. I received materials from a number of settings, visiting the one which looked to be the most viable alternative, but eventually came back to my original decision to start with her home school. Because she was already in the special education system, a whole battery of tests and observations then began.

First, the teachers at her preschool tested Lydia. Then she was observed and tested by the school district personnel. Last, I finally got an appointment and took her for an assessment at the nearby University hospital's Center for Developmental Disabilities. Oh, and there was also the childcare center's assessment.

For the school testing, we went first to an initial screening. The test results did not look so good. We did, however, continue on together to the Young K classroom to see the space and meet the teacher. At this time I was telling Lydia, *this* will be your school; *this* will be your classroom and teacher. Following the school assessments, I was called to come in and meet with the "team" prior to the meeting transitioning Lydia from the CPSE to the Committee on Special Education (CSE), the school-age decision-making body for children with special needs. At this meeting, I heard the results of the team's assessment.

The news was not good. In fact, said one team member bluntly, "there's no way Lydia would make it in a regular kindergarten." I also got the distinct impression that they did not think my parental insights or those of her preschool teachers had much validity. They gave some lip service to addressing her strengths and my concerns, but the bottom line seemed to be that they thought she should be in a full-day, self-contained classroom in another of the district schools where "her needs could be better met."

We went back and forth on this for some time with me asserting my belief that her home school ought to be able to serve her and that she ought to be able to ride the bus to school with her friend and neighbor, Lainie. Labeling a child and putting him or her in a special education setting is a serious concern because of how unlikely it is once a child is identified (or "coded") as having special needs that he or she will ever be returned to regular classes. For example, in western New York only 1.7 percent of children ever make it out of the special education system. I teach my students about the Continuum of Services model where students are placed in the least restrictive placement and only moved to a more restrictive one when it is shown to be necessary, and then my daughter's school tells me, "sorry, we can't meet her needs here"—without even having tried! As Bailey, McWilliam, Buysse, and Wesley note rather dryly, ". . . services for children with disabilities still tend to be organized separately from those for typically developing children [which] makes the idealized continuum difficult to put into practice, and transitions from one system to another can be particularly challenging" (1998, p. 33).

One of the team members called and left a message about showing me a "wonderful" 12:1:1 classroom (12 children, one teacher, and one aide) with a "wonderful" teacher, never addressing the fact that it was clearly a self-contained special education classroom in opposition to my expressed wishes. Again, after much soul-searching and dialogue with friends, family, and colleagues, most of whom, by the way, counseled me to stand firm for an inclusion setting, I consented to visit the special education classroom. It did in fact look like a place where Lydia would thrive, so I went into the CSE meeting reluctantly agreeing to the proposed placement. At the meeting I heard the details of my daughter's assessment, the proposed IEP for the following year, and the programming planned. I took the opportunity, while acceding to their plans, of critiquing the school district's inability to adequately educate my daughter in her home school. I expressed my disappointment and frustration, but summed up by saying that although I had

personal and professional problems with the projected scheme, I was not
going to make Lydia fight my battles for me. I believed that it would not be
to her advantage to be placed where people obviously did not want her or
know how to deal with her. I know the CSE was glad to not have to deal
with this "difficult" parent any more—at least for the time being.

Time marched on. Over the summer we visited the playground of her new
"new school" and talked about how she would not be attending the *other*
school after all. We answered the questions of family, friends and colleagues
about where she'd be going, and why it was a full-day program, and which
bus she would be riding, me always feeling uncomfortable that I had to do all
this explaining, and also feeling bad for Lydia. We went to the school to meet
the teacher and see the classroom. Our visit was another rude awakening: No
longer was there the warm and caring preschool atmosphere Lydia and I were
used to. Now the teachers had very specific and high expectations for behavior, the children would be eating their lunches with aides in the cavernous
school cafeteria, homework would be coming home each day, and, worst of
all for Lydia, there was to be no "dress-up" play.

Then, after almost a week's delay due to storm damage, school finally
opened. I sent Lydia off wearing a nametag with her name, the teacher's
name, and two bus numbers, carrying both a backpack and a lunch bag, and
seemingly not at all weighted down with my fears and concerns for her. All
day long I worried about her, thinking, if this was preschool, I could call or
even stop by to see how she's doing. Since this was no longer an option, so I
suffered until I finally retrieved her that afternoon. We went out to dinner to
celebrate her first day of school—she shared some of her experiences and
seemed none the worse for the day—and then I anxiously peered into her
backpack to see how things went from the teacher's perspective.

Lydia *did* receive a "blue ticket" for having a "great day" (although it was
not clear just what the day entailed or what exactly constituted a great day);
many forms were sent home; and there was a very brief and, I thought, curt
note to the effect that some parents needed to get with the program. The two-
pocket folder that I had purchased per instructions, filled with helpful first-
day papers, and clearly labeled with her name and put in her backpack, was
returned untouched. There was instead another school folder inside with additional papers but no explanation for why the original folder had been returned. So I called the teacher at home that night. Fortunately, she seemed re-
ceptive to my call, and she cleared up my confusion. I also received a telling
reminder that expectations for this room were tough. When I told the teacher
about the folder situation, she replied, "Lydia probably forgot to take her
folder out. That wouldn't surprise me." I thought, but didn't say, *This is the*

first day of kindergarten, damn it! Of course she "forgot"! Isn't it your responsibility to help her learn to do this?

It was the evening of the second day of kindergarten. Lydia seemed to be enjoying herself at her "new school" and I had received no negative notes, yet when I received the message from her teacher to call her, I was worried. Perhaps the teacher thought Lydia wasn't "right" for that class. Perhaps she was going to suggest that Lydia needed to go on Ritalin; she is, after all, very active, impulsive, and has difficulty attending at times. While it is true that I may be an overly concerned parent, and it is also true that many parents experience anxiety when a teacher calls, I think that for parents of children with special needs these situations are more challenging. After all, I have been receiving bad news from education professionals for some time now, and for an equal amount of time, I've been trying both to defend Lydia and myself, as well as to make what I think are the best decisions about her education.

As it turned out, the teacher wanted to convey some information and make a suggestion. She also had some "concerns about Lydia's behavior." It seemed Lydia was having trouble "following directions" and "staying on task." She was "easily distracted" and often needed one of the aides to "keep her focused on what she is supposed to be doing." Her teacher wanted to know what I do in similar circumstances and would I support the use of a "point system" which she had found to be effective with other students who are also easily distracted. Now, I know Lydia and this report did not surprise me. On the other hand, this was only the second day of a school, and her IEP and other parts of the voluminous paperwork accompanying Lydia clearly described these characteristics of hers. This seemed too much, too soon, and I worried about her losing "choice time" if she lost points. I also began to worry that this might be a classroom where children's hearts and souls [were] being silently destroyed in the name of good management (Ayers, 1993).

Before school one morning the first week Lydia cried seemingly without provocation. Then came an increasing number of indicators that all was not well. She was crying often, she was being much more aggressive than usual, and she was expressing fears, acting out, and using negative words and phrases that I knew came from adults at school. She was not thriving. After two weeks of school, I met with the teacher to express my concerns about what I considered the negative atmosphere of the class. The teacher was quite defensive, and instead of responding to my concerns, suggested that Lydia be reassessed for ADD/ADHD and said she'd be requesting a one-to-one aide to help Lydia stay on task. I felt as if I was not being heard, one of the most common and aggravating experiences of parents who have children with special needs.

It was at this point that I began working to have her placed in a different setting. The extensive focus on rules and following directions and doing things the "right way" (the teacher's way), the need to earn approval (to be seen as "good"), and the focus on punitive child guidance (for example, time out and taking away points and choice time)—it was all too much for Lydia, and for me. This classroom used a "melting pot" view of classroom culture where there is a group norm to be followed. In contrast, I support (and teach my education students about) a pluralistic view of classroom culture—where the classroom is viewed as a group consisting of many diverse individuals.

My worries surfaced in the questions I kept asking myself: *Will Lydia's spirit be squashed by the need to conform, to always listen to the teacher, to do what the teacher wants her to do instead of what she wants to? Will she lose what the pediatric neurologist described as her "wonderful flamboyance?" Will she experience school as a dull and joyless place to be dreaded and only survived?* I didn't want to be another ". . . devastating, but all-too-true, and too typical, story" like that of Darlene and her daughter (Greenberg, 1998, pp. 70–71) where a child's initial enthusiasm for learning was eradicated by an uncaring and overly academic early school experience.

Two CSE meetings later (in addition to numerous calls, observations, and an educational evaluation) I got the placement for Lydia I had wanted in the first place! She went back to her home school in the Young Kindergarten class with a one-to-one aide to help her adjust. More importantly, she was in a setting where learning occurred in the context of functional activities and was embedded in play, with a warm and caring teacher, and with her peers. Lydia had a great year and went on to have a good Kindergarten year, too!

She is now in sixth grade, included in a general education classroom after much fighting (or "advocating," as the CSE chair would have it) every year to have her included. It has become clear that this is a fight that will be ongoing. Despite our stated preference for an inclusive middle school placement, Lydia and I were pushed to once again consider a self-contained classroom where "she would be with other children with the same classification!"

What have I learned from these experiences?

First, we mothers should stick to our convictions and utilize our intuition. Education is not a one-size-fits-all proposition (Ohanian, 1999). Teachers and schools need to recognize and respect the uniqueness and potential of each child. Parents have valid ideas about desirable education practices, and we should not let others (the "experts") try to convince us that they know better. If I had been stronger in my convictions from the start, perhaps Lydia and I would not have had to go through all that we did. Confronting the system was not easy or comfortable for me, but my love for her—as well as my background in education—gives me the strength to do things that are difficult or uncomfortable, and to advocate for what I believe is best for her.

Second, and related to the above, enlist the support of others. We all have friends and colleagues to whom we can turn when we are fighting for our beliefs. For instance, I am certain that taking colleagues with me to the CSE meetings provided legitimacy for my claims and strengthened my stance. Further, they were invaluable in terms of moral support in the face of a phalanx of professionals. Use whatever power you have!

Third, we need to do a better job of preparing teachers of young children with special needs. In New York, where an ECE certification has just recently been added and the general and special education certifications are separate, I find teachers are often unprepared to work with the Pre K to grade two population and especially with young children with special needs. It has become a mission of mine to revamp teacher education programs so that teachers are better equipped to deal with children such as Lydia—in inclusive settings. Early childhood (special) educators must take a strong and positive stance on inclusion. After all, the full participation of young children with disabilities in early childhood classrooms designed for typically developing children reflects recommended practices in both the early childhood and early intervention fields.

Fourth, schools need to view all children as of promise rather than at risk and build on their strengths; each child should be viewed as a whole, special person who is strong, capable, and rich in potential. And, we must keep the joy in education, even (perhaps *especially*) for children with special needs. We mustn't be so concerned with specific goals and outcomes, narrow academic tasks, classroom management, behavior modification and the like. Rather, we should utilize and revel in the hundreds of languages of children (Edwards, Gandini, & Forman, 1993) and attend to each child's development of autonomy, individual needs and successes, sense of wonder, and happiness (Abery, 1994; Noddings, 1992; O'Brien, 1999).

Also, we need to think about education as a true partnership between home and school. As Yelland avers, "When mutual sharing occurs, teachers are no longer colonizers, and parents need no longer resent what teachers have to give. They become partners" (2000, p. 108). It behooves all of us to consider the voices of parents when we plan for schooling young children. I've become a more vocal parent advocate and activist since Lydia's entry into the world of early care and education. I now challenge students, teachers, and schools to really demonstrate a commitment to the concept of partnership. Schools often say they want parents involved, but actively resist all but the most limited forms of connection. Barnes and Lehr write, "traditionally parents have been viewed by some teachers as outside the decision-making process of education and, at worst, as adversaries" (1993, p. 85). In opposition to these often negative and adversarial approaches to parent involvement, I want the teachers and teachers-to-be with whom I work to do more than give lip service to the oft heard "Parents are the child's first teacher" or "Parents are the experts on their child." I want them to believe in and act on these premises in ways that serve to support on-going collaborations in the care and education of young children.

"Building positive and trusting relationships with parents begins with respecting their love and hopes for their child, soliciting and listening to their ideas and concerns, and sharing one's own questions. It also requires an understanding of what parents can realistically do given all the demands on their time and energy" (Barnes & Lehr, 1993, p. 85). I want teachers to really listen to the voices of parents! Writes Marsh, "the professional can at least *hear*. It doesn't require superhuman power; it just requires attention" (1995, p. 27).

Ultimately, I want my students to understand that teaching, like parenting, is not a scientific, but a human endeavor, the nature of which is conversation, a dialogue between teacher and student, and the aim of which is an intellectual and moral development of which only humans are capable (Deering, 1998). I don't think Mem Fox is out of line when she asks teachers to be as human as parents. She contends, "Parents . . . are such naturally good teachers that we need to copy what they do and how they behave. We need to emulate the affectionate attitudes and relationships of happy families" (1995, p. 15). I am reminded here of Jane Roland Martin's (1991) call for schools to be more home-like and believe this can only occur if we move past the factory model of schooling which has clearly outlived its usefulness.

Finally, spread the word. I have taken every possible opportunity to share my experiences with others, especially with my teacher education students. I think it is important for teachers and teachers-to-be to hear an insider's perspective so that they might work to create more just, caring, and inclusive schools. I am also asking teacher educators to be role models and examples for their students. I can now more confidently, and honestly, address advocacy and inclusion and parent involvement after all I've been through. If we are asking teachers to not only talk the talk but—in the face of myriad obstacles and constraints—also walk the walk, then we teacher educators must do the same.

Thoryk, Roberts, and Battistone (2001) argue persuasively that hegemony, domination, and power persist, unconfronted and pervasive, within the institution of education. Despite good intentions, caring personnel, and (seemingly constant) educational "reform," the same power relations between those who are typically developing and those who are not are modeled and re-enacted, and so the same roles are perpetuated. We educators need to broaden our perspectives and open our minds to examining how assumptions are played out in classrooms; we need to push for an honest and open assessment of the purpose/s of education; and we need to initiate open dialogue between those at the center and those on the fringes of society. Teacher education programs should discuss varying perspectives on issues of oppression and disablement; myths and assumptions need to be aired; analytic and self-reflective skills must be honed. More diversity needs to be seen at all levels of the education system and multiple perspectives need to be both validated and valued. Some parting thoughts on my continuing journey as a mother and teacher educator.

Kohn (1998) calls for a move away from a school culture that emphasizes competition and credentialing, to one which attends to developing each individual's capacity to act as a free and thoughtful agent, striving to explore and master his or her world, within a caring community. He notes that it is often not until parents have a child with special needs that they raise questions about educational emphases on sorting and classifying. That is, having a child with special needs changes their perspective from one where they are sacrificing other children to their own, to one where they support an equity agenda and equity pedagogy.

No doubt in part because of my "experience-near" perspective on disability (Gustavsson, 1999), I share Sapon-Shevin's concern about the "disruption of community" (1994): "When children who are identified as 'gifted' or children who are identified and labeled as 'handicapped' are removed from the classroom to 'have their needs met,' the concept of classrooms as inclusive communities is challenged" (p. 6). Excluding students because of a label and differing learning needs leads inevitably to the belief that community membership is available only to those children who are typically developing.

In contrast to this model, I am looking for schools where *everybody* belongs, is accepted, supports, and is supported by, his or her peers and other members of the school community in the course of having his or her educational needs met. I am looking for classrooms "in which students can legitimately act on a rich variety of purposes, in which wonder and curiosity are alive, in which students and teachers live together and grow" (Noddings, 1992, p. 12). I am looking for teachers who believe that every person has the right and the dignity to achieve his or her potential within the school and larger community; who believe that education ought to encompass the many facets of the whole child; who believe that education should be germane and relevant for each child, attending to multiple spheres of development; and who are willing to work to bring the vision of full inclusion to reality. And I want teachers to understand that "to be included is not merely to be present, but to participate, to influence, and to be influenced by the communities in which one lives, works, and learns" (Mallory & New, 1994, p. 11).

I want Lydia to have teachers who believe she has something to offer, teachers who know that all children have special gifts that we adults have an obligation to develop. With Fox,

> I am asking . . . for a loving atmosphere in which students and their interests are treated with dignity; an environment in which they are seen as exciting, fascinating beings who are alive with anticipation and longing for real communication . . .; a system in which they never sit in corridors and suffer lovelessness; a classroom . . . in which there is a throbbing heartbeat of passion connecting the class to itself and the teacher to the class (1995, p. 13).

John Dewey said it well many years ago: "What the best and wisest parent wants for his [or her] own child, that must the community want for all its children. Any other ideal for our schools is narrow and unlovely; acted upon, it destroys our democracy" (1900, p. 7). And in his opinion, the best and wisest parents want for each of their children an education that matched his or her needs, capacities, and interests (Noddings, 1992, p. 44). I don't think that's asking for too much.

In a democracy, not only should all citizens have access to the mainstream, but diversity and heterogeneity should be valued as well. Successful teachers guide and encourage children to be all that they can be, not necessarily what we expect them to be. As Wien puts it, the choice is between developmental appropriateness and teacher dominion. "[D]evelopmentally appropriate practice celebrates and tries to be responsive to differences. . . [whereas] . . . teacher dominion . . . aims for obedience, conformity, and reduction of differences" (1995, p. viii). When teachers use the latter approach, they are choosing to hold all or most of the power. My dream is that teachers can learn to share power with others and move to a model that leads to empowerment, to children taking action in the world, of having agency. In this view, adults and children are seen as co-constructors of knowledge who jointly, in dialogue, conduct inquiries about the world. Children are quite capable of and willing to be active participants in their learning, if we give them the opportunities and guidance needed to do so. Liberatory praxis can and should include children with special needs.

I hope my students begin to re-think and think otherwise, as Derrida asks us to do, and at least aspire to be the kind of teacher described above. It has been my ongoing learning as a parent of a child with special needs that has caused me to feel so strongly about this orientation. I cannot and will not take off my "mommy hat" as a teacher educator, but perhaps it is just that dual role which will allow me to have an impact on the teachers who work with our children. I hope so, for Lydia's sake.

REFERENCES

Abery, B. H. (1994). A conceptual framework for enhancing self-determination. In M.F. Hayden &

Abery, B. H. (Eds.), *Challenges for a service system in transition: Ensuring quality community experiences for persons with developmental disabilities* (pp. 345–380). Baltimore, MD: Paul H. Brooks.

Ayers, W. (1993). *To teach: The journey of a teacher.* New York: Teachers College Press.

Bailey, D. B. (1994). Working with families of children with special needs. In M. Wolery & J. S. Wilbers (Eds.), *Including children with special needs in early childhood programs* (pp. 23–44). Washington, D.C.: National Association for the Education of Young Children.

Bailey, D. B., McWilliam, R. A., Buysse, V., & Wesley, P.W. (1998). Inclusion in the context of competing values in early childhood education. *Early Childhood Research Quarterly, 13* (1), 27–47.

Bakley, S. (1997). Love a little more, accept a little more. *Young Children, 52* (2), 21.

Banks, J. A. (1998). The lives and values of researchers: Implications for educating citizens in a multicultural society. *Educational Researcher, 27* (7), 4–17.

Barnes, E., & Lehr, R. (1993). Including everyone: A model preschool program for typical and special-needs children. In J. L. Roopnarine & J. E. Johnson (Eds.), *Approaches to Early Childhood Education* (2nd ed.) (pp. 81–96). New York: Macmillan.

Bateson, M. C. (1989). *Composing a life.* New York: Penguin Press.

Booth, E. (2001, July). The John Washburn Memorial Lecture. Paper presented at the Memorial Art Gallery, Rochester, N.Y.

Bredekamp, S. (Ed.). (1987). *Developmentally appropriate practice in early childhood programs serving children birth through age 8.* Washington, D.C.: National Association for the Education of Young Children.

Bredekamp, S., & Copple, C. (Eds.). (1997). *Developmentally appropriate practice in early childhood programs.* Washington, D.C.: National Association for the Education of Young Children.

Brown, F., & Cohen, S. (1996). Self-determination and young children. *Journal of the Association for Persons with Severe Handicaps, 21* (1), 22–30.

Burdell, P. & Swadener, B. B. (1999). Critical personal narrative and auto-ethnography in education: Reflections on a genre. *Educational Researcher, 28* (6), 21–26.

Carson, R. (1956). *The sense of wonder.* New York: Harper & Row.

Cartwright, S. (1999). What makes good early childhood teachers? *Young Children, 54* (4), 4–7.

Deering, T.E. (November, 1998). *The social sciences and the decline of teacher preparation.* Paper presented at the American Educational Studies Association annual conference, Philadelphia, PA.

Dewey, J. (1900/1990). *The school and society.* Chicago, IL: The University of Chicago Press.

Edwards, C., Gandini, L., & Forman, G. (1993). *The hundred languages of children: The Reggio Emilia approach to early childhood education.* Norwood, N.J.: Ablex.

Elswood, R. (1999). Really including diversity in early childhood classrooms. *Young Children, 54* (4), 62–66.

Ferguson, P. M., & Ferguson, D. L. (1998). The future of inclusive educational practice: Constructive tension and the potential for reflective reform. *Childhood Education, 74* (5), 302–308.

Fox, M. (1995). *"Like mud, not fireworks." The place of passion in the development of literacy.* Paper presented at the symposium "Teaching as an art, writing as a craft," The English-Language Arts Consortium of the Greater Bay Area, Redwood Shores, CA.

Fuchs, D., & Fuchs, L. S. (1998). Competing visions for educating students with disabilities: Inclusion versus full inclusion. *Childhood Education, 74* (5), 309–316.

Gandini, L. (1993). Fundamentals of the Reggio Emilia approach to early childhood education. *Young Children, 49* (1), 4–8.

Gardner, H. (1983). *Frames of mind: The theory of multiple intelligences.* New York: Basic Books.

Goldstein, L. S. (1997). *Teaching with love: A feminist approach to early childhood education.* New York: Peter Lang.

Goodman, J. F. (1992) Preschools for slow children. *Education Week, 4/22,* 33 & 40.

Greenberg, P. (1998). Warmly and calmly teaching young children to read, write, and spell. *Young Children, 53* (5), 68–82.

Greene, M. (1973). *Teacher as stranger: Educational philosophy for the modern age.* Belmont, CA: Wadsworth.

Greene, M. (1986). Reflection and passion in teaching. *Journal of Curriculum and Supervision, 2* (1), 68–81.

Gustavsson, A. (1999). Experience-near perspectives on disabled people's rights. In F. Armstrong & L. Barton (Eds.), *Disability, human rights, and education: Cross-cultural perspectives* (pp. 149–160). Buckingham, UK: Open University Press.

Jipson, J. (1991). Developmentally appropriate practice: Culture, curriculum, connections. *Early Education and Development, 2* (2), 120–136.

Kanpol, B. (1998). Confession as strength: A necessary condition for critical pedagogy. *Educational Foundations, 12* (2), 63–75.

Katz, L. G. (1984). *More talks with teachers.* Urbana, IL: ERIC Clearinghouse on Elementary and Early Childhood Education.

Kellor, K. S. (1999). Her-story: Life history as a strategy of resistance to being constituted woman in academe. In L. K. Christian-Smith & K. S. Kellor (Eds.), *Everyday knowledge and uncommon truths: Women of the academy* (pp. 25–44). Boulder, CO: Westview Press.

Kemple, K. M., Hartle, L. C., Correa, V. I., & Fox, L. (1994). Preparing teachers for inclusive education: The development of a unified teacher education program in early childhood and early childhood special education. *Teacher Education and Special Education, 17* (1), 38–51.

Kincheloe, J. (November, 1998). Whose practice? Whose knowledge? Practitioner research and the formal vs. practical knowledge debate. Paper presented as part of a panel at the Annual American Educational Studies Association conference, Philadelphia, PA.

Kohn, A. (1998). Only for my kid: How privileged parents undermine school reform. *Phi Delta Kappan, 79* (8), 568–577.

Kulak, A. (1998). A teacher's responsibility—To be enthusiastic about teaching fast and slow learners alike. *Young Children, 53* (2), 43.

Lubeck, S. (1998). *Is* developmentally appropriate practice for everyone? *Childhood Education, 74* (5), 283–292.

Mallory, B. (1994). Inclusive policy, practice and theory for young children with development differences. In B. Mallory & R. New (Eds.), *Diversity and developmentally appropriate practices: Challenges for early childhood educators* (pp. 44–61). New York: Teachers College Press.

Marsh, J. D. B. (Ed.) (1994). *From the heart: On being the mother of a child with special needs.* Portland, ME: University of Southern Maine.

Martin, J. R. (1991). The contradiction and the challenge of the educated woman. *Women's Studies Quarterly, 1&2,* 6–27.

Miller, R. (1997). *What are schools for? Holistic education in American culture* (3rd Rev. ed.). Brandon, VT: Holistic Education Press.

Mumford, L. (1946). *Values for survival: Essays, addresses, and letters on politics and education.* New York: Harcourt, Brace and Company.

National Association for the Education of Young Children. (1998). *Code of ethical conduct and statement of commitment: Guidelines for responsible behavior in early childhood education.* Washington, D.C.: Author.

National Association for the Education of Young Children (1998). *Guidelines for the preparation of early childhood professionals: Guidelines developed by the National Association for the Education of Young Children and the Division of Early Childhood of the Council for Exceptional Children and by the National Board for Professional Teaching Standards.* Washington, D.C.: Author.

New, R., & Mallory, B. (1994). Introduction: The ethic of inclusion. In B. Mallory & R. New (Eds.), *Diversity and developmentally appropriate practices: Challenges for early childhood educators* (pp. 1–13). New York: Teachers College Press.

Noddings, N. (1992). *The challenge to care in schools: An alternative approach to education.* New York: Teachers College Press.

Noddings, N. (2003). *Happiness and education.* Cambridge, UK: Cambridge University Press.

O'Brien, L. M. (1991, October). Turning my world upside down: How I learned to question developmentally appropriate practice. Paper presented at the Reconceptualizing Research in Early Childhood Education conference, Madison, WI.

O'Brien, L. M. (1993). Teacher values and classroom culture: Teaching and learning in a rural, Appalachian Head Start program. *Early Education and Development, 4* (1), 5–19.

O'Brien, L. M. (1996/7). Turning my world upside down: How I learned to question "Developmentally Appropriate Practice." *Childhood Education, 73* (2), 100–102.

O'Brien, L. M. (1999). I love Lydia: Mother as early childhood teacher educator. Journal of Early Childhood Teacher Education, 20 (2), 105–119.

O'Brien, L. M. (2000). Engaged pedagogy: One alternative to 'indoctrination' into DAP. *Childhood Education, 76* (5), 283–288.

O'Brien, L. M. (2001). Juggling scarves or Inclusion for what? Young children with special needs in an era of school 'reform.' *Contemporary Issues in Early Childhood, 2* (3), 309–320.

Odum, S. L., & Diamond, K. E. (1998). Inclusion of young children with special needs in early childhood education: The research base. *Early Childhood Research Quarterly, 13* (1), 3–25.

Ohanian, S. (1999). *One size fits few: The folly of educational standards.* Portsmouth, NH: Heinemann.

O'Loughlin, M. (1991, October). Rethinking early childhood education: A sociocultural perspective. Paper presented at the Reconceptualizing Early Childhood Education Conference, Madison, WI.

Paley, V. G. (1997). *The girl with the brown crayon.* Cambridge, MA: Harvard University Press.

Reed-Danahay, D. (1997). *Auto/Ethnography: Rewriting the self and the social.* New York: Berg.

Rosen, E. (1992, September 17). Lighten up on special education kids, study says. *Democrat and Chronicle,* p. 3C.

Sapon-Shevin, M. (1994). *Playing favorites: Gifted education and the disruption of community.* Albany, NY: State University of New York Press.

Soriano-Nagurski, L. (1998). And the walls came tumbling down: Including children who are differently abled in typical early childhood educational settings. *Young Children, 53* (2), 40–41.

Swadener, E. B. (Fall, 1990). Children and families "at risk": Etiology, critique, and alternative paradigms. *Educational Foundations,* 17–39.

Swadener, B. B. & Lubeck, S. (Eds.) (1995). *Children and families "at promise:" Deconstructing the discourse of risk.* New York: State University of New York Press.

Thoryk, R., Roberts, P., & Battistone, A. M. (2001). Both emic and etic: A view of the world through the lens of the ugly duckling. In L.J. Rogers & B.B. Swadener (Eds.), *Semiotics and dis/ability: Interrogating categories of difference* (pp. 187–208). Albany, NY: State University of New York Press.

Walsh, D. (1991). Extending the discourse on developmental appropriateness: A developmental perspective. *Early Education and Development, 2* (2), 109–119.

Wien, C. A. (1995). *Developmentally appropriate practice in "real life:" Stories of teacher practical knowledge.* New York: Teachers College Press.

Wolery, M., & Bredekamp, S. (1994). Developmentally appropriate practice and young children with special needs: Contextual issues in the discussion. *Journal of Early Intervention, 18,* 331–341.

Yelland, N. J. (2000). *Promoting meaningful learning.* Washington, D.C.: National Association for the Education of Young Children.

Chapter Two

E is for Education:
Telling Ourselves, Telling our Worlds

Sue Novinger

My granddaughter Hannah was born when I was 39 years old. I was thrilled; filled with joy, crazy in love with her. I was a grandmother! A grandmother? How could I be a grandmother?!?! How could I fit this new identity, this notion of grandmother, with the other "I's;" the "I's" that were divorced, a single mother, a daughter, a sister, a runner, an early childhood teacher educator, a campus school director? How would becoming Hannah's grandma change who I was — in my own eyes, in the eyes of my family and friends, in the eyes of the world? How might my emerging image of myself as a grandmother fit with my images of my own grandmothers?

Now, ten years later, I know the answers to those questions aren't simple ones. I've come to understand that our identities are not constant or static, but are instead dynamic and multiple (Grieshaber & Cannella, 2001), constantly shifting and changing (Ryan, Ochsner & Genishi, 2001). Becoming Hannah's (and now Leah, Kirsten, Alex, Trevor, and Eli's) grandma has changed who I am, is still changing who I am, how I am positioned by others, and the identities I choose to take up. "Grandmother" and "educator" aren't separate and distinct identities I inhabit at different times. Rather, my evolving grandmother identity both shapes and is shaped by my evolving educator identity. In this chapter, the "I" who is a grandmother and the "I" who is an educator are inextricably linked as I tell and reflect on a story of Hannah learning to read.

Hannah and Sue

CONSTRUCTING STORIES /
CONSTRUCTED THROUGH STORIES

Reflecting on shifting and overlapping identities, I've also learned something about the power of stories to both create and understand ourselves and our worlds. Thomas King (2003) asks us to "wonder how it is we imagine the world in the way we do, how it is we imagine ourselves, if not through stories" (p. 95). Stories "make people" (Shannon, 1999, p. 397) and we strive to construct ourselves and define who we are through the stories we tell about our lives (e.g., King; Taylor, 1997). It is through stories that we project our multiple, shifting identities into the world, through stories that we reach out to others reaching out with stories of their own (Dyson, 1994). Our stories inter-animate each other, creating connections, weaving ever more richly textured webs of stories, constructing us as family, as community.

Susan Florio-Ruane (2001) writes that our stories are like mirrors. As such, we can use our stories to examine and reflect on our lives, even as we use our stories to tell ourselves and our worlds into being. Through telling and listening to stories, through thoughtful examination of stories, we can weave together the many threads of our lives, to search for coherence in the fabric that emerges, to ask questions, to seek new possibilities. In the process, we attend selectively to the reflections, to the events in our lives; the stories we construct are partial truths, imperfect representations (Bailey, 2001), interpretations of possible multiple realities. Moreover, our stories and our constructed identities are reflexively related. As such, our stories are shaped by our current understandings of self, and, at the same time, those stories work to further create and recreate who we are.

As "scenes of learning" (Florio-Ruane, 2001, p. 32) then, stories are one of the primary ways we make sense of ourselves and our worlds. But the scenes of learning created through our stories, and what it is that we learn as we consider such stories, are social constructions, shaped and constrained by the overlapping discourses in which we live our lives (e.g., Dyson & Genishi, 1994). Discourses can be thought of as

> . . . socially organized frameworks of meaning embodying particular values and practices that stipulate rules and domains of what can be said and done, by whom, and when. Thus, discourses have a material, social, and linguistic existence and enact particular power effects. (Ryan, Ochsner & Genishi, 2001, p. 51)

Discourses shape ways of knowing and what can be known. What stories mean, then, is dependent upon the discourses in which those stories—and our interpretations of them—are embedded. Put differently, stories embody the values and knowledge of particular discourses, and shape both our experiences and our interpretations of those experiences (Florio-Ruane).

And, situated as they are in overlapping, often contradictory discourses, stories are profoundly political (e.g., Shannon, 1999). Stories are told in particular ways and for particular purposes by particular people. "Stories can control our lives" (King, 2003, p. 9) and "set the parameters for our thinking" (Shannon, p. 397), and so it is imperative that we do our best to critically read the stories we tell and are told. We must do our best to understand the beliefs and values that are reproduced through the stories that inhabit our lives, and to understand who benefits from their telling (Shannon).

Such critique creates opportunities for us to use our stories to take action in the world. Grounded in our critical readings of the discourses that seek to control us, we can use our stories to cross borders among discourses, to complicate our understandings of ourselves and our worlds, and to resist the ways that particular stories seek to position us. We can use our stories to try to make our world a better place.

READING COMMUNITY TEXTS: READING THE WORD AND THE WORLD?

I tell the stories that follow from my multiple identities as grandmother, early childhood literacy educator, and activist. Through the telling, I seek to make sense of Hannah's experiences as a reader in her kindergarten class, and of the larger discourses in which those experiences are immersed. I want to use these stories to critique the discourses of market-driven education (McLaren, 1993) in general and the discourse of instrumental, back-to-basics literacy (Edelsky, 1999; Macedo, 1994) in particular. In order to do so, I have chosen to juxtapose two very different stories about early literacy learning and teaching, such that each story might become a lens through which to view the other. In each story an early childhood teacher involves young children in using similar kinds of community texts, albeit in very different ways and for very different purposes. Embodying, as they do, two different discourses about literacy learning and uses, these two classrooms act to shape children's own stories about themselves as literate persons in different ways.

As does Shannon (1999), I know that all stories are political, and I have a political agenda, rooted in my identities as a grandmother and early childhood literacy educator, in sharing and critiquing these particular stories. To quote Freire (1998), "I am not impartial or objective; not a fixed observer of facts and happenings" (p. 22). Rather, I've chosen these two stories because I'm worried and I'm angry. I'm worried and angry about what I think the reductionistic literacy discourse of Hannah's school might teach her about herself as a reader and as a person. I'm outraged at the ways the mainstream discourses of instrumentalist literacy learning and teaching (Coles, 2000; Macedo, 1994; Shannon, 1999, 2001) shape and constrain what teachers and parents come to believe about literacy learning and teaching, and shape educational policy at local, state and national levels. And I'm mad as hell about the ways such discourses serve to silence dissent, and narrow the possibilities for the identities that children and teachers might construct.

"E" IS FOR ESCAPE: HANNAH "READS" THE PAPER

Hannah, just home from morning kindergarten, unzipped the top of her backpack, and pulled out a black and white photocopied, stapled booklet with the title, "My E Book," printed across the front. Several pages were already filled with the upper and lower case E's Hannah had traced over dotted lines. She had filled two pages with rows of upper and lower case E's and e's. She had drawn lines connecting the E in the middle of a page to the pictures of things whose names begin with an E: things like eggs, elephants, and elbows. "E is for *ecchh!*" I mumbled to myself, but only to myself. After all, even if as an early childhood literacy educator I found the project devoid of meaning, as Hannah's grandma I wanted to support her efforts to engage with the literacy practices of her classroom.

"This is my homework," Hannah told me. She gathered up scissors, a glue stick, and a stack of magazines and newspapers—all of which were full of holes where words and pictures had already been cut out of them. "It's what we always do. We have to find letters and words that start with the letter, E this time, and then we have to cut them out and paste them in the book. You can help." A perfect example, I thought, of what James Britton calls "dummy runs" (1993): engaging in decontextualized practice exercises with bits of language instead of learning to read through really reading.

We each took a section of the paper, and started scanning. "Hey, look. Here's a story about an elementary school in town. Elementary starts with E," I said. "Let's see what it's about." I started to read the story aloud, but got no further than the first sentence when Hannah laid her hand on mine. I lowered the paper and looked at her.

"We don't have to *really* read the paper," she told me as she gently patted my hand. "We just have to find the letters and words. Where's the word you found?" she asked, scissors at the ready.

"Wouldn't you like to hear the story, anyway?" I asked.

Shaking her head, Hannah took the paper and peered at *elementary*. "The letters are too little to cut out and paste in right. I like big words and letters."

Big letters and words will fill up the pages more quickly, at least, I thought, as I shifted my attention to headlines and advertisements. The size of the print, or more specifically of the E's, was to be the salient feature of the text as defined by our task. So we looked for BIG words and BIG letters. Because Valentine's Day had just come and gone, the week-old paper was full of ads and flyers for jewelry, perfume and other cosmetics, flowers, restaurants, and lingerie. When we found an E or a word that began with E, I read the bit of surrounding text to Hannah: *Enchant her with long-stemmed roses. General Electric dishwasher. Enjoy dining elegance.* Hannah repeated each word as she cut it out and glued it in to the book.

We tried talking a little about the texts we were poring over. For instance, using a video store advertisement, we talked about the merits of the movies we had seen. We talked about the words we were cutting out—but such talk didn't go far. Since, as Hannah had explained, we didn't need to "really read" the text, such talking about the text seemed forced and artificial. The "E Book" slowly began to fill up with words—*entertainment, enchantment, Energizer Bunny, elegant, elaborate, enough, electric, escape*—and with upper and lower case E's in a wide variety of fonts. It looked, I thought, like one of those notes you see in movies, where the kidnappers cut letters from newspaper clippings to construct a ransom note. The big difference, of course, is that a ransom note, even in a movie, is a coherent, meaningful piece of text. All we were creating was a list of decontextualized words.

What meaning potential might these isolated words, ripped from headlines and ads have for Hannah? I entertained a little fantasy about creating such a patchwork note to Hannah's teacher (and the publishers of the reading series from which the E-Book assignment was drawn), demanding the children's release from mind-numbing homework.

As we scanned and cut and pasted we talked of Hannah's friends and the Valentine party held at her school several days before. Along with three-year-old Leah, who was sitting at the table with us drawing pictures, we talked about what we would make for dinner that night, what time Daddy would come home from work, what we would do next. We talked about playing in the snow and about our favorite colors. We talked about Leah's pictures and the stories they told. What we didn't talk about in any real or serious way was the pasted together text of "E words" Hannah and I were so industriously creating.

We knew the E Book was finished, finally, when there wasn't room to glue any more letters or any more words. Hannah tossed the booklet on the table. "Shall we read the words you glued in?" I asked.

"Nope," Hannah replied. "Let's read *books*."

And so we did.

WHAT DO MOTHERS REALLY WANT?

Young Children Reading the World and the Word

This account tells a very different kind of story. Jennifer O'Brien, then a teacher in a multi-age primary classroom in Australia, tells about her own work helping her five to seven year-old students critique community texts (O'Brien, 2001). Mother's Day was fast approaching, and the children's homes were inundated with catalogs advertising gifts for sale. O'Brien saw this as an opportunity to help her young students look at the catalogs through a critical lens. She writes,

School reading practices, which involve literature and books written for use in the classroom, rarely take account of texts like these . . . I wanted the [children] . . . to use [the] catalogs as reading material and to consider junk mail as texts that construct specific versions of the social world in order to persuade people to spend money . . . I wanted students to think about who benefited from texts like these, to think about how junk mail created a limited range of truths about women's lives, and to challenge these versions of women's lives by coming up with other possibilities. (O'Brien, pp. 47–48)

Before they read the catalogs, O'Brien asked the children to draw and write about the presents they would expect and not expect to find in the catalogs, and to consider how the mothers in the catalogs were both like and unlike real mothers. She asked them to examine what kinds of people were depicted as gift-givers, and to design a Mother's Day catalog full of "fun things instead of clothes and things for the house" (Luke, O'Brien & Comber, 2001, p. 118) Finally, O'Brien asked children to think about who produced the catalogs and for what purposes they produced and distributed them. Through their critique, the children discovered that the catalogs were produced by major retailers, and that "catalog mothers" (O'Brien, 2001, p. 49) were shown as slim, well-groomed, and as engaging in a limited range of activities. In contrast, in the catalogs they created, children drew and wrote about mothers engaged in a variety of activities (for example, going out to dinner, jumping on trampolines), and in diverse settings.

As Mother's Day approached the following year, O'Brien reexamined her goals for children's learning. What had been missing, she decided, was that she had not invited the children to think about the cultural practice of Mother's Day alongside issues of race, class, and culture. Now teaching in a different primary school, O'Brien writes that,

> [D]iscussion revealed that for many children in the class Mothers' Day was not a familiar institution; others simply could not afford to buy presents. I wanted to . . . [begin] a wide ranging discussion of Mothers' Day as a cultural practice and to [raise] questions of how race and culture are represented in everyday mass-advertising texts. So I decided that we should look for the groups of mothers who were not included in the catalogs, and to explore what that exclusion meant for the construction of the ideal woman in capitalist consumer society. (2001, p. 49)

O'Brien posed questions such as the following to focus the children's examination of the catalogs:

> What happens on Mother's Day? Why do we have Mother's Day? What is Mother's Day for? What part do [mothers, children, fathers, grandmothers, teachers, restaurant owners, shopkeepers] play in Mother's Day? Whose family celebrates Mother's Day? What do fathers have to do with Mother's Day? Where do children get the money to buy presents? Where do presents come from? (O'Brien, 2001, pp. 49–50)

As the children categorized the kinds of women represented and the kinds of gifts recommended for them by the catalogs they "investigate[d] how mothers' desires are constructed through the gifts included in them" (O'Brien, 2001, p. 50) and they "explored the ways in which textual practices construct gendered identities and produce a limited but purposeful versions of what mothers are like and what they do" (Luke et al., 2001, p. 119). Children explored who was present and who was absent in the catalogs, and discovered that the catalogs represented mothers as "young, Anglo-Australian and pretty" (O'Brien, p. 50). Mothers who were Greek, Lebanese, Cambodian, Vietnamese, Aboriginal, older, heavy-set—the real mothers of the real children in O'Brien's classroom—were not represented in the catalogs.

O'Brien's students then surveyed their own mothers, grandmothers, and aunts to discover their preferences for Mother's Day presents. They found that their mothers desired activities and gifts that weren't advertised in the catalogs, including rest, leisure, horror novels, and roller blades. Through this process, children learned that "the women's world constructed in the text was narrow, but one among many possibilities and, as importantly, that the catalog represented only those aspects of women's lives that resulted in consumer spending" (Luke et al., 2001, p. 120).

READING THE STORIES:
WHO SAYS WHAT IT MEANS TO BE LITERATE?

On the surface, these stories share some similarities. Both Hannah's teacher and O'Brien sought to use community texts as pedagogical tools. They even chose similar kinds of texts—holiday advertisements and catalogs, and newspapers—texts that are likely to be present in many, although certainly not all, children's homes. Looking below the surface, however, these stories demonstrate that Hannah and her classmates were immersed in very different literacy discourses than O'Brien's students, and as a result, had very different opportunities to construct particular identities of themselves as literate people. In Hannah's classroom, literacy use and literacy learning were situated within what Macedo (1994) calls an instrumentalist literacy discourse. In contrast, Jennifer O'Brien grounded her literacy teaching within the discourses of critical literacy. In this section I want to take a close look at the distinct discourse practices in which these stories are situated. I begin by considering how literacy and literacy learning are understood and practiced, and how children and teachers are positioned within each of these discourses. I then examine how, for what purposes, and in whose interests these different literacy discourses are constructed and perpetuated.

Barbara Comber invites us to consider classroom literacy practices with the following question: "If you only knew about literacy from being in this classroom, what would you think it was for?" (Comber, 2001) In classrooms such as Hannah's, instrumentalist, "back-to-basics" discourses frame and define the practice of literacy as decoding text in order to comprehend the author's intended meaning, which resides in the text (Macedo, 1994). Comprehension is understood as a skill, and is said to develop as readers become increasingly fluent decoders (Cunningham, 2002; Garan, 2001). Texts are understood as neutral, and children's texts are controlled through decodability and leveling of texts (Allington & Woodside-Jiron, 2002). Learning to read and write is conceptualized as a linear process (Dyson, 2001), and so instruction is sequenced through commercial materials that control not only what children read, but when and how teachers teach particular skills (e.g., Coles, 2000). As Hannah understood all too well, 'school reading' becomes reading for reading's sake, mere practice in preparation for real reading (Britton, 1993; Macedo, 1994). As a matter of fact, *learning to read* is understood as something very different from *real reading* or from *reading to learn*.

Within such discourses, teachers are positioned as technicians who implement instructional strategies using materials developed by "experts" (e.g., Allington, 2002; Coles, 2000; Macedo, 1994). As a matter of fact, commercial reading materials such as Open Court are even 'teacher proofed,' providing scripts that teachers must follow as they implement highly structured lessons in a predetermined order. The positionings children might take up within these discourses are likewise constraining. As Macedo puts it, instrumentalist literacy discourse practices theoretically may construct technically proficient readers, but not readers able to critically question what they read. As a matter of fact, critical examination of texts, and of the worlds in which those texts are produced, is usually thought to be "developmentally inappropriate" (Bredekamp & Copple, 1997) for young children. Children in classrooms immersed in such discourses are regulated and disciplined through materials that control the pace of their learning and the content of what they read, and through evaluation tools that categorize and stratify them (Shannon, 1999), constructing them as either successful or unsuccessful readers. Kept busy practicing reading skills, children have few, if any, opportunities to engage in personally and socially meaningful literacy experiences. Because of the limited ways in which literacy is constructed and may be used, Macedo names instrumental literacy "literacy for stupidification" (1994, p.9), claiming that the fragmentation of skills and knowledge serves to "anesthetize the mind" (p. 16) of readers and prevent critical thinking, the ability to read the world (Freire, 1970).

How and why are instrumentalist literacy discourses constructed? Who benefits? Macedo (1994), McLaren (1993), Edelsky (1999), and Shannon (1999, 2001), among others, argue that instrumentalist literacy discourses serve the needs of capital. As Giroux puts it, "literacy in this perspective is geared to make adults more productive workers and citizens within a given society" (cited in Macedo, p. 18). Simply put, instrumentalist literacy is designed to create compliant workers and citizen/consumers. Power elites, including George W. Bush, the U.S. Secretary of Education, members of the Business Roundtable, and agencies such as UNESCO, link literacy learning and achievement to national needs within a competitive global economy as well as to individual economic betterment. State and national legislation mandates back-to-basics skills approaches, grounded in the language of standards in the name of educational equity (Coles, 2000; Shannon). Publishers leap to create and sell materials aligned with these mandates and standards, as well as the high-stakes tests that are used to enforce the mandates (e.g., Allington, 2002; Shannon, 2001).

In contrast to the instrumentalist discourse in which Hannah's teacher seemed to be immersed, Jennifer O'Brien situated her work as an educator within critical literacy discourses. While there is no one critical literacy (Green, 2001), critical literacy discourses share some common threads. Texts are understood to have meaning potentials, as opposed to inherent, unitary meanings, and meanings are constructed in the transactions between and among readers and texts. Both readers and texts, however, are situated within complexly overlapping discourses, which shape and constrain the multiple meanings that might be constructed. Learning to read, then, involves not only reading the word, but reading the world (Freire, 1970). Indeed, Macedo (1994) argues that reading the world must come *before* reading the word. Learning to read the world involves learning to recognize and name the discourses in which texts are created, to evaluate the purposes that texts are created to achieve. *Learning to read* is not seen as something separate from *real reading*. Rather, literacy instruction engages young children in reading for real purposes. In the process, skills and strategies are taught in the context of personally and socially meaningful literacy events (O'Brien, 2001). In essence, from a critical literacy perspective, the instrumentalists' purpose for literacy instruction is turned on its head: Rather than practicing skills as an end in themselves, children are supported in developing skills as they use literacy to ask critical questions and to take action in their worlds.

Teachers and children are positioned very differently within critical literacy discourses than they are within instrumental literacy discourses. Instead of taking up identities as technicians who deliver prepackaged curriculum to passive learners, teachers working within this perspective have opportunities to take up identities as intellectuals and cultural workers (Edelsky, 1999; Giroux, 1988). As Vivian Vasquez puts it, such teachers engage incon-struct[ing] a critical curriculum that is socially just and equitable, where issues such as race, class, gender, and fairness are constantly on the agenda. The kind of curriculum I have in mind is one which cannot be prepackaged or preplanned because it is built on children's cultural questions about everyday life. Rather, it arises as teachers and children tune in to issues of social justice and equity unfolding through classroom conversations and begin to pose critical questions. Conversations like these lead us to ask in what ways we are already readers and writers of the world and in what ways can we equitably and democratically reread and rewrite the world in order to move toward becoming the literate people we want to be. (2001, p. 56)

Teachers working from a critical literacy perspective know that literacy isn't apolitical, and they know that curriculum and pedagogy aren't neutral, either (e.g., Comber & Nixon, 2001; Macedo, 1993; O'Brien, 2001; Shannon, 1999). Their work is situated in the social, cultural, and historical contexts of their students' lives, and such teachers create spaces for children's outside-of-school ways of knowing to inform and support their learning *in* school (e.g., Dyson, 2001; Vasquez). In classrooms grounded in such perspectives, children learn that texts are never neutral and that they themselves are not passive subjects. Instead, they learn to problematize both public and classroom texts, to question whose purposes are served by particular texts, and to consider how texts might be written differently from different perspectives and for different purposes (Green, 2001). As McLaren puts it, children learn to "critically read the narratives" (1993, p. 203) that are already reading them.

And, critical literacy is not just for 'older' children. Writers such as O'Brien (2001), Vasquez (2001), Dyson (2001), Comber (2001), Compton-Lilly (2004), and numerous others, have taken us inside classrooms where teachers engage young children in reading the world. Indeed, Comber "question[s] any suggestion that critical literacy is a developmental attainment rather than social practice which may be excluded or deliberately included in early literacy curriculum" (p. 92). To deny young children early critical literacy experiences by claiming 'developmental inappropriateness'—or because they 'must learn the basics first'—is to ignore the reality of children's lives and to severely underestimate young children's intellectual curiosity and courage. Doing so also ignores the notion that schools for young children might be places of personal and social transformation, by denying children and their teachers opportunities to interrogate their worlds and construct and use strategies for taking social action.

Critical literacy discourses didn't develop in a vacuum, any more than did instrumentalist literacy discourses. Rather, critical literacy discourses have developed (and are developing) as counter-narratives to the discourses that construct and perpetuate marginalization and oppression along lines of gender, race, ethnicity, class, sexual orientation, ability, language, and so on. Edelsky (1999) tells us,

> Learning to see these systems of domination requires a critical pedagogy . . . [that] examines what is taken for granted . . . and what is accepted as business-as-usual.

Further, a critical pedagogy works at figuring out where the taken-for-granted, business-as-usual came from, what it's connected to, and whose interest it serves. (pp. 14–15)

Those who teach from a critical literacy perspective aim to create spaces where children and adults might "mount a personal critique of all those issues which surround us as we live, learn and work—to help us understand, comment on and ultimately control the direction of our lives" (Withers, cited in Green, 2001, p. 7). Critical literacy practices are grounded in the notion that social justice is the purpose of education, and those who enact such practices aim to support children in constructing a range of strategies for taking action to make the world more just.

These stories of literacy practices in schools are constructed through the interpretive lenses of the discourses in which I am immersed, through my own lived experiences. It is my grandmother-educator's story that is told here; not Hannah's story, and certainly not her teacher's. They would tell different, equally valid stories of living and of literacy learning in that kindergarten classroom. In the telling, I have exposed something of who I am, who I am becoming, as grandmother / educator [above you use a hyphen to link]. And I've exposed something of the discourses I have taken up, of the discourses that speak through me (Bakhtin, 1981).

I've also learned something through telling these stories about how becoming / being a grandmother is shaping my stance as a teacher. Ayers (1998) writes that "teaching must be toward something; it must take a stand; it is either for or against" (p. xviii), and this is true, I think, for grandmothering, as well. Through telling and interpreting these stories I take a stand for the kinds of literacy experiences I want for Hannah and for all children. I take a stand for the creation of classroom spaces wherein young children and their teachers have opportunities to construct identities as active meaning makers, as social actors, able to read and take action in their multiple worlds. And, through telling stories such as the ones I've told here as part of my teaching, I might create spaces where my own students, practicing teachers and teachers-to-be, might come to value and tell their own stories, as they take stands for what they believe about young children's literacy learning and their own work as teachers.

ONE MORE STORY: LEARNING TO *REALLY* READ

The good news is that children are not passively positioned by the stories they're told, by the discourses in which they are immersed. They can, and often do, resist the positionings of master narratives, and choose to take up alternative identities, to construct alternative stories of themselves as literate people. I was reminded of this when Hannah and her family visited me in New York the summer following her kindergarten year. One afternoon I asked her to tell me about learning to read in kindergarten.

"I didn't learn to *really* read," she said. "But I *can* read books that are good."

"What are good books?" I asked.

"Like *I Went Walking* (Williams, 1990) and *Brown Bear, Brown Bear, What do you See?"* (Martin, 1992) she replied, naming books that are highly supportive texts for emergent readers because of their predictable, rhythmic language, and congruence of pictures and text.

"And what did your teacher do to help you learn to read?" I asked.

Hannah replied, "Well, she read us lots of books and at choice time I'd go to the book corner and I'd try and try to read the books she read, and I could do it pretty much."

"What about the worksheets she had you do? Did they help you learn to read?"

"Well, that's just stuff they want you to learn, matching upper and lower case letters and sounds and stuff," Hannah offered. "Reading books to us is how she taught us to *really* read."

According to Hannah, isolated skills on worksheets are "just stuff [teachers] want you to learn." Learning to read is about attending to the demonstrations of what real readers do, and then trying it out, by ourselves and with others, with supportive text. Hannah tells herself a story about learning to read that constructs for herself an identity as an active meaning maker. I wonder how long she'll tell herself that story. What identities as a literate person will she construct for herself if her subsequent classrooms fail to engage her in critically examining texts, in reading the world?

TELLING STORIES AND CREATING POSSIBILITIES

Hannah and I often end our phone conversations by telling each other, "I can't wait until I see you again." "I can't wait" conveys our eagerness, our joy in sharing each other's company. It speaks to the pleasure we find in sharing our stories and living new experiences out of which we'll craft new stories. It speaks to our desire to continue to construct the ongoing intertwined narrative of our lives. We know we will wait, that we have to wait, but our waiting is filled with the stories we tell each other over the miles and days and weeks we are apart.

But the phrase *I can't wait* has yet another meaning potential. *I can't wait* conveys a sense of urgency, the need to act *now*. I can't wait to tell stories— as a grandmother, as a teacher, as an activist for and with children. I can't wait to support Hannah and my students in the telling of their stories. Hannah and millions of other children are right now immersed in classrooms shaped by discourses that position children as technically, but not critically literate. Thousands of teachers are right now constrained by the discourses that position them as technicians, not as transformative intellectuals (Giroux, 1988; Macedo, 1993).

We can't wait to tell our stories. I wrote earlier that I chose to tell these stories because I was worried and angry. But I also chose to tell these stories because I am hopeful. Our stories are a potentially powerful form of protest, a way of naming and critiquing the reductionistic discourse of instrumentalist literacy, a discourse that marginalizes children, families and teachers. It seems, at times, that stories situated in this dominant discourse take up all the space, that there is no room for challenges to such regimes of truth (Butin, 2001). But left unchallenged, such stories become uncontested truth (Florio-Ruane, 2001). We can't wait—we must not wait—to tell our stories that challenge such truths, stories that position children and teachers as active meaning makers, able to question and challenge dominant discourses.

Bruner (1993) writes that "world making is the principal function of the mind" (p. 28). What worlds might we imagine, what alternative identities might we be able to create through our stories? What better gifts can we give and receive, as grandmothers, granddaughters, teachers, and students, than stories that help us tell ourselves and our worlds into being?

Acknowledgments: I would like to thank Catherine Compton-Lilly, Cindy Novinger, Jason Novinger, Leigh O'Brien, and Robin Umber for their critique and collaboration. I especially thank Hannah for sharing her thoughts and feelings about reading and learning to read with me—and for making me a part of her story and for being part of mine.

REFERENCES

Allington, R. (2002). Troubling times: A short historical perspective. In R. Allington (Ed.), *Big brother and the national reading curriculum: How ideology trumped evidence* (pp. 3–46). Portsmouth, NH: Heinemann.

Allington, R., & Woodside-Jiron, H. (2002). Decodable text in beginning reading: Are mandates and policy based on research? In R. Allington (Ed.), *Big brother and the national reading curriculum: How ideology trumped evidence* (pp. 195–216). Portsmouth, NH: Heinemann.

Ayers, W. (1998). Foreword. In W. Ayers, J.A. Hunt, & T. Quinn (Eds.), *Teaching for Social Justice* (pp. xvii-xxvii). New York: Teachers College Press.

Bailey, C. (2001). To speak: Problematizing of the use of personal stories in early childhood research. In J. Jipson & R. Johnson (Eds.), *Resistance and representation: Rethinking childhood education* (pp. xvii-xxvi). New York: Peter Lang.

Bakhtin, M. (1981). *The dialogic imagination.* Houston, TX: University of Texas Press.

Bredekamp, S., & Copple, B. (1997). *Developmentally appropriate practice in early childhood programs serving children birth through age 8* (Rev. ed.). Washington, D.C.: National Association for the Education of Young Children.

Britton, J. (1993). *Language and learning* (2nd ed.). Portsmouth, NH: Boynton-Cook.

Bruner, (1994). Life as narrative. In A. Dyson & C. Genishi (Eds.), *The need for story: Cultural diversity in classroom and community* (pp. 28–37). Urbana, IL: National Council of Teachers of English.

Butin, D. W. (2001). If this is resistance I would hate to see domination: Retrieving Foucault's notion of resistance within educational research. *Educational Studies, 32* (2), 157–176.

Coles, G. (2000). *Misreading reading: The bad science that hurts children.* Portsmouth, NH: Heinemann.

Comber, B. (2001). Classroom explorations in critical literacy. In H. Fehring & P. Green (Eds.), *Critical literacy: A collection of articles from the Australian Literacy Educators' Association* (pp. 90–102). Newark, DE: International Reading Association.

Comber, B., & Nixon, H. (1999). Literacy education as a site for social justice: What do our practices do? In C. Edelsky (Ed.), *Making justice our project: Teachers working toward critical whole language practice* (pp. 316–352). Urbana, IL: National Council of Teachers of English.

Compton-Lilly, C. (2004). *Confronting racism, poverty and power: Classroom strategies to change the world.* Portsmouth, NH: Heinemann.

Cunningham, J. (2002). The National Reading Panel Report [a review]. In R. Allington (Ed.), *Big brother and the national reading curriculum: How ideology trumped evidence* (pp. 49–74). Portsmouth, NH: Heinemann.

Dyson, A. H. (2001). Where are the childhoods in childhood literacy? An exploration in outer (school) space. *Journal of Early Childhood Literacy, 1* (1), 9–39.

Dyson, A. H. (1994). "I'm gonna express myself": The politics of story in the children's worlds. In A. Dyson & C. Genishi (Eds.), *The need for story: Cultural diversity in classroom and community* (pp. 155–171). Urbana, IL: National Council of Teachers of English.

Dyson, A. H., & Genishi, C. (1994). *The need for story: Cultural diversity in classroom and community.* Urbana, IL: National Council of Teachers of English.

Florio-Ruane, S. (2001). *Teacher education and the cultural imagination.* Mawah, NJ: Lawrence Erlbaum Associates.

Freire, P. (1970). *Pedagogy of the oppressed.* New York: Seabury Press.

Garan, E. (2001). What does the report of the National Reading Panel really tell us about teaching phonics? *Language Arts, 79* (1), 61–70.

Giroux, H. A. (1988). *Teachers as intellectuals: Toward a critical pedagogy of learning*. South Hadley, MA: Bergin & Garvey.

Green, P. (2001). Critical literacy revisited. In H. Fehring & P. Green (Eds.), *Critical Literacy: A Collection of articles from the Australian Literacy Educators' Association* (pp. 7–14). Newark, DE: International Reading Association.

Grieshaber, S., & Cannella, G. (2001). From identity to identities: Increasing possibilities in early childhood education. In S. Grieshaber & G. Cannella (Eds.), *Embracing identities in early childhood education: Diversity and possibilities* (pp. 3–22). New York: Teachers College Press.

King, T. (2003). *The truth about stories: A native narrative*. Toronto, ON: House of Anansi Press.

Luke, A., O'Brien, J., & Comber, B. (2001). Making community texts objects of study. In H. Fehring & P. Green (Eds.), *Critical Literacy: A Collection of articles from the Australian Literacy Educators' Association* (pp. 112–123). Newark, DE: International Reading Association.

Macedo, D. (1994). *Literacies of power: What Americans are not allowed to know*. Boulder, CO: Westview Press.

Martin Jr., B. (1992). *Brown bear, brown bear, what do you see?* Illus. E. Carle. New York: Henry Holt & Co.

O'Brien, J. (2001). Children reading critically: A local history. In B. Comber & A. Simpson (Eds.), *Negotiating critical literacies in classrooms* (pp. 37–54). Mahwah, NJ: Lawrence Erlbaum Associates.

Ryan, S., Ochsner, M., & Genishi, C. (2001). Miss Nelson is missing! Teacher sightings in research on teaching. In S. Grieshaber & G. Cannella (Eds.), *Embracing identities in early childhood education: Diversity and possibilities* (pp. 45–59). New York: Teachers College Press.

Shannon, P. (2001). *iSHOP you shop: Raising questions about reading commodities*. Portsmouth, NH: Heinemann.

Shannon, P. (1999). Sociological imagination, stories, and learning to be literate. *Theory & Research in Social Education, 27* (3), 396–407.

Taylor, D. (1997). Foreword. In L. Winston (Ed.), *Using family stories in elementary classrooms* (pp. ix–xi). Portsmouth, NH: Heinemann.

Williams, S. (1990). *I went walking*. Illus. J. Vivas. New York: Harcourt Brace.

Chapter Three

Moral Feminists:
Caring for Themselves and Others

Ann Monroe-Baillargeon

*This was our goodbye—she will now exist only in my memory. I will not
see her again or learn her story, but in my memory she remains and in my
life she guides me; I can only hope that the smiles we exchanged meant as
much to her.*

—Emma Baillargeon (December, 2004)

How is it that such a brief encounter—with a person whose name she did not
know, whose life experiences were so different from her own, and whom she
will likely never see again—touched her so deeply? Not until my daughters
Emma and Martha recently chose to write about their experiences working
with internally displaced refugees did I begin to comprehend the significance
of these events. Recently, Emma again wrote about the impact of her experiences as "opening my mind, soul, and heart to such amazing people—an [en-
counter] that continually guides and shapes who I am and the choices I make"
(January, 2005).

My daughters' reflections have in turn challenged me to consider a moment or event at a similar time in my life which has shaped me. However, in
my reflections,[1] I see a difference. These reflections of life-shaping events,
unlike my daughters', recall my futile urgency to have family members recognize me in the reciprocal relationship of caring for others. My recent
awareness of being guided by women—my mother, siblings, and teachers—
whose beliefs in "selfless acts of caring" has illuminated through these experiences what I struggled to understand years ago. The dissonance that continues to permeate my relationship with family members who encouraged
me to succumb to their ideals does not exist in my relationship with my

Martha, Ann, and Emma

teenage daughters. I contend it is in my role as mother/educator that I have nurtured our shared beliefs as "moral feminists," a term I adopted from Harriet Anderson (1992), which draws my daughters and me together, and continues to allow us to have common understandings of our experiences, ourselves, and the world around us.

My theory of moral feminism examines women's moral development as simultaneously seeking to care for themselves and others, rather than sacrificing oneself in the service of others. In particular, women as daughters, mothers and educators highlight moral development from a feminist perspective. I examine my narrative account of an experience when I was 18, and my daughters' experiences in Thailand at around that same age, to further develop my theory of young women's development of "moral feminism."

A THEORY OF MORAL FEMINISM

The theory of moral feminism I propose—considering mothers, daughters, and educators—has seldom been discussed in women's studies. However, Anderson (1992) writes of moral feminism as part of the feminist imagination in literature. Through analysis of several authors' works, Anderson supports the position that in imaginative literature, feminists' lived experiences provide truths:

Such insistence on the personal suggests that the inner life as the outer is regarded as real and true, and from there it is only a small step to seeing the psyches as the seat of a truth which is not that of objective reality (p. 213).

After proposing that truths exist in both inner and outer lives, Anderson then goes on to analyze an autobiography in which the author supports the existence of two truths, two realities:

There is the objective truth and reality of facts and external life as opposed to untruthful convention. And there is the subjective truth and reality of the inner life, which is not artistic fantasy but the truth of the 'struggling soul' (p. 213)

Through her analysis of literature, Anderson makes it possible to understand moral feminism as one of many struggles in which feminists seek to find truths in both their external and inner lives.

In her discussion of moral feminism Anderson (1992) suggests that the morality under which woman suffer (a morality thousands of years old which safeguards men from self-reproach), is made by men, and it is this limited moral system that is at fault, not the morality of the individual. Carol Gilligan, a feminist psychologist, and Anderson would agree that we must understand the moral and the psychological development of women as different from men. One such example of this difference is Gilligan's (1993) understanding of young women's moral development not as achieving separation but as nurturing connections, while Anderson understands them not as faithfully following what Gilligan (1993) refers to as a moral code, but as living generally in authenticity and frankness.

Gilligan (1982, 1993), through her work, *In a Different Voice,* expanded psychological theories of moral development by giving voice to young women who had been silenced not only by men, but by women as well. Gilligan notes that it is not enough to have something to say, you must have someone willing to listen. By listening to women's words, Gilligan validated a different voice and created a different reality by more fully understanding moral development through women's lived experiences. In so doing she has provided an opportunity for those who follow her—like me—to analyze women's stories and experiences not as compared to others but as valid in their own right; unique, powerful and informative. As Gilligan gained access to the understandings of young girls by listening to and analyzing their stories, I too listen to the voices of my daughters and draw meaning from their words. Women have illuminated our understanding of the tie between relationship and responsibility, the ethic of caring, and the importance of attachment throughout the human life cycle. It is with this understanding of women's moral development we look more closely at the relationship of caring.

Caring as defined by Nel Noddings (1996) "is a particular kind of relation between two people—a carer and a 'cared for.' It may occur in a brief episode or in a relationship over time"(p. 160). In many cases, the relationship of caring between two individuals is reciprocal allowing both parties to participate in both roles (albeit unequally as in parent-child or teacher-student relations). Noddings's theory of caring suggests that when an individual takes on the role of carer, she is motivated to consciously focus on the needs of the cared-for and are enveloped in the other's pains, needs and hopes, not her own. These two conditions precede all individual acts of caring, although subsequent actions the carer chooses to engage in may be contingent on many factors.

The cared for—the recipient of care—engages in the relationship by responding to the actions of the carer in a positive way. It is this response that not only completes the relation between the two but also provides feedback through which the carer can analyze the effects of her caring. Noddings believes these elements of caring to be "universally true" although, as she notes, the specific interactions are individually unique:

> In the moments of care, carers attend and feel their motive energy flowing toward the cared for; the cared-for makes some form of response that completes the relation. But beyond this basic description of two consciousnesses meeting in a caring relation, what actual, concrete people do varies with the situation; further, it varies across time and cultures, even across personalities and moods. This variance is indeed part of what it means to care. (p. 161)

This notion of variance that Noddings speaks of in collaboration with Gilligan's validation of women's voice and lived experiences provides support for further developing the theory of moral feminism through an analysis of the individual care experiences of young women.

Integrating the work of these three feminist theorists helps us to understand women's development as a process of seeking authenticity and frankness, through nurturing connections, while in a caring relationship. This work provides the foundation from which I will advance the discussion of young women's development of moral feminism through an examination of my experiences and that of my daughters. Just as Anderson has analyzed literature, so too will I analyze my own narrative reflections as a means of revealing my own early development of moral feminism. I purport that in analyzing my own experiences and that of my daughters I have come to understand how we as young women have, as Anderson suggests, found truths within our "struggling souls." Through our struggles to remain authentic and speak frankly we have come to acknowledge the reality within our inner and outer lives. I now see how in validating the reciprocal nature of our lived experiences in caring, we are free to acknowledge both what we have given and what we have received through these relationships. Moral feminism, the validation of caring for one's self while simultaneously caring for others, provides a theoretical understanding of the moral development of young women in caring relationships which celebrates and promotes the positive development of all.

OUR EXPERIENCES IN THAILAND

The occasion or event that precipitated an opportunity to evaluate my theory of moral feminism in my daughters and me came with our three visits to Thailand. My daughters and I had the opportunity to travel to Thailand during the summers of 2001, 2002, and 2004. Each time, I traveled to Bangkok to teach university courses to teachers at the International School, and the girls joined me toward the end of my professional commitments. Before, during and after these trips, they talked with me at length about our shared experiences as mother and daughters. I soon became aware of the depth of our conversations and the impact of these experiences and asked if I might tape record our reflections; they refused.[2] It was not until after our most recent trip that both girls elected to write about their experiences and agreed to my including their words for reflection within this chapter. It is through my analysis of their writings, and my memories of experiences at a similar age that I have come to a deeper understand as a woman, mother and educator, their development of moral feminism, and my own.

Emma (14) and Martha (13) first joined me in Bangkok, Thailand during the summer of 2001. In this first visit, the girls both volunteered to assist in a summer school program for young Asian students who were learning English as their second language.[3] In the summer of 2002 the girls again joined me as my teaching responsibilities were finishing. A former student invited the girls and me to her home in Northern Thailand and to accompany her in visiting the refugee camps as part of her work with a local Non-Government Organization (NGO).

Hot and sweaty, we traveled by pick up truck to Mae La refugee camp along the border between Thailand and Burma. Entering the camp, we were warmly greeted by several thin, scantly clothed, smiling children who are among the 40,000 people displaced from their homes in Burma, who now call Mae La home. Our two days in the refugee camps were spent delivering supplies purchased in a nearby town, singing with orphaned children and visiting simple dwellings they call home, school and church. We climbed steep muddy hills, crossed streams of water used for drinking, cooking and cleaning, and hiked deep into the woods to remote parts of the camp to assess needs for medical care and materials. Finally, exhausted, sore, and speechless, we began our journey home.

The girls were not able to return in the summer of 2003, but joined me again in summer of 2004. In this, our third trip, we came prepared to visit the refugees by bringing supplies we knew were desperately needed. In a University newsletter article that summarized our 2004 trip, I shared how we defined our purpose:

> "We did not want to go simply as visitors or tourists. Each year we look to increase our involvement both in terms of learning and service. As we planned this year's trip, we asked ourselves what we could do for the people we had come to know there" (Blakeslee, 2005, *Warner Educator*).

Inspired by a recent NGO newsletter, we urged friends and local businesses to donate school supplies that we could deliver during our trip. Thanks to generous donors, we personally delivered 150 school packs to children and paid the annual salaries of five teachers.

Our shared experiences—coming to know the lives and needs of internally displaced Burmese refugees now living in Thailand—prompted me to wonder how the girls understood their acts of caring for others, and if caring for themselves was part of the experience. It was not until they elected to write about these experiences that I had a means for analysis. How, then, have these experiences contributed to my daughters' development of moral feminism, and what implications do such experiences have for me and other mothers, daughters, and educators[4] as we explore ways and means of nurturing the development of moral feminism in others? And as a teacher educator, how might I facilitate in my students—as I have in myself and in my daughters—a deeper understanding of their own lived experiences, the experiences of others, and the reciprocal nature of these relationships?

MY MEMORIES OF LONG AGO

Experiencing with my daughters the excitement of leading them out into the world, empowering them to travel independently, exploring with them ways to give meaningfully, and to hear what these events meant to them, brought me back to this time in my life, to reflect upon my family circumstances and one event in particular that I now see as significant in developing my moral feminism. I share with you my memories:

> *"Be a life long or short, its greatness depends on what it was lived for"* is the quote by an unknown author published next to my senior picture in the 1978

Parapet: Beaumont School for Girls yearbook. I wondered then as I do now what my life has been lived for and in my eyes and the eyes of others what might be considered greatness. As a young woman and now an adult I have taken great joy in nurturing my sister Lisa. As a child, I learned to care by singing Lisa[5] to sleep at night, searching the neighborhood when she wandered from the yard, and being her supporter in the absence of my parents. As a daughter, I learned of a mothers' love as I accompanied mom to speech and hearing clinics, physical therapy appointments, and listened as she pondered the most difficult decisions of sterilization and group home living. Ann Monroe-Baillargeon (December, 2004)

It was these acts of nurturance so common in young women's moral development that defined for me how my life might be lived for others. However, they did nothing to define for me how my life might be lived for *me*. Reflecting now on these experiences, I have come to understand that one can live her life for others only while living her life for herself. It has been in my development as an adult, and as a professional educator that I have faced this challenge to care for myself while also caring for others. The first of the developmental transformations—which I painfully refer to as confrontations— occurred 27 ago:

At 18 years old, I was excitedly sending out college applications, dreaming of life beyond my family, and pursuing my dreams of becoming a teacher when my sister, 10 years older than I, interrogated, "How can you think of going away to college?" I was confused and did not know why she was questioning my endeavors. I expected that this would be a time in which my siblings would support and encourage me. I had been clear with my family of my intent to choose a college that I felt would best prepare me to teach children with significant disabilities, and no such program was offered at local colleges. I had met no resistance to these ideas until now. She went on, "Who will help mom with Lisa?" I was stunned, and had no reply. Throughout my childhood and adolescence, I had given tirelessly both emotional and physical support to my parents, especially my mother whose gendered role it was to care for Lisa. My sister seemingly decided that this was to be my lifelong vocation; I found this intolerable. Ann Monroe-Baillargeon (December, 2004)

In this brief encounter, I was challenged to envision caring for my mother and sister as separate from caring for myself. My sister had developed her morality and was expecting my moral view to be the same. I am sure she was later surprised to find that her efforts to propose shared familial expectations so that I might faithfully follow the moral code had quite a different effect. Rather than succumbing to her suggestions to remain home and go to college, I soon relocated from Ohio to Wisconsin. In these actions I found what Gilligan calls "my voice" and what Anderson refers to as an authenticity and frankness. I now know the significance of this event in my development of moral feminism and understand that it was this event which began a 27-year journey that has included becoming a wife and mother, achieving a doctoral degree in education, and legally taking on my role as Lisa's life-long advocate and guardian. Not for one moment have I ever stopped caring. My professional knowledge and skills have allowed me to accomplish for Lisa an independent lifestyle, with purpose, excitement, and security equal to my own. And in so doing, I have allowed my parents the financial and emotional freedom from Lisa's care. My parents, now in their 80s, continue to live independently. As a moral feminist, I now know that I could not care for others in the absence of caring for myself, and in pursuing my needs and dreams, I have increased my capacity to do this for others one hundred fold.

MY DAUGHTERS' WORDS

My own experiences caused me to wonder how moral feminism might be developing in my two teenage daughters, Emma and Martha. True to their adolescent nature, they ensured their confidentiality by refusing my requests to keep a journal of life events, or allowing me to interview them. I respectfully took this to include not allowing me to keep field notes on our mother-daughter conversations regarding pivotal moments in their lives. Our relationship was much more valuable to me than the opportunity to further my understandings. It was not until after our third summer in Thailand, in the fall of 2004, when Emma began writing about her experiences in college applications and Martha began her not-for-profit business, that they openly expressed their interpretations of these experiences.

Emma's Voice

The following excerpt from a scholarship essay provides a powerful representation of Emma's beliefs:

> On January 27, 1965, Dr. Martin Luther King Jr. spoke words of wisdom when he declared that "The ultimate test of a man is not where he stands in moments of comfort and the moments of convenience, but where he stands in moments of challenge and moments of controversy." Dr. King not only spoke these words but his actions defined them. With him as an example and influence, I too work to define these words in the way I speak, think and act.
>
> When faced with challenge and controversy, it is human nature to revert to instinct and our core values as a person. In general, we act as we truly are. What Dr. King said reflects contemporary realities. When measuring a person we must

measure them on their honest beliefs and actions, and who they actually are not something they pretend to be. In situations of comfort there is time to analyze what people are expecting of you, who you will offend, and what you "should" do socially speaking. This process diminishes who the person really is to who the person thinks they should be. A person should be defined by what they genuinely think, say, or do rather than on their ability to act a part that society dictates to them. Emma Baillargeon (taken from the Dr. Martin Luther King, Jr. Scholarship Essay, December 1, 2004)

In this essay, Emma speaks of Dr. King as her role model in facing challenges in moments of controversy and accompanying his word with actions. It is clear in her account that she will be asked to speak what she believes in and to act upon those beliefs, even in controversy. It is in this challenging of beliefs that she will refuse to adopt another's moral code, but instead create her own authentic code. Rejecting what one "should" do, she defines people by what they authentically think, say, or do, rather than their ability to act a part. Her notions of authenticity and frankness resonate with Anderson's analysis of moral feminism in others' literature, and her integration of beliefs and actions calls upon Noddings's notions of caring through actions. A more specific reference to the reciprocity in caring is provided in this excerpt from her application essay on a topic of her choice[6]:

Our days are defined by relationships with our neighbors, whether they are neighbors in family, work, play, or passing. These relationships, crucial to our society, require cooperation achieved through understanding. Sometimes it takes accepting differences in people to realize our similarities.

Looking into the eyes of a young Karen[7] girl, orphaned by war and persecution, living in a Thai refugee camp made the existence and strength of such similarities clear to me. As I spent the day singing songs with the children and delivering supplies this girl commanded my attention. She was about my age, fifteen at the time, and though language barriers prevented our speaking our eyes and hearts spoke for us. Looking at this Karen girl, I saw myself in her eyes. I could not begin to imagine the struggles life served her; yet I knew that she had hopes and dreams of health, success, love, joy, and security. In these dreams we were the same, in these dreams all people are the same. As a people we need to be loved, accepted, and needed by the people around us. Leaving the orphanage, I waved to the girl and she smiled in return. This was our goodbye—she will now exist only in my memory. I will not see her again or learn her story, but in my memory she remains and in my life she guides me; I can only hope that the smiles we exchanged meant as much to her. Emma Baillargeon (taken from the common application personal statement, November, 2004)

In this essay, Emma confirms what Gilligan (1982/1993) describes as young girls' moral development being accomplished through nurturing relationships, not separation. She powerfully portrays the connection she feels with this young girl as an opportunity to see herself in what she describes as shared hopes and dreams. In support of Noddings's (1996) theory of caring, she describes her conscious focus on this young girls needs and hopes, and is motivated to wave, a gesture of caring, and receives a smile in return. Similar to my own experiences, she recalls a powerful moment in her development of moral feminism; however, hers is different in that she readily identifies herself in this reciprocal relationship of caring. In her final essay, she goes on to describe how she envisions her life's work:

> *My plan is to foster a future in which I can solve problems, help people, challenge myself, and be happy through a career in Biomedical Engineering. My experiences working and living with people affected by mental and physical disabilities also fuel my passion for such a field as Biomedical Engineering because I am drawn to its capacity to improve people's quality of life. I have seen my share of suffering and am and driven to make a difference—life is good, it should be enjoyed.* Emma Baillargeon (taken from the Boston application essay on engineering November, 2004).

Lived experiences have shaped her beliefs as a moral feminist as she pursues in her life a career of caring in which she finds happiness in challenging herself to improve people's quality of life. In seeking her own happiness through her career goals, she includes herself when she speaks about enjoying life.

Martha's Voice

Martha (16) recently wrote of her experiences in Thailand in her application for admission to the National Honor Society and her business plan to create a not-for-profit organization she named *Global Advocates*. In both documents, Martha specifically identifies caring as a central element. In her self deposition she states, "throughout all of my activities and responsibilities I work to exhibit respect . . ., caring, and concern for others." She uses caring to describe her own character as well as what clients will find in her organization: "a strong and significant connection with a caring and compassionate organization that is always willing and eager to support small international organizations." As with Emma's words, the following excerpts provide a representation of how experiences have shaped Martha's beliefs:

> *I earn respect. I strive to obtain significant positions within school and my community that allow me to express myself and influence others, simultaneously. I demonstrate positive Leadership throughout all of my obligations and activities. However, leadership should never be used as a means to achieve power and au-*

thority. A leadership position can only be reached by earning the respect and support of those who surround you. Authority is not characterized by receiving power, but by influencing others, while supporting positive change. Martha Baillargeon (excerpt from National Honor Society essay, December 20, 2004)

Martha's passionate words embody and add to Anderson's self-truth (1992), Gilligan's feminist, moral voice (1982/1993), and Noddings's (1996) reciprocity of care, all characteristics of moral feminism. In her opening words and later in her essay she describes respect and support, necessary in leadership roles, as earned through relationships with others not achieved in isolation. Her use of the word *simultaneously* describes her on-going relationship with others and the dual outcomes of self expression and influence. Martha powerfully articulates her goal to achieve a significant position in a leadership role achieved only through a reciprocal relationship resulting in positive change. In the two excerpts that follow, she provides in greater detail her leadership plan through her creation of *Global Advocates*:

Global Advocates is a non-profit, sole-proprietorship Non-government organization (NGO), which works to support existing small international organizations by increasing awareness and support simultaneously. This is done by connecting these organizations with the supportive community of Rochester, NY through the administration of events, fundraisers, and services. Global Advocates works to increase awareness along with support by creating events that allow the volunteers and donors to understand where their support is going and how it is being used. At all major events or fundraisers, a presentation will be made about Global Advocates and the international organizations. Martha Baillargeon (excerpt from Global Advocates business plan, November, 2004)

Sprinkled throughout this mission statement are multiple relationships that, as creator and leader of this organization Martha hopes to facilitate. The caring which she envisions benefits both the carer and the cared for, through *simultaneously increasing support and awareness.* Through her lived experiences provided for and influenced by me—her moral feminist mother/educator—Martha, too, has come to position herself as both the carer and the cared for in her relationships and the relationships she facilitate for others. In so doing she has, in her development as a young woman, adopted her *own* moral feminism and has embarked on her journey as educator through the sharing of her story, and the stories of those she meets. In her final words she ties it all together:

The creation and directing of this organization embodies my dreams to make a difference and as a result change the world in a small way. Ever since I took my first trip to the refugee camps in Thailand, my eyes were opened and I knew that

I had to do something. With your support my dreams and hopes are blossoming into reality. Thank you for helping me [to] help the world. Martha Baillargeon (excerpt from Global Advocates business plan, December 2, 2004)

Nurtured and supported in her development as a moral feminist, Martha, like Emma, has spoken and been listened to, allowed what she has experienced to influence her, and has envisioned future endeavors in which she too is cared for while caring for others.

CONCLUSION AND IMPLICATIONS

As I return briefly to my memories, and the quote that accompanies my senior yearbook picture, I have a much clearer understanding of what makes a life "great." As I move on in my life as a daughter, mother, and educator, I have come to know myself as a moral feminist and adapt the original quotation, claiming as my own: "Be a life long or short, its greatness depends on caring for oneself and others"—Ann Monroe-Baillargeon (February, 2005).

As have feminist theorists including Harriet Anderson, Carol Gilligan, and Nel Noddings, I have used feminist, qualitative research methodologies to analyze the lived experiences, narrative texts, and girls' "voices" through my reflections and the writings of my daughters. A theory of moral feminism which draws from feminist theories of moral development and caring relies primarily on the lived experiences and voices of young girls and women. This analysis allows for an understanding of how lived experiences in caring help to shape the moral development of those who participate. The further development of the theoretical understanding of moral feminism requires continued analysis of women's experiences specifically in care relationships. As we continue to interrogate women's lived lives, our understandings of this complex theory will evolve. This work offers implications for the lives of daughters, mothers, and educators.

Confirmed through this work is an understanding of the intersection between women's personal and professional lives. As daughters, mothers and educators, we play a significant role in providing for and engaging in these experiences with our daughters and students. I am encouraged to explore the ways in which I provide such opportunities for young women, specifically my students in teaching professions. I am compelled to ask, how do I facilitate in my students a deeper understanding of their own lived experiences, the experiences of others, and the reciprocal nature of these relationships? In their experiences in teaching, an analysis of the relationships of teacher and student, student and student, and teacher and parent will provide great insights. Giving voice to my lived experiences and those of my daughters through these reflections and critical analyses has been essential to furthering the theoretical understanding of moral feminism. My wish, as an educator, is that through this reading you may be encouraged to do the same. Best wishes in your endeavors.

NOTES

1. These reflections come 27 years after the actual event and are filtered through 27 years of life experiences and knowledge. I know now what I could not know then.

2. During their adolescence, I have been fortunate that my daughters continue to share with me their feelings and thoughts. However, this seldom happens in a face to face conversation, but rather "on the fly." As though they are unable to speak reflectively when looking at me directly, they often speak most openly with me when we are in planes, trains or automobiles, and even more often, when on the phone.

3. At the time, the girls spoke of how pleased they were that the young children were so willing to work with someone they did not know and trust. Whatever hesitations they had in working with children different from themselves were quickly forgotten as they recalled how "easy" it was to get to know the children, and how eager they were to practice their English with a native English speaker. They had fun. I believe the children's unconditional acceptance offered what Nel Noddings refers to as an affirmation of their caring. It was in these early positive interactions between carer and caree from which the girls became open to other opportunities to care.

4. "Educate" comes from the Latin word *educere* meaning to lead forth. How might we as mother/educators lead forth our daughters and others we seek to educate into the world?

5. Lisa is three years younger than I, the last of eight children. At her birth, Lisa was diagnosed with severe mental retardation and was not expected to survive, much less live a healthy and happy life long into adulthood. Lisa is now 42 years old and living independently with supports.

6. On the common application, Emma had six choices of personal statement topics from which to choose. I confirmed with her that this essay was topic #6, a topic of her choice. She explained she chose this option because it allowed her "more freedom." She elaborated: "What I was thinking was that they might be expecting students to write about diversity, and expected diversity to be defined as difference. I wanted to write about our similarities amidst our diversity and found this choice topic did not confine me."

7. Karen people, an ethnic minority group, constitute approximately seven percent of Burma's 42 million occupants. Since 1988 the actions of a violent military regime have resulted in well over one million internally displaced persons and additional millions of refugees and economic migrants fleeing to neighboring Thailand, India, and Bangladesh. Thailand alone houses over two million Burmese, with only a fraction allowed into refugee camps. As long as this regime remains in power, it is unlikely that refugees can return to Burma and live in safety and dignity (http://www.refugeesinternational.org).

REFERENCES

Anderson, H. (1992). *Utopian feminism: Women's movements in fin-de-siecle Vienna.* New Haven, CT: Yale University Press

Belenkey, M., Clinchy, B., Goldberger, N. & Tarule, J. (1997). *Women's ways of knowing: The development of self, voice and mind.* New York: Basic Books

Blakeslee, P. (In press). *The Warner Educator.* Rochester, NY: University of Rochester,Warner Graduate School.

Gilligan, C. (1982/1993). *In a different voice: Psychological theory and women's development.* Cambridge, MA: Harvard University Press.

Noddings, N. (1996). The caring professional. In S. Gordon, P. Benner, & N. Noddings, (Eds.), *Caregiving: Readings in knowledge, practice, ethics and politics* (pp. 160–172). Philadelphia, PA: University of Pennsylvania Press

Orr, D. (2000). *Mothers as moral educators: Teaching language and nurturing souls.* In A. O'Reilly & S. Abbey (Eds.), *Mothers and daughters: Connection, empowerment, and transformation* (pp. 161-173). Lanham, MD: Rowan & Littlefield.

Chapter Four

Stories I Tell My Daughter

Suzanne Lamorey

I chose to become a single adoptive mother at age 41 and I received my infant daughter, Maggie, from India. Twelve years later, my daughter and I are preparing to receive a baby boy from Guatemala. In preparing for the coming little brother, my "tweener-aged" daughter reminded me to be sure to tell him all of the "Jimmy and Poppa" stories, "Naughty Grammy" stories, and the series of "Baby Momma" stories that I told her (over and over) as she was growing up. In retrospect, I fondly think back on those spur-of-the-moment stories told during road trips and holidays when my parents, Maggie, and I were all together. Those were times before my father died and before my daughter began migrating towards the world of peers, spending less time in my world and the world of family.

I have taken this opportunity to reflect upon role of those family stories and the meanings of those stories that I was communicating to my daughter. I think that perhaps these family stories have been particularly important to my daughter and me as the two of us comprised a unique little family building a life geographically distant from grandparents, aunts, uncles, and cousins. And I think these stories provided something important for my daughter as she struggled to find her own meanings as an Indian-American single child growing up without a father and with an older Anglo-American mother (i.e., very different from the families of her friends as well as the stories of families portrayed in books and media).

My daughter has always hungered to hear the "growing up stories" about my parents, my grandmothers, and me. (I wasn't close enough to my grandfathers to include them in my family stories.) These stories have evolved as a mix of fiction and non-fiction, and for the most part are situated in geographic

Maggie and Suzanne

locales in and around San Francisco where my parents grew up and where I spent summers as a child. They began as descriptions about the typical activities of families that encompass accidents, successes, and mistakes in school, play, and work, and feature pets, friends, and family relationships. Initially for me, the stories functioned as pacifiers on long trips and served as treats prized more by my daughter than candy or money.

Now I am aware of them as providing a sense of a heritage of some kind between a white, Anglo, mid-life adoptive mother, ghosts of important memories of childhoods re-interpreted, an emerging sense of family and family values, and an East Indian baby-girl's developing sense of self. For my daughter and me, this is our Motherline. It is a connection and communication that spans generations, distance, time, and cultures. When our immediate family is mother and daughter, and visits with extended family require a five-hour plane trip, our Motherline stories have become the virtual family scrapbook. I think of these stories as a scrapbook of what I wanted to explain to my daughter about the journey to come into one's own identity and about the extended family she knows only as adults and senior citizens. It is a "living" scrapbook (or for this generation of children a "living video"). It includes many of my own semi-biographical stories about a mean 5th grade teacher, getting stuck under the house, or shoplifting a roll of Lifesavers (my first and last offense of its type). It includes my semi-fictional depiction of my mother as risk-taking run-a-way on a bicycle and a struggling child of the Depression. It is my fictional depiction of my father (now deceased) as a vital and active boy with a make-believe life rescuing zoo animals, witnessing bank robbers, and getting lost late Halloween night in Golden Gate Park.

Over time, the stories began to be Maggie's stories, too, as some of her questions about right, wrong, and accidental might begin with her saying to me, "Remember when you were a little girl in Grammy's old house, and you accidentally rolled the car down the street? Tell me about what happened afterwards." Our shared family stories could be interpreted as the Lamorey Family Book of Virtues that explains our version of the whys and wherefores of appropriate behaviors and favorable outcomes. In this way our stories are ways to communicate the importance of the good effort, how hard work and perseverance can pay off, how parents have been less-than-perfect children, the value of being and having good friends, how fears can be overcome even in the dark, and in general how to survive growing up.

My stories were not planned morality plays or lessons to the wise. They were serendipitous. At the time I told them, I don't remember that the stories had a certain moral point to communicate, but of course they did. As my daughter undertakes to launch herself into adolescence, and as I undertake the journey of starting to "grow another child," I appreciate the opportunity to explore what it is that I have been saying in my stories. What have I been telling my daughter; what have I been teaching her? What are the stories that mothers tell their daughters? What do they mean? Who is our own Little Red Riding Hood? Who is our personal Cinderella? What themes did I find important to tell about, and what themes did she value and subsequently ask to hear over and over? Who and what am I asking or advocating my daughter to become?

THEORY AND RESEARCH ABOUT
FAMILY STORIES AND THEIR MAKING

In seeking to make sense of the stories that have meant so much to my daughter and me, I found that family narratives and their analysis comprise an evolving research literature (e.g., Fiese & Bickham, 2004). For example, the use and meaning of family stories have been analyzed in cultural contexts of East and West (Wang, 2001), in understanding individual identity development (McAdams, 2001), as a measure of marital satisfaction (Oppenheim, Wamboldt, Gavin, Renouf, & Emde, 1996), as a reflection of family satisfaction (Vangelisti, Crumley & Baker, 1999), and a means of the transmission of family values (Kandell, 1996; Norris, Kuiack, & Pratt, 2004).

According to Reiss (1989), families tell narrative stories in order to make meaning out of the social world. Black (1991) investigated the role of family stories through analysis of the functions of family stories as well as the topics of those stories. Her analysis of family story interviews indicated that there were six major story themes: traumatic events, births, individual roles, vacations, good deeds, and what the authors called "coupling" (how couples met and important points in their relationships). The functions of families emerged as (a) an identity in terms of who we are as a family, (b) relational maintenance relative to bonding and importance of family, and (c) family values. Family stories thus are teaching tools used to foster a sense of family identity as well as to communicate family values and beliefs to members.

Research by Fiese and Bickham (2004) has also shown the existence of content themes in parents' stories about family life. They reported themes of (a) kinship and affiliation, (b) achievement and hard work, (c) independence and autonomy, and (d) getting into trouble. The affiliation theme noted by Fiese and Bickham is similar to the theme of relational maintenance found by Black (1991), and the themes of hard work and achievement as well as independence and autonomy can be viewed as family values as articulated by Black.

Fiese, Hooker, Kotary, Schwagler, and Rimmer (1995) found that 96% of parents told stories to their children about their own childhood experiences. These authors also reported that specific themes distinguished fathers' stories and mothers' stories. Achievement themes were common for fathers, whereas mothers' stories were likely to involve affiliation themes. Chance and Fiese (1999) examined gender-stereotyped themes in family stories told by mothers and fathers. This research indicated that mothers' stories were characterized by emotional content particularly in stories directed to their daughters, while fathers' stories were more instrumental to sons as well as daughters. In this way, and perhaps not surprisingly, mothers and fathers seem to be communicating differential sets of values to sons and daughters.

THE STORIES AND THEIR MEANINGS

Our stories emerged from occasions when my parents, daughter, and I were all together. In retrospect, most stories were about my father's childhood. One example included the tales about Pinky, a little white mouse that my father never really had, but who, to my mind, added quite a bit of excitement and mischief to the imaginary life I gave my dad. A mouse was the last thing my grandmother would have allowed in her orderly house, and the juxtaposition of a controlled and careful home environment with this creature who could be a supportive friend as well as a tiny outlaw created opportunities to comment on the challenges of childhood and parenthood. In my stories, Pinky escaped at home and in school, at church, and at the mall with embarrassing results for mothers, girls in dresses, older women in the pews, and female English teachers. Although my dad would always eventually recapture Pinky, that little white puff of wildness was a force to be reckoned with, as she humorously ran rampant through different settings upsetting the adults to no end.

Some of my daughter's favorite tales were the "Jimmy and Poppa" stories. This series of foibles was fictional but based upon the characters of my dad and his best friend Jimmy. There were at least two dozen of these stories that were generally about two youngsters who needed to make some money, and in so doing were involved in harrowing adventures. Their friendship was a constant as was the mischief they invariably found themselves in. There were dog-walking stories of lost ghost dogs, stories of cowboy treasure seen buried under a park windmill, stories of bush burglars that the boys tried to capture in Sutro Forrest, a housecleaning (for pay, of course) episode that occurred during an electrical outage at crazy Mrs. Coit's tower home. There were ghostly shipwrecks off Land's End, and Boy Scout merit badges earned while sailing with old "Doc" in his un-seaworthy dinghy in San Francisco Bay. I made sure that the stories inhabited places that actually exist, that we could and did visit, to fill out the story/experience in order to make it real. And to my delight, my father developed a habit of concluding many of my Jimmy and Poppa stories with the reminder that "Now this was a true story!"

What are the implications of these stories as my daughter's (and my) favorites? I think a part of the love of these stories for me was experienced when during my father's funeral, Jimmy stood up during the open eulogy and described how my dad was always his best friend, and in a sense for me the stories came true. My father *had* been that young and *did* have that much fun and camaraderie. When I told the Jimmy and Poppa stories, perhaps I knew that my father was declining, and I wanted my daughter to have some positive memories of him. She didn't know him when he was in his prime and active days. She knew him only as an old man, a confused man sometimes. I wanted her to know this senior citizen as a vital person who had had childhood adventures that she would have liked to have shared with him. And I myself wanted to know him in this way too, particularly to remember him (and perhaps reinvent him) in a way that was humorous, brave, and "white-mouse" wild.

The stories about my mom were titled the "Naughty Grammy" stories and comprised only about four or five stories in all. These stories were about my mother as a child—a risk-taker, an explorer, and free spirit, the determined young girl who was constantly getting lost and then finding her way home again. Naughty Grammy was the character who was always venturing out around the edges of a child's life. She crossed busy streets without the assistance of adults. She climbed towering trees, and rode less-than-broken horses in Golden Gate Park. Her pets were black cats that followed her everywhere (one was named "Me Too") and would daringly hide in the warm oven during cold nights. At times, my mother emerged as a historical figure, Naughty Grammy of the Depression days, surviving hard times, with homeless men asking at the backdoor for sandwiches (which she always gave to them) and the only little girl without a dime to go to the movies. These stories had a defiant tone to them, and a strong sense of personal autonomy. Naughty Grammy broke the rules. She looked for adventure, and wasn't afraid when she found it.

In terms of themes, perhaps these stories were to emphasize that the "Lamorey women" were tough and strong in the midst of difficult circumstances. In terms of relationships, these stories were to help Maggie experience the approachable and fun-loving side of my mom and to depict my mother as an adventuresome alter-ego and amicable advocate for Maggie. What has been surprising to me is that it seems like over the years my mother has kind of become more like the young woman in stories I told about her—more outgoing, more spontaneous, and more risk-taking. Perhaps story telling gives family members a way to remember the more spirited parts of ourselves and to find them inside, and to live them out. Indeed, the stories seem to have a transactional dimension wherein the storyteller, the characters, and the "audience" can experience personal change and gain insights into self.

I also told stories about my mother's mother. Grammy Maggie was born in rural Utah, lost an eye as a child, traveled to San Francisco on the train, and made a home near Chrissy Field (my daughter's favorite place to run and play) in San Francisco's Marina District. She is the relative whom my daughter was named after. Grammy Maggie was elegant and self-made. A descendant of wagon-train pioneers, she was strong and hardworking. She dreamt of living in San Francisco, and was fearless in her journey to the big city by herself.

The Grammy Maggie stories were told more in terms of history rather than the day-to-day life stories I told about my parents. I told stories about her grandparents coming across the plains in covered wagons. I told stories of the handmade toys that Grammy and her siblings created and the dirt canals that they swam in during hot summers. There was a story of how she lost her eye and had to ride on a horse-pulled wagon to the eye doctor in a far-away town. There was the story of how she met her husband on vacation in San Francisco, and how she later invested in the stock market to make money.

Many of the attributes and experiences associated with Grammy Maggie (hard work, perseverance, trauma, poverty, and dreams accomplished) are those that I would like to have my daughter value as I do. We visited my grandmother's grave outside of Salt Lake City when my daughter was about eight or nine years old, and she brought a short autobiography about herself to leave on Grammy's gravestone—so that Grammy could get to know her, she said. Perhaps the stories did serve to connect the generations over time and the naming-after meaning created a sense of connection. Perhaps my daughter did come to know about this Grammy of mine, as she remembered that Grammy's old house was near our favorite beach in San Francisco during a recent visit there. She also asks occasionally about facts in the Grammy stories, and if Grammy really did grow up in a dusty valley and made her dreams come true in San Francisco ("Go west, young woman!").

I didn't tell many family stories specifically about Grandma Muriel (my Dad's mother) although she did function as adult backdrop throughout the Jimmy and Poppa stories. Poppa and Jimmy functioned on their own in those stories, yet Grandma was always there behind the scenes ready to rescue the boys should they need help. In these stories, she was the adult who would leave the house to go grocery shopping, yet, upon her return home in the evening, was non-judgmental when finding furniture legs trimmed, evidence of small chemical fires, or impressions of skateboards that had raced down the carpeted stairway to the garage. Married to a travelling salesman, Grandma was a single mother of sorts, a somewhat gullible yet wise character in an apron who kept a home up and running. I think her role was to show acceptance of children's search for adventure and autonomy. She celebrated Poppa and Jimmy's cleverness and rewarded their quixotical efforts with the smell of baked cookies and a hug.

As I recall, I told very few family stories about myself. Those that I told were specifically about my doing something embarrassing and self-effacingly humorous, and were told to quickly counteract some particular disaster or problem that had come up for my daughter. They were along the lines of embarrassing first dates, dropped flyballs, burned dinners, lost glasses, frightening dogs, ripped pants, teacher misunderstandings, lost homework, and tummy aches during school exams. In general, these were stories that were comedic, commonplace, and meant to take the burn out of something not going well for my daughter. They were vignettes about everyday difficulties and fears that were ultimately survive-able, although perhaps not immediately survive-able in the eyes of a 5th or 6th grade girl. They were meant to release tears and relieve tensions, and put a smile onto the face of someone I love dearly.

CONCLUSION

In understanding these family stories and their meanings, there are at least two perspectives that seem appropriate to use. One perspective is illustrated in Fiese's work which details the role of family stories as providing family meanings about (a) personal identity, (b) belonging and affiliation, (c) relationships, and (d) beliefs and values. From this perspective we approach family stories as a means to understand who we are and from whom we came. The second perspective includes the agenda and motivation of the storyteller. These two perspectives will be discussed in an effort to understand and summarize the uses of family stories.

According to Fiese, Sameroff, Grotevant, Wambolt, Dickstein, and Fravel (2001), the content, themes, and connections among the stories told by family members reflect the views of the family. These views include values, truths, lessons, relationships, identities, and meanings that are specific to each family group. Oral histories have been used to provide instructive lessons in life as well as provide a sense of order and meaning to the world and times occupied by the group, tribe, village, or congregation. As spiritual elders and community leaders repeat the stories of how to live the "right kind" of life to new generations, so do families as fathers and mothers choose different stories to tell their sons and daughters about their roles in a social and cultural sense. The stories I tell my daughter fit into this framework of the roles of stories. My stories function to communicate family values, self-identity, family truths, and meanings to my daughter, particularly in the absence of on-site relatives and siblings.

The second perspective in which to understand family stories is to understand the storyteller. The storyteller is the meaning maker. I felt that it was my job to stitch together attributes of my daughter with attributes of her adopted family members in order to create more and deeper layers of belonging. I wanted to create some sense of shared "history," and to story about how we all overlap in our identities, values, and care, even when we do not know each other or have not met each other. I created a backdrop of personalities who would have loved her had they lived to know her.

I also desired to address issues of gender limitations of the media and other cultural sources that suggest to children "who it is okay to be." The emphasis upon strong and resilient women in the family stories serves to send a repeated message of female power and bravery. Furthermore, I attempted to create a sense of children as adventure-seekers, fearless and resourceful in their dealings with wildness (dogs, tigers, ghosts, storms, robbers). In this way I sought to promote child resilience in the face of violence, wars, and crime that children are exposed to in contemporary times.

In my reflections on family stories, I have decided to create a new series of stories for the new baby boy we have recently adopted. My daughter and I will journey to Guatemala to receive this new little brother later this summer when he is about eight months old. The new series of stories will be the Big Sister stories and will be all about the adventures of a sister 12 years his senior, who rode not-yet-broken horses, captured escaped tigers at the zoo, crossed streets without an adult, raised a mischievous mouse named Pinky, survived mean 5th grade teachers, and sometimes got tummy aches during school exams.

REFERENCES

Black, M. (1991). A phenomenological case of study of family stories and the relationship to identity. *Dissertation Abstracts International, 51* (12-B, Pt1), 6139–6140.

Chance, C., & Fiese, B. (1999). Gender-stereotyped lessons about emotion in family narratives. *Narrative Inquiry, 9* (20), 243–255.

Fiese, B., & Bickham, N. (2004). Pin-curling grandpa's hair in the comfy chair: Parents' stories of growing up and potential links to socialization in the preschool years. In B. Fiese & M. Pratt (Eds.), *Family stories and the life course: Across time and generation* (pp. 259–277). Mahwah, New Jersey: Lawrence Erlbaum Associates.

Fiese, B., Hooker, K., Schwagler, J., & Rimmer, M. (1995). Family stories in the early stages of parenthood. *Journal of Marriage and the Family, 57,* 763–770.

Kandell, S. L. (1996). Grandparents' tales: Stories our children need to hear. *Dissertations Abstract International-Section A: Humanities and Social Sciences, 57* (1-A), 0028.

McAdams, D. P. (2001). The psychology of life stories. *Review of General Psychology, 5* (2), 100–122.

Norris, J. E., Kuiack, S., & Pratt, M. W. (2004). "As long as they go back down the driveway at the end of the day": Stories of the satisfactions and challenges of grandparenthood. In B. Fiese & M. Pratt (Eds.), *Family stories and the life course: Across time and generation* (pp. 353–373). Mahwah, New Jersey: Lawrence Erlbaum Associates.

Oppenheim, D., Wambolt, F. S., Gavin, L.A., Renouf, A.G., & Emde, R. N. (1996). Couples' co-construction of the story of their child's birth: Associations with marital adaptation. *Journal of Narrative and Life History, 6,* 1–21.

Reiss, D. (1989). The practicing and representing family. In A. J. Sameroff & R. Emde (Eds.), *Relationship disturbances in early childhood* (pp. 191–220). New York: Basic Books.

Fiese, B. H., Sameroff, A. J., Grotevant, H. D., Wambolt, F. S., Dickstein, S., & Fravel, D. L. (2001). Observing families through the stories they tell: A multidimensional approach. In K. Lindahl & P. Kerig (Eds.), *Family observational coding systems: Resources for systemic research* (pp. 259–271). Mahwah, New Jersey: Lawrence Erlbaum Associates.

Vangelisti, A., Crumley, L., & Baker, J. (1999). Family portraits: Stories as standards for family relationships. *Journal of Social and Personal Relationships, 16,* 335–368.

Wang, Q. (2001). "Did you have fun?" American and Chinese mother-child conversations about shared emotional experiences. *Cognitive Development, 16,* 693–715.

THE IMPACTS OF ACADEME ON TWO GENERATIONS OF WOMEN

Emilie and Mimi

Chapter Five

Cultural Histories and Multi-generational Tales: The Power of Stories by Mothers and Their Daughters

Emilie Bloch Sondel and Marianne Nieman Bloch

What generally happens when we tell a story from our own life is that we increase our working knowledge of ourselves because we discover deeper meaning in our lives through the process of reflecting and putting the events, experiences, and feelings that we have lived into oral expression. It has always been this way. That may be why we have a need to make our lives coherent, understandable, and meaningful. Telling the story of our lives is so basic to our nature that we are largely unaware of its importance.

—Atkinson, 1998, p. 1

WHO ARE "WE"?

We are daughter and mother. We are both Euro-American females, middle class, English speaking, both with graduate degrees (though in different fields), married, and heterosexual. In general, and specifically in our jobs, we share an interest in anthropology, psychology, education, and working with others. One of us, Marianne—hereafter known as Mimi—Bloch, has had two children: Ben, age 31, and Emilie, age 26, while the other, Mimi's daughter, Emilie, expects to some day be a mother herself. We are not the same as each other in many other ways, 'though we share a bond of love, history, educational background and interests, and a sense of continued, hopefully positive, long-term relationships. We've been asked to share the experience of writing about the *Motherline* which we interpret as an invitation to talk to each other (and others) about our own lives together—situated as they are within particular cultural and historical contexts.

AUTOBIOGRAPHY, PERSONAL NARRATIVES, AND MOTHERS AND DAUGHTERS AND THEIR EDUCATION

What knowledge might be important to tell? Which stories about our lives make "sense"? What is too intimate to tell? What is too mundane, and only important to "us"? Having never written together before, we have chosen to orient our own stories in the framing of narratives as complex representations of our "selves" and others, with several ways of telling our own stories, and multiple interpretative lenses making sense of the stories that are told. These include, in this case, Emilie Bloch Sondel's and Mimi Bloch's own sense of their stories, as well as the sense made of these stories by each other and the reader(s).

The idea of writing publicly about our intimate, private lives and experiences is not only unusual for us, but also difficult to interpret in terms of what is important to tell. In addition, we are still governed by the discourses of modern thinking and science as objective and impersonal, *and without emotion*, although we certainly try to open up new ways of reasoning as our stories certainly embody subjectivity and emotion.

What counts as valuable knowledge, or important knowledge, as we perceive the "audience" for these stories also has affected what we think we might say, and what seems unimportant, except to us. But several recently published edited volumes reinforce the worth of personal stories in reconstructing the "subject" of mothering, education, and stories of child-rearing (e.g., Hauser and Jipson's (1998) *Intersections: Feminisms and early childhoods,* Mutua and Swadener's (2004) *Decolonizing cross-cultural research: Critical personal narratives,* and David's (2003) *Personal and political: Feminisms, sociology and family issues;* also see, Apple & Golden, 1997 for a broader literature.) It is from this perspective, and with the experience of telling stories that we venture forward. We hope that this time by writing together, we can choose things that make sense to others and we can respond and interact with each other, rather than the story of parenting being one-sided (see Bloch, 1998, for the first, one-sided example of personal story-telling about childrearing).

The experiment of writing together for the first time—the fun of it. Despite the public nature of our family stories here, we are interested in the experience of writing together, and finding out how well we can do this thing called collaborative story-telling. The following writing is experimental for us; we hope a beginning, not an ending of our work and writing together.

A DIALOGUE ABOUT SELECTED
CHILDHOOD/PARENTHOOD MEMORIES

Written by Emilie:

Mothering a daughter—and being a daughter of a mother. In thinking about the "motherline," I focus on the idea of examining "how mothering a daughter or daughters impacts women educators' beliefs and practices" (O'Brien & Swadener, from the Introduction to this volume). As a co-author with my mother, I feel somewhat confused by this idea, as I cannot tell how mothering me has impacted my mother's beliefs and practices—at least not without writing a chapter with her! My take on this concept is that I am a daughter of a mother who is a professor of education, and it is helpful, at least to me, but hopefully to others, as I begin my own life and career in counseling psychology to understand or make meaning of my experiences in this role of "daughter." I also hope this will help us—my mother and me—make meaning of our joint experiences as mother-daughter. How have we taught each other different "ways of being"?

It may be important for me to outline how I view my mother. To me, she is a teacher, a feminist, a culturally sensitive human, and an observer/researcher of human behavior and learning. These are all self-made traits that she seems to have reached through years of experience and pursuit of unanswered questions. All my life I've seen my mother battle gender stereotypes and go above and beyond what is expected of her. Now, these are just my observations, so she may disagree.

Something that stands out to me about what this book is meant to illustrate is the power of stories. I realize that my mother uses stories often in her qualitative research and teaching methods. In the past, she has attempted to have her subject(s), the "other," provide her with an inside look into the group, culture, or institution that she was studying. Through my experiences, I have also learned the value of using stories, and have now begun my career in counseling psychology where storytelling is one of the most critical aspects of my work. Many of the stories of my mother's life have also become some of the teachings of my life. I will attempt to tell a few of the more important stories here to illustrate the power and weight of how mother/daughter stories are interconnected.

Memories of growing up: Education in and out of school, or cross-generational education in my family. I grew up in a family that valued education. This is partly due to the fact that both of my parents are professors, but also due to the strong cultural and multi-generational value in education as a form of success that I learned very early and consistently while growing up.

My great-grandfather on my mother's side of the family, Max Kalin, immigrated to America from Lithuania in order to escape the persecution of the Russian Army. Because he was a Jew, he was not allowed to finish even his elementary school education. Once he got to America and had a family, he decided that all of his five children, including his three daughters (one, my maternal grandmother) were going to be well educated and go to college. Even though this was during the depression, it was still incredibly important to him. It was not a time that many women went to universities. However, my maternal great-grandfather, who had been denied this "right," thought this was very important. In the end, all five of his children, including three daughters, completed a university degree, with my grandmother receiving an education degree from the Pennsylvania State University in 1933.

On my father's side, formal and higher education were clearly also important. My grandmother and grandfather were born in Germany in the early 20th century and were both forced to immigrate to the United States in the mid- to late-1930s. They were fortunate in being able to bring out all their parents, sisters, and brothers by 1940. Despite the time, and the discrimination against Jewish people finishing their schooling in the 1930s, my grandmother had still completed high school and one year of University before she immigrated to the United States. She was lucky that she had learned English in her language courses in high school in Germany and that she had supportive relatives in the U.S. ready to help her immigrate and find a job in refugee services in New York city. My paternal grandfather was forbidden to continue his studies in physical chemistry in 1936 in Munich, and moved to Switzerland where he received a Master's degree before being told he could not continue into a doctoral program there. Through his perseverance, and with luck, he was able to immigrate to the U.S. where he completed a doctorate in biochemistry at Columbia.

Clearly the valuing of education and schooling was something I learned as a child from both sides of my family. I think the stories of my great-grandparents as well as the stories of my grandparents are retold time and again so that my family will not forget where we have come from and how we got to where we are now. These stories echo in my mind as I make decisions about my next directions (both personal and professional).

The lessons I have learned from these stories are sometimes a problem, as well as a gift, in that pressure to become highly educated, as well as to achieve has surrounded me since birth. It was a gift that I have realized not all people were "given," while, at the same time, it was also a pressure to succeed that not all people feel from their families. As I have just completed my own work in a graduate program in counseling psychology, these two "influences"—the pressure toward more education, and the gift of support toward that end—have become even more apparent to me.

My mother. My mother grew up in a different time than I did; she was born in 1946, while I was born in 1978. My mother grew up in a family and at a time when, much like for her mother, she and her two sisters were expected to go to college. My mother, like her mother before her, graduated from the Pennsylvania State University, in the same town (State College, Pennsylvania) where her own mother, aunts and uncles had grown up, gone to college, and still lived. Then she moved away, first to Washington, D.C., where she met my father; eventually she (they) went to northern California for graduate school in child development and early childhood education (my father in economics). A generation later, she took me to visit colleges in California and I fell in love with the University of California at Santa Cruz where I decided to do a bachelor's degree in psychology and child development, with a cross-cultural emphasis.

Written by Mimi:

My daughter. Reading how Emilie sees her father's and my own family history as one of educational success as well as pressure, I am struck by ways in which our stories coincide, and also feel intrigued as one person's understanding of her context is reinterpreted and experienced in a very different way during another generation, in another context.

I love reading her written stories above. For the first time, I can see how she thinks about some of the implicit/explicit supports and pressures she's had, and how she's willing to discuss these things more publicly as a daughter and as a professional counselor whose training has taught her to be able to use her life experiences (and others') as an important part of her work. It's interesting to me to see how she is integrating her different family influences, and her undergraduate, cross-cultural, and graduate education. Yet at the same time, I feel it is still my daughter, whom I love dearly and would never intentionally hurt, telling me that she grew up in a relatively pressured environment, one that I helped to create. She is also suggesting that we are still dealing with how to appropriately balance, support, help, and, the most difficult thing for me, let go. I am beginning to realize that, in addition to recognizing her strength, beauty, independence, and creativity, I also need to understand that she has the ability to make her own decisions, and to stumble through mistakes as I have done, and to enjoy her own successes.

My own mother asked me more than once: "Why do you ask for advice if you never take it?" My daughter has this right—to ask for counsel and support, and also make her own decisions. While this "lesson" seems trite, it is a challenge for me to follow. Many times I try to remember that my own mother learned *not* to stop me from trying new, sometimes risky, and somewhat "abnormal" (for their time and place) adventures, including my trips for work to Africa with my two young children, after graduate school. As I try to remember my mother and my father as parents, I think they knew more about how to be quiet—to let go, to accept that I would have to live and learn on my own. Or perhaps they had little choice, as I do in my turn as a parent/mother.

My life, growing up. When I was growing up in Pennsylvania, I knew that it was important that my sisters and I were "well educated" and did well in school. Having seen Emilie and my son Ben struggle at times with these expectations, I understand that my own educational expectations and the history of our families' (my husband's as well as my own) academic achievements have made it difficult at times for my children to feel they have had all the choices open to them that they might have wanted.

Gender was important in my family of origin, as gender has been important in the raising of my own two children. I was the middle child in a family of three girls, while Emilie was my first daughter, as well as the second and last child. My family joked about my father's reaction to having three girls and no sons. The story was that when my father gave up on having a son, he started to treat all of his daughters as though we were "boys" who could achieve anything we tried. In my memory of him, he always believed in our abilities, and thought we would do well in school. Was this because he only had daughters and no sons? What would have happened had there been a son? I will never know.

Socioeconomic class, social networks, and cultural capital were also important, and they are for my children, too. When I went to high school, I was oblivious to the fact that I was in the college track. Only later did I realize that not everyone in central Pennsylvania in the early 1960s completed high school. Indeed, as State College is in a fairly rural area of Pennsylvania (a part of Appalachia), many did not go on to college. In high school in the early 1960s, I was part of a male/female peer group of students almost all of whom went on to college, many across the nation. I assumed I would go on to college and, in some ways, was living in a "bubble" (State College is nicknamed "happy valley" for a reason). I overlooked what was happening around the world, and I didn't question why many people had fewer "home advantages" than I had (see Lareau, 2000). As I look at Emilie's and Ben's childhoods, and as I've worked with many students who have less opportunity to go on to college and university than I had, I realize more and more that there were good and bad aspects to my life in that bubble, and I've tried to help my children have more awareness of the inequalities in the world than I had growing up.

But there were other factors that affected me as I moved into college and later into graduate school and a career. My high school bubble deflated when, during my senior year in high school, my father very suddenly passed away.

The shock of a sudden pin prick (or more) to my bubble is still painful forty years later. The shock waves also reached my children in a variety of ways which I can see more clearly after reading Emilie's story relating the pressures she's felt from all of us in growing up, thinking about careers, marriage, and how to start and balance her own marriage and career.

After my father died, I went to Penn State in my home town largely because it was more affordable than other colleges. I majored in psychology and math, but I also wanted to travel, and I went to France in my junior year for a study-abroad experience. My interest in traveling, and my curiosity about other people and places may have influenced both of my children, perhaps Emilie more than Ben. Her interest in cross-cultural work with children and adults comes from many things, but no doubt in part from her father's and my own international traveling and work, first in France, and after graduate school, through our work and living in West Africa.

Marriage, family, and careers. Because I'd seen my mother struggle economically after my father's death, and in contrast to many other women graduating from university in the mid-to-late 1960s, I felt it was important to have an independent career. I wanted to work and then go on to a graduate program. I wanted to be prepared to take care of myself economically. I also felt that if I got married, which many of my friends were doing immediately after college, I would never continue with graduate school or have the possibility for a "career." This had been a lesson from my mother's experience when my father died; this was also a lesson of the late 1960s second wave of feminism.

However, when I graduated from college, I'd had little other preparation for any career except my degrees, and perhaps getting married and having a family. Despite positioning my identity as one who should be a "high achiever" in school and college, I also felt that I was a young woman, and to be "normal" (i.e., similar to peers, living up to my perceptions of what my family assumed young women out of college would do), I was expected to get married. Indeed, as I took my first job in Washington, D.C., in the summer of 1968 at the U.S. Census Bureau as a "mathematical statistician" (a low-level but "professional" civil service position), I felt there was a black hole in front of me that I needed to fill in some way—marriage, job, graduate school; I wasn't sure what.

Some other reflections about Emilie and me. As Emilie has described her perceptions of our families' background and orientation toward school achievement, I recognize that there was little else I knew to do as a mother than to repeat some of the familial patterns toward school achievement that I learned. Yet, I know that I deviated from the normal pathways for girls and young women as I was growing up. I certainly hope that I have provided some support for Emilie to do the same.

I learned to reflect more on these influences, however, only by listening to Emilie's stories of how she perceives things somewhat differently today, and through questions she's asked me, and finally by watching her make her own choices at a somewhat different period. As I think back, I can see how important it is for her to make her own pathways, her own choices. It is difficult for me to separate my life from hers—something about mothers and daughters. I wonder if it's difficult for her, too.

As I watched Emilie struggle with whether or not to get married shortly after college herself (four years ago), and now with job-hunting after her graduate program, I can see these are common transition issues for most people. However, it is also a gendered issue. As a woman, I felt I had expectations and training to get through college, but that, beyond the expectation of getting married after college, expectations for my achievement in other domains were never clear.

The opportunities for women who complete college or graduate school are quite different today compared to the 1950s and even the 1960s, but I still worry that things haven't changed that much. As more and more discussion of a family "values" politics and the pros and cons of a "mommy track" occur, with many young women putting their careers on hold to raise children, I am concerned that young women in general and Emilie in particular still feel and will feel many of the same pressures I did in balancing the desire to be married, have a family, and to work and/or to have a career. But again, I will have to leave much of this to her and them. She and they will find their own way; it's not clear that my/our way was right.

My post-college shift into education and marriage. When I moved to Washington, D.C., in 1968 for my first job after college, it was during the Viet Nam War. Women were not being drafted, but many men were agonizing over whether or not to go to war and some friends had already died in the war. I felt I should be more involved in something that would relate to "caring" or social services, rather than the more technical scientific career in math for which I'd prepared myself. I began to tutor young children in a Washington inner-city public housing area in 1968–1969. With advice from a former professor about the increasing importance of early childhood education, I applied for graduate school in that area. Against my Census Bureau colleagues' advice (who thought moving from mathematics to *early childhood* education was a fatal error), I moved to the west coast with my future husband in 1969, and we both began doctoral programs. It was the height of the Viet Nam war protests on the West Coast. It was an era of major civil rights protests (Dr. King was assassinated in 1968). It was during what is known as the "second wave of feminism" when largely middle-class Euro-American women were demanding equal opportunities and rights with men. It was also the time of the "hippie" generation. Finally, in early education and child care, it was four years after the federal Head Start program had begun and it was two years before Nixon's 1971 veto of legislation on federal child care standards.

Talking about the cultural historical contexts that were coming together and surrounding my ideas of who I thought I was and who and what I thought I might be represents a part of my story. No one event by itself affected me or positioned me in terms of what I did in the future. Each context— changing expectations about women's and men's roles, the discourse of opportunity and, sometimes radical change, of protest, and new discourses and practices surrounding the importance of child care and early education— made its own impact on my personal/professional identities. These, together, have helped me to make meaning of my stories, envision new possibilities, and share the stories now with others, including Emilie.

Another reflection on mothering my daughter. I can see better, after talking with Emilie, reading her stories above, and thinking about how my son and daughter grew up, how much we are all a product of our own cultural historical moments, the languages of our time, the ways of understanding what we were and are to do, and how we were and are to behave. We are positioned by our moments, the languages of our times, what it means to be a girl or a woman, a wife, a mother, a daughter, a "worker" inside as well as outside our homes, what we should do, and shouldn't. But these are ideas that I am learning again by listening to both of my children, especially watching Emilie's experiences as a young woman now. As a mother, I have great pride in so much of what Emilie has become, and pride in imagining all the different pathways she will take and things she will choose to do as she moves through her own life. I hope for a world filled with possibilities for her, and others.

It has been difficult to say directly to her that I am so very proud of her, that I trust her judgments for herself and others in her own future, and that I love her so very dearly. This is also part of our cross-general story telling, I see now. My own mother seemed to praise us (my sisters and me) to others, but rarely directly to each of us; my sisters and I have spoken of this together 'though never with my mother before she died recently. I am pleased that this chapter provides one opportunity to "speak" directly to Emilie about how I feel about her.

Written by Emilie:

Educational/Professional Identity Development. In reflecting upon my childhood, growing up with a mother who worked was instrumental in influencing my own development and thinking. What I observed was important in my personal career development as well as my development in becoming a woman who is an independent thinker and motivated to achieve academic success.

When I first started my undergraduate education, my ambition was to become a scientist, like my grandfather, and like my mother had wanted to be. The life stories of my family members, specifically those from my mother, made me feel as though I needed to deviate from what was "expected" of me as a woman. Therefore, the field of science seemed to be leading me in the right direction. However, soon after taking my second course in chemistry, I took my first psychology course. Based upon my own choice and interests, I changed directions and decided that I was most interested in human development and interactions. I struggled with this decision for some time because the last thing I wanted to do was to follow in my mother's footsteps when she had specifically instructed me to be independent and break gender barriers. With all of these ideas and lessons that I had internalized during my childhood, I found myself in what developmental theorists such as Erikson would call a "developmental crisis." It didn't take long for me to accept that I had chosen this area of study (psychology) of my own free will and that I was not just settling for what my mother had done before me.

Despite the acceptance of my decision, I still felt internal pressure to do something more or something different from my mother. I found myself searching to find my place in this land of psychology. Based on some motherly advice, I took a course from Professor Barbara Rogoff on the cultural nature of human development, as part of my undergraduate studies in psychology at the University of California at Santa Cruz on the cultural nature of human development. It was in this course that I deepened my interest in psychological studies of human behavior and development and how these things are influenced by a person's cultural context. The experience of learning about the cross-cultural context of human development from Professor Rogoff propelled me into the next stage of my academic and personal experience.

Shortly after the end of this course I decided that I would take an opportunity to study abroad. This decision gave me the chance to experience a new place and a new culture. It is for this reason, I believe, that I chose to go to Ghana, West Africa, to study at the University of Ghana at Legon.

My experience of studying abroad was something that I chose on my own; however, something that has occurred recently has shown me that this decision was once again an example of how my mother's, and in this case my father's, life stories have influenced how I have chosen to live. A short time ago, a close friend of mine questioned my reasons for studying in Ghana. It has been five years since I went to study for about six months in Ghana and people seem to still be puzzled by my decision. The other day my friend asked me, "If you could choose to go anywhere in the world, why Ghana?" To me it was a no-brainer. If I could go anywhere in the world, why *not* go to Ghana? I grew up in a household filled with African art; my older brother was born in Senegal while my parents were conducting research; I lived there while a baby; and my parents continued to spend a great deal of time during my childhood working in Africa. Moreover, I've seen pictures of my self as a young child playing soccer in Senegal, so maybe it's not such a new place for me to go. These are some of the reasons to push myself into an experience so seemingly far away from my comfort zone. Additionally, I have always been taught to go "above and beyond the norm" in the way I choose to live my life. This means to succeed academically and make all of my experiences "count" in some note-worthy manner. Was this always the best way for me to develop? Probably not, but it gave me a great deal of drive as well as a rich array of experiences.

My time in Ghana further encouraged my passion for understanding and examining cultures. On one of the first days of my first term back in college after my time abroad, I ran into Professor Rogoff. I explained to her how much I appreciated what I had learned from her course and how my experience in Ghana boosted my interest in cross-cultural work. It was at this point that I began to work with her on creating my own student-lead seminar which gave me and some other students an opportunity to delve further into the cross-cultural nature of human development. As I went through this new learning process I realized more and more how fascinated I was with individual experiences. I believe it was around this time, my senior year in college, that I realized that I wanted to get involved in the field of counseling psychology.

My interest in counseling has led me to the graduate program which I have just completed. This particular field of psychology includes much of what I have been interested in all along: human development, socio-cultural influences, research, and learning about the individual. Once again, it fascinates me to think about the fact that all of these aspects of counseling which I value are also those which are integral aspects of my mother's world of work and our life together.

STORIES ABOUT FAMILY AND
CHILD-REARING: STRIKING A BALANCE

Written by Mimi:

Beginning in graduate school, I became interested in child care research and its effects on child development, in the effects of mother's employment outside the home on children's development, and in the organization and public financing (or lack thereof) of child care in the United States. I became interested in the fact that the United States, one of the richest countries in the industrialized world, was one of the few without paid universal prenatal health services or paid maternity or parental leave. While all of this was in the early 1970s, later I had direct experience (for years) with the difficulty of balancing family/work and professional/work. The pity is that I still remain concerned about these very same issues today because so little has changed in these thirty years of my career. Now I am worried, however, about Emilie and her children to be, as well as other peoples' children.

I wonder how Emilie will negotiate her own life now. She chose to spend four years in California for undergraduate education, one semester in Ghana as a study-abroad student, and two years in Portland, Oregon, for her master's degree in counseling psychology. Now, with her husband, they have chosen to return to Madison, Wisconsin, where they both grew up, to start their careers, and eventually a family. I think she learned by watching me that it wasn't easy to be so far from family. While it is a true joy to have her move close to where I am, she will have to find her own balance between her desire to explore new places and things, and the desire to not be so very far away. I know she can do it. For my own part, I must remember that she needs freedom to explore and create her own life, as I did myself as a young woman. I must remember that my mother, who must have wanted her three daughters closer to home than they ended up being, allowed us to spread our wings in so many ways and places. Can I learn from the examples of Emilie's grandmothers to support her explorations and adventures in the same ways they have done for me?

Written by Emilie:

From my own perspective as a child growing up, I think that my mother's desire to be mother, wife, and professional in a university setting, without much support from her environment (time, family, geographical location, etc.), pushed her to attempt to provide the environment she would have liked to have had for me—had there not been so many constraints on her or my father. While finances were not as constraining as the other cultural and contextual issues mentioned above, time was always an issue, and lack of a geographically close, extended-family support system (grandparents, aunts and uncles were in Boston, New York, and Pennsylvania; we were in Wisconsin) was always a constant in my parents' dealing with child care issues.

For my mother, these contextual and historical events were important to our stories for this chapter (and, of course, our lives). It is important to reflect on both the privileges my parents had by both being well-educated academics. It is also important to understand the political, economic, and social environments they traversed in trying to make work outside the home and work inside the home at rearing a family successful. Many of the stories which I have told and will continue to tell are based on my mother's life events and how the stories of those events have shaped my life.

Psychology and the observation of the other, and being the other. One story that always seemed to stand out for me was about my childhood bedroom. When I think back to the time when I was in preschool I can see my room filled with everything a kid could want and more. I see my puppet theater, my block corner, my book station, and my pretend kitchen. What I didn't realize at the time was that I was living in an experimental preschool. I have recently discovered that at the exact time I was enjoying my room, my mother was teaching a course about preschool design at the University of Wisconsin-Madison. I was her research subject, validating or thwarting her theories of preschool-age education. I think back to that time and wonder how those experiences influenced my growth and how strange to be the "other" that my mother was observing for some sort of personal ethnographic study.

This story surfaced for me during my course work in my Lifespan Development course which included a lot of personal processing of my childhood, family, and life. As in any development course, Piaget's study of his own children is always a favorite for discussing his genius, as well as the controversies about how he did his research. Was I too an "other" in my mother's informal study of preschool environments and their effects on young children?

But education is not a one-way street: Sexuality and mother-daughter educational experiences. Based on the time in which my mother grew up, it seemed as if she was not given certain information, so therefore she hoped to make that information more available to me. For instance, we began discussing sexuality starting at an earlier age than may be typical. I believe her intent was to have a more open, honest, and non-judgmental stance on a stigmatized topic. From this openness, perhaps, I was able to have a healthier attitude towards sexuality and being able to talk about it. In college I felt that others had not been able to have the same honest discussions with their mothers as I had with my own and I felt the need to share my experience through my assignments. Despite attending a well-known liberal university, I still felt that I should "push the envelope" with sexuality information to make this topic more normalized. It wasn't that I felt that I knew it all or was comfortable with all discussions of sexuality; it was that I felt that there should be no, or at least less, shame for women when attempting to be open and comfortable with issues around sexuality. In this light, I began work to give strength to the feminist aspects of sexuality by writing an informational book about female masturbation. This book was not as radical as it may be perceived. I wasn't saying anything new about the particular topic of female sexuality; it was just that I was presenting it to women as knowledge, rather than shaming it or celebrating it.

At the time (late 1990s), I didn't feel that women were getting the opportunity to hear this type of information. I even went a step further by researching the gender differences in social perception of masturbation and presented a video documenting the interviews I had compiled from male and female identified students from my university. My grandmothers were horrified by this as a course project while my mother and aunts were, in their own turn, intrigued. My mother also encouraged me to think about a graduate program in San Francisco on human sexuality. While I never went in that particular direction, she was clearly accepting of and interested in my work.

Without a strong base of support and knowledge from my mother, I would have never had the "balls" to take on such a provocative line of study. In my childhood, the lessons, teachings, and stories my mother shared with me made me feel that I had the right, and the duty, to be an independent thinker and make sure to share my feelings to that effect with others, as well as to open up new spaces for dialogues that aren't easy to have.

A SORT OF ENDING AND INTEGRATION

Written by Mimi:

Listening to Emilie in these last stories, I can't help but realize how much our lives have been an interaction—from her birth through today, she is constantly making me rethink how I act, what to think, and challenging me in ways that no one else really can. She's my daughter. She makes me laugh, she makes me cry, and she sometimes makes me want to pull my hair out with frustration—because she wants to go her own way, make her own decisions, and, unlike many graduate students that I work with, she doesn't have to listen to my advice. But the wonder of watching her teach me new things, or her being ready to experiment on her own is exciting. The fact that many of her interests and my own have coincided makes this even more special, though it wasn't necessary. I am thrilled for her as she makes her own paths, and, I can only hope to ease some of them for her, when I can, and when she asks.

Written by Emilie:

For us, writing together has been a chance to experiment with a new form of talking or communicating with each other. It is part of our mutual and interdependent education of each other, part of our growing relationship as mother-daughter and as two adult women from similar backgrounds, with shared histories. It is becoming apparent to me that the decisions that I have made in the way in which I am living and will continue to live my life are influenced by similar decisions my mother has made in her life. Furthermore, I am also realizing that my mother's decisions, since my birth in 1978, have been influenced greatly by me. Thus our mother-daughter relationship is a circular and fluid, and somewhat symbiotic, process. It is a process based on our collective historical and experiential life stories.

This process I speak of seems related to the concept of how a culture influences human development. Barbara Rogoff explains that there are "overarching orienting concepts" for understanding and explaining cultural processes. One of her initial concepts was that "humans develop through their changing participation in the socio-cultural activities of their communities, which also change" (Rogoff, 2003, p. 11). This overarching concept can be applied to the cultures of mothers and daughters. In the case of this chapter, we are presenting a look into one of these cultures. In writing this chapter with my mother I am beginning to see the evidence of how our participation in one another's lives (or our collective "community") has affected and will affect our ever-changing and adapting life constructions. While this is the end of this particular story and this chapter, our stories will continue, for both of us, for a long time to come.

REFERENCES

Apple, R .D. & Golden, J. (1997). Introduction: Mothers, motherhood, and historians. In R. D. Apple & J. Golden (Eds.), *Mothers and motherhood* (pp. xiii–xvii). Columbus, OH: Ohio State University Press.

Atkinson, R. (1995). *The gift of stories: Practical and spiritual applications of autobiography, life stories, and personal mythmaking.* Westport, CT: Greenwood Press.

Atkinson, R. (1998). *The life story interview.* London: Sage Publishing Company.

Bloch, M. N. (1998). Cross-cultural contexts of mothering and child care: Linking the personal and the professional. In M. Hauser & J. Jipson (Eds.), *Intersections: Feminisms and early childhoods* (pp. 303–323). Peter Lang Publishing Co.

David, M. E. (2003). *Personal and political: Feminisms, sociology and family issues.* Stokes on Trent, Staffordshire and Sterline, VA: Trentham Books Unlimited.

Hauser, M. & Jipson, J. (1998). *Intersections: Feminisms and early childhoods.* New York: Peter Lang Publishers.

Lareau, A. (2000). *Home advantage: Social class and parental intervention in elementary education.* Lanham, MD: Rowman and Littlefield Publishers, Inc.

Mutua, K. & Swadener, B.B. (2004). *Decolonizing research in cross-cultural settings: Critical personal narratives.* Albany, N.Y.: State University of New York Press.

Rogoff, B. (2003). *The cultural nature of human development.* New York: Oxford University Press.

Whiting, B. B. & Whiting, J. W. (1975). *Childrearing in six cultures.* Cambridge, MA: Harvard University Press.

Witherell, N. & Noddings, N. (Eds.). (1991). *Stories lives tell: Narrative and dialogue in education.* New York: Teachers College Press.

Chapter Six

Two Sides of the Story: Living an Academic Life

Janice Jipson & Jennifer Jipson

When we were invited to contribute a chapter to *Writing the Motherline: Mothers, Daughters, and Education*, Leigh O'Brien and Beth Blue Swadener asked us to reflect on academic mothers and daughters from our perspectives as university faculty members. They further suggested that since we had collaborated on several research projects we might consider some of the issues that had emerged from our professional work together. As we discussed the possibilities for such a chapter we kept coming back to the differing experiences we had had learning to transit academic environments and, in particular, learning to use academic discourse. An earlier collaborative research project on gender dynamics in classroom communication suggested itself as a starting point, one that would allow us to explore how gender-related issues impacted our teaching, but also how our reciprocal influence on each other as mother and daughter have influenced our work as researchers and teacher educators.

Our relationship as professional colleagues and co-researchers, who are also mother and daughter, has spanned the past ten years as we have shared the frustrations and pleasures of our research and teaching. Jennifer's mother, Jan, has worked as a university professor of early childhood education for over thirty years. Jan's daughter, Jennifer, is beginning her third year as a professor of psychology. Parallel histories in academe began when Jennifer was born during Jan's first year of college teaching and continued as Jennifer started elementary school the same year Jan began her doctoral studies program. Since that time our work together has been characterized by long phone conversations and e-mail messages as we consulted each other on teaching strategies, recommended books to each other, and designed and conducted several research projects.

Janice and Jennifer

In this chapter, in order to vivify our relationship as mother/daughter teacher/researchers, we would like to share our experience in doing a collaborative research project on academic discourse, an issue that has long permeated our personal conversations on living an academic life. De Lauretis (1986) suggests that an individual's personal history is "interpreted or reconstructed by each of us within the horizon of meaning and knowledge available in the culture at given historical moments" (p. 8). To contextualize our work together, we each begin by telling a story of how we separately became aware of the issue of discourse in our personal and academic lives. Since each of our lives connects with each other's as well as the lives of so many others, we then connect our individual stories to create a code with which we decipher the meaning of both our academic lives and our collaborative research, a kind of meta-narrative we construct to explain our academic existence. By telling our individual stories and by describing our first collaborative research project, we hope to illustrate some of the tensions and understandings underlying our work together and bring into focus the process of cross-generational professional collaboration between mother and daughter.

FEBRUARY 2005, ANGELIQUE CAFÉ, WEST VILLAGE, NYC

Jan: How to start? A man across the way sits drinking his latte or cocoa or something and reading Wittgenstein . . . very absorbed in his thoughts. Is he a student? A teacher? Some inspired professional intellectual? I think to myself, that is what academics are supposed to be doing on a grey March Sunday afternoon. It sometimes seems I have spent my whole adult life noting what it is academics are supposed to do; how they are supposed to think, and talk.

I always used to blame my public silence on my mother and on all that adolescent girl-development stuff. I'm not saying that it's not part of the truth of who I am, but now I am thinking about how I haven't learned the academic discourse "naturally," even now. I need scripts, preparation so that I can play out my part—and then I usually do it just fine. But catch me unaware, with no time to think through or mentally rehearse, and I am incoherent, self-conscious, struggling to speak in even the simplest way.

I grew up in a rural, northern Wisconsin community of Scandinavian and Eastern European immigrant families who communicated in a taciturn, almost dour fashion. Punctuated with "don'tcha know?" and "nicht wahr?" their language was direct, depending on the listener to fill in nuance and implications, or perhaps not caring beyond the delivery of the simple message. Plain speaking, I believe they call it.

From a very early age, I was also surrounded by stories. My grandmother, who was my primary caretaker while my mother taught school, would gather my sister and me up on her lap and lull us with paper dolls cut out of the Sears catalog and memories of blueberry picking and bears from when she was a girl. My grandfather even answered questions with stories, biblical parables alongside riddles, rhymes and tales about individual cows in the barn (usually the ones named after my sister and me). In my community, truths were directly and tersely expressed, but words were allowed to flourish in the range of the imagination. Perhaps I learned this distinction as a frame for understanding how to use language—the public and the personal, the actual and the poetic.

I was a quiet, shy child . . . often caught daydreaming rather than listening. Playing in the front yard of our house, I was a cowgirl riding the range on my pony; perched on the boulders in front our cabin on Cedar Rapids, I was a pioneer girl in the "Big Woods." In first grade, distracted from my reading lesson by one dream or another, I recall my frustrated teacher, Mrs. Wise, admonishing me to pay attention. In fourth grade I was sketching horses, and in fifth, designing prom dresses for my imagined future. Even so, by the time I completed elementary school I had established myself as a good student, one who did her work and seldom caused problems.

But then came seventh grade—my mother was my seventh grade teacher and that was a major trauma for an eleven-year-old girl. I remember realizing that it was best not to talk in class . . . that way I neither could be accused of being the teacher's pet by my classmates nor be criticized by my teacher/mother if my answers weren't exactly right. My friends and I passed notes back and forth and I suppose I learned then that it was better to be a writer than a talker. Psychology has since taught me that it was not simply being silenced by my mother/teacher but a more complex process of adolescent identity development, but I did not know that then. What I discovered was that it was best not to speak.

My self-conscious silence persisted through high school ("Janice would be an excellent student if she would only talk in class," my Sophomore year English teacher told my mother), through the large lecture classes of college, and even into graduate school, where I finally realized that it was not that I did not have anything to say, but rather that my thoughts did not seem to comfortably translate themselves into the words that other people understood. My ideas often formed themselves as images in my mind and when I tried to describe them, I became entangled in long, contextualizing anecdotes. When I did hesitantly venture to speak, I was often met with confused glances from my peers, or even worse, totally ignored.

As long as I wrote good papers, however, I succeeded. For unknown reasons, my writing seldom suffered from the discordant hesitancy of my spoken words. There was magic to putting pen to paper that let my ideas flow out in "intellectual form." Committed to liberating myself from the rural working class environment in which I grew up, I decided to become a writer. Instead, several years later, I found myself married, with two daughters, a Master's degree, and a job teaching at a small local college. I happily discovered that I enjoyed working with students who were near my own age—perhaps our shared cultural experience of the sixties gave us a common ground from which to speak.

Not surprisingly, the hardest part of being a faculty member was participating in meetings. Like other women in my department, I would remain docile and quiet until ultimately frustration broke through restraint, and I would shakily blurt out my contribution to whatever was being discussed, only to be once again cut off by my mostly male colleagues. For a time, in order to avoid being implicitly censored in this way, I took to writing "DO NOT TALK" in big block letters on my notepad—but that did not work either so I reverted to writing notes, venting my frustration to a colleague sitting next to me. Once another colleague and I did an informal count of the number of times males and females spoke during a meeting and for how long. When we presented our results to the group, they were appropriately aghast and for a time respectfully deferred to each other with comments such as "Oh, I'm sorry. Was I interrupting you?" or "Did you have something you wish to say?" Shortly after, the meetings reverted back to 'normal' and I once again reserved my contributions for things that I considered really important, but always fearing censure.

Recently, however, several woman colleagues and I agreed to "run interference" for each other, neutrally re-opening space for each other to speak by interjecting into the mostly-male dialogue comments such as: "I think Nancy is trying to make a point here" or "I don't believe Mary has finished talking yet." But it makes me think, warily, about what Adrienne Rich (2001) writes about "the tone of a woman determined not to appear angry, who is willing herself to be calm, detached, and even charming in a roomful of men where things have been said which are attacks on her very integrity" (p. 14). I still wonder, however, what the real problem is for me. . . . is it my lack of cultural capital or one of differing gendered discursive practices? Or is it, as Rich suggests, an underlying issue of power relations? And why do I always find myself in the middle of it?

MARCH 2005, FACULTY OFFICE, SARAH LAWRENCE COLLEGE

Jennifer: A student's unexplained absence from our weekly conference meeting allows me the opportunity to begin to document my reflections on how I came to be sitting here in a small office in North Hall, a professor in my second year at a small, coeducational liberal arts college. My entire life has been spent training for this position; I gave no other career possibility serious consideration. In the language of psychology, one might call this "foreclosure." Marcia (1966) explains that the foreclosed individual has avoided the uncertainty of the identity crisis by committing herself to whatever role parents or influential friends have prescribed with little questioning of whether it really fits the individual. At times I feel that this description fits, that I have adopted the role of academic without contemplation of any alternatives. But the concept of foreclosure elicits negative connotations of passivity and I prefer to think of my career choice due to a process of socialization, of enculturation. Throughout my life I have been immersed in the language and culture of academia. Living in a petri dish of scholarly thought and activity, it is no wonder that I developed the skills and ambition that ultimately led me to construct an academic identity.

My mother is a scholar. My earliest memories are of her working late hours in her home office as my sister and I played quietly nearby, not wanting to alert her to our presence and the fact that it was long past our bedtime. Other memories involve attending parties and gatherings where I became an unintentional eavesdropper, overhearing conversations about theory, analytic strategies, and the rewards and frustrations of academic life. My mother and her colleagues often invited me into these conversations by asking me about my viewpoint and challenging me to defend my ideas. As a result, I became comfortable sharing my thoughts and ideas about a variety of topics, and I was insulted when "impolite" adults failed to ask for my opinion. I also engaged in the academic world in other ways. I was the voice of 4th graders everywhere in a guest appearance in my mother's class and a guinea pig as she practiced the administration of psychological tests. Thus, the world of academe was my world; I was a participant long before I started my own performance as an academic.

In high school I began my one-woman act. I excelled partly because I was attentive and thoughtful, but also because I knew how to play "the game." The years of peripheral participation in my mother's academic life had taught me how to phrase comments, pose questions, and construct arguments. I was particularly articulate in my writing and consistently produced papers that received high grades. I was less confident about sharing my ideas in class discussion. I felt that having to express myself "on the fly" would reveal that I was an imposter, that I had appropriated a discourse that allowed me to make my mundane ideas seem intelligent. I felt that although I had successfully adopted my mother's language, my thinking could never be as complex or profound.

In my junior year at Smith College, this began to change. As I moved from larger introductory courses to smaller advanced seminars, I found myself participating in class more often, contributing to discussion of my own accord. I felt that my ideas had value and trusted that others would listen with respect and, if they disagreed, would do so in a considerate way. After graduating, I looked forward to going to graduate school to continue to construct understandings and engage in meaningful conversation. I felt prepared, having already lived my life in the world I was about to enter. I thought I knew what to expect. I was wrong.

My first graduate seminar was uncharted territory. To speak, I would have had to interrupt another student, and expect to be interrupted myself. No one invited me into the discussion with a friendly, "Jennifer, what do you think about this?" And I was not about to offer my opinion as I had seen others face direct challenges, challenges not tempered with the respectful "I can see what you're saying, but . . ." I withdrew. But why? It struck me that perhaps I really was not ready for this; perhaps my life had provided me with a completely different model of what academic discourse should be.

Only recently, as a college teacher myself, have I discovered that I can play a role in shaping the dynamic of the intellectual conversations of which I am a part. I have resisted adopting what I see to be counterproductive tactics of interrupting and grandstanding. My colleagues commend me for my "calm, professional presence." I don't have insight into what I am actually doing, but I take pride in somehow having figured out how to have a voice on my own terms. And yet, at a recent academic conference, I found myself paralyzed during Q&A periods despite my interest in and curiosity about the topics. I can't help but wonder what it was about this context that silenced me. Or, possibly, what it is about me that allows me to be silenced. This past term, in a perhaps self-serving manner, I chose to develop a course on gender, language and learning that allows me to indulge my curiosity about the variables that influence styles of interaction, while at the same time increasing student awareness of classroom conversation dynamics and encouraging them to reflect on their own engagement patterns.

SUMMER, 1996, SOMEWHERE IN WISCONSIN

Jan and Jennifer: It was no surprise, given our similar professional interests and shared history that we decided to collaborate on a research project. Partially because of our personal histories but also because of similarities between our doctoral dissertation topics, we decided to focus on the educational socialization process and specifically, the construction of academic discourse. We were interested both personally and professionally in the nature of women's experiences in academic environments and in the construction of academic identity. We decided to focus on women graduate students' transit of academe—for us a 'detour to the self through the other,' as suggested by Paul Ricoeur (1977). Perhaps, we thought, by examining the experiences of other women, we could better understand our own. It occurred to us that our project, like all research, was autobiographically informed—for Jan as a teacher of women graduate students, for Jennifer as a women's college graduate now teaching in a liberal arts college with a predominantly female student body. We believed that by examining the academic socialization experiences of other women, we could better understand our own.

We began our research on a late summer afternoon, motivated by an impending conference proposal deadline. The participants in our initial project included six women who graduated from all-women's colleges including Smith, Wellesley, Mills and Mt. Holyoke and then went on to coeducational post-baccalaureate programs. At the time of the study, five of the women were enrolled in doctoral programs and one was in medical school (in a combined MD/ Ph.D. program). We conducted extensive interviews with each participant, asking questions that encouraged each interviewee to talk about her educational experiences in her own words. One recurring topic brought up by our participants and echoing our own personal experiences was the overall nature of communication among women and men. Popular accounts of gender differences in communication suggest that whereas women tend to use language to focus on maintaining connections with others, men use language to assert dominance and to establish independence (e.g., Gray, 1992;

Tannen, 1990). Leaper (1994) characterizes these behaviors as emphasizing either interpersonal affiliation or self-assertion.

The interview with Hilary, a doctoral candidate in geology, reveals her interpretation of discourse in all–female classroom settings as affiliative: "Um . . . well, the exchange of ideas in a classroom. I felt like there was so much mutual respect and, as a group of women in a classroom setting, we really listened to each other and respected each other and just had a thoughtful exchange of ideas. " She went on to say: "Plus, this comfortable, supportive all-female, like I keep saying, mutual respecting environment where you were free to come up with new ideas and say things and NOT feel stupid."

Hilary, like Jennifer, found the experience of an all women's environment supportive and affirming. She went on to discuss her transition into a coeducational setting: "And now, I'm back in a mixed group and so it's a mixed conversation style and I tend to get very frustrated with trying to work with males. They interrupt more and they kind of just want to skip over the thought process; it's just different conversational dynamics. It's a little faster paced, um, and I felt like we never get to really follow through with a thought or a subject that we, then, have to quickly move on."

A second interviewee, Michelle, also talked about her transition to a coeducational setting from a women's college: "I forgot how much guys dominate discussion and how confident they are in their answers and how they're willing to just use up other people's time to discuss their ideas. But, they are really willing to talk and so part of it for me was coming to the realization that this is what I'm up against. But I also felt prepared and I remember going through my first quarter here. I was getting frustrated because I was used to thinking methodically and listening to everyone's points of view and then coming to my own conclusion and speaking up on that. Then I realized that the pace of the discussion was going so fast that I wouldn't get things in."

Issues of conversational pace were also expressed by Melody: "I think that maybe men tend to make a conversation—it's like, a little bit more of a race." Jennifer echoed these impressions: "The fast pace of conversation was something I noticed in my first graduate seminar at UC-Santa Cruz. I realized that to engage in the discourse one had to interrupt someone else and expect to be interrupted as well." Jan's experience in faculty meetings confirms this pattern of interruption in academic discourse.

Some aspects of these personal accounts of experiencing an emphasis on self-assertion in a mixed gender setting are consistent with results obtained through more experimental methodologies. For example, a meta-analysis conducted by Anderson and Leaper (1998) integrated the results of numerous individual studies on gender differences in the use of intrusive interruptions (in contrast to overlapping speech). Findings support the notion that men interrupt more often and more intrusively than women. Interestingly, however, this effect is minimal in conversations between two people and substantial in conversations including three or more persons (such as occurs in meetings or classroom contexts). We remarked to each other how consistent this pattern of intrusive interruptions was with our own experiences.

In addition to being frustrated by interruptions in mixed-gender conversations, several of our participants had noted the tendency for male peers to focus on the main point of a topic without elaborating, thereby reflecting an instrumental communicative strategy. Academic discourse assumes the ability to distance one's self from the situation, to recognize boundaries; to differentiate one's self from the subject of discourse, to focus on the categories-dichotomies-roles-stasis-causation. According to Tannen (1990) and Belenky, Clinchy, Goldberger, and Tarule (1986), a feminine style[1] includes intuitive analysis, use of personal experiences, the non-generalizable, the particular, ambiguities, pluralities, processes, continuities and complex relationships. Considering all of this in the context of our own experiences, we concluded that the instrumental, masculine style, which seemed to be synonymous with accepted academic discourse all too often excluded what might be described as a feminine style. Perhaps, Jan speculated, this explained why her mostly-male colleagues seem to get impatient with her in meetings.

Within the interview narratives, we also identified issues of gender as they relate to power and status. By interrupting, talking fast, and focusing on conclusions, men seemed to attempt to control the scope of the discourse. Often women, as Hilary admits: "just let the other people do the talking—I take it as a good opportunity to stop listening," suggesting her partial complicity in men's assertion of dominance. Hilary went on to say: "I really feel I have more confidence, more faith in myself and what I know and what I'm capable of and I don't feel I have to play the game of trying to prove that I'm smart or trying to dominate the conversation and instead I can be reflective and also think about what other people's thought processes are, so even though we don't all get to take turns sharing ideas, I can use the time in class to try and understand where people are coming from."

Hilary may be enacting and affirming an aspect of women's relational perspective as she considers seriously the words and ideas of others. This, however, echoes Jan's concerns about whether women' often silent relational practice discounts their agency, thereby privileging the contributions of their male colleagues. Adrienne Rich (2001) suggests that we know "that men tolerate, even romanticize us as special, as long as our words and actions [don't] threaten their privilege of tolerating or rejecting us and out work according to their ideas of what a special woman ought to be" (p. 15).

Their initial experience in a mixed-gender setting caused several women to question the reality of their own experiences: "If this is what the real world is like, I hate it!! I want to go back to Smith and be around chicks!" Jane, another women's college graduate commented, "My first impression right out of college was that we were really in a total bubble." Lisa, another participant, commented: "Eventually you have to get back to the real world and there are all those dynamics in the real world. You can't ignore the fact that there are power differentials between men and women. Um . . . so I guess the one thing I would criticize about women [women's colleges] is that you get insulated from, kind of withdrawn from the real world. But one thing that was nice about my women's college is you could take classes at MIT and Harvard, and I did classes at MIT which was nice because I still felt like I had some connection to the real world."

The difficulty, of course, with defining mixed-gender settings as the "real" is in the implication is that women's colleges offer "unreal" and therefore somewhat inadequate experiences and that the women who attend them communicate in inadequate ways. By denying the legitimacy of interactions among women only, do these women also devalue their educational experience as a whole? Such a sentiment is expressed by a participant in work by Sadker and Sadker (1994) who stated, "I think a single-sex school prepares students poorly for a double-sex world" (p. 237). We wonder why women, despite expressing satisfaction in their single-sex educational experiences, suggest that these same experiences put them at a disadvantage in mixed-gender contexts. Was this a variation on our own personal difficulties with mixed-gender discourse?

Doing this research project allowed us each to examine our own academic socialization and to reconsider the complex interrelationships of gender, social class, and experience in each of our constructions of our academic identities. Alcoff (1989) cites Lauretis's 1984 assertion that "women can (and do) think about, criticize, and alter discourse and, thus, that subjectivity can be reconstructed through the process of reflective practice" (p. 315). Our cross-generational reflection on our own experiences and those of the women who participated in our research led us to new understandings of the gender dynamics of academic discourse but it also took us further into the identification of other important factors.

Maxine Greene (1978) writes of her concern with "enabling individuals to reflect upon their own lives and the lives they lead in common with one another, not merely as professionals or professionals-to-be, but as human beings participating in a shared reality" (pp. 54–55). She encourages women to create "the kind of conditions that make possible a critique of what is taken to be 'natural,' of the 'forms of illusion' in which persons feel so completely at home" (p. 54). The opportunity to collaboratively reflect on our lives as mother/daughter and as academics in similar careers was, perhaps, one of the most powerful benefits of our work together. As mother and daughter, we had shared an initial immersion into academic life during Jen's childhood. Having grown up in a home where academic discourse was part of dinner-table conversation gave Jen a very different set of discursive skills and perspectives from those Jan acquired in her rural, working-class upbringing. While gender dynamics may have been experienced in a similar way across both our lives, important differences in our understandings of work and personal agency also existed. Identifying these differences as aspects of the cultural capital we each bring to academic life, we sought both to understand how they had been constructed and how they contributed to each of our comfort and facility with any particular form of discourse. This led us back to our experiences as mother and daughter and then, perhaps inevitably, to our own distinct teaching practices.

For Jan, it was always a question of what does a mother do to provide her daughter with that (cultural capital) which she could never quite access for herself? This naturally extended into her professional life and compelled her to offer the same opportunities and personal mentoring to her women students. Perhaps, then, Jan's negation of her own working class upbringing contributed to Jen's ability to succeed within the academic world? But how did Jen experience the discursive environment her mother created? And in what ways did Jen's familiarity with academic environments from childhood on confront Jan's continuing discomfort with that discourse? Did Jen's facility with academic discourse help provide a "family of origin" where Jan could finally internalize it?

We also considered these questions in light of Adrienne Rich's (1979) urging that women claim, rather than receive an education. Embedded in the different meanings of 'claim' and 'receive,' is a strong message about women's agency to change the discourse of their experience. In what ways, as mothers or teachers, do we alter the discourse of the environments in which we live and work?

MARCH 2005, POLKA DOT BAKERY, BLEEKER STREET

No talk. Jan reads Walter Benjamin, Jen reads Swift and Miller's *Gender and Language: A Handbook of Non-sexist Writing* (1988), and we share green tea and chocolate cake as the 5 p.m. traffic creeps by. The sound system suggests "smile, though your heart is breaking," then "on the street where you live." A lot has happened since our initial work: We presented our research project at a Vygotsky conference in Moscow; Jennifer finished her Ph.D. and a postdoc and is now, herself, a professor. It seems as though we have become each other's academic mentor. We talk on the phone almost daily, share teaching and reading suggestions, vent our frustration with our professional worlds, wonder where we will ever find the time to "do normal stuff." We continue to do research together, finding common questions that cross our separate fields and allow us to try to understand the complicated nature of being women in an academic environment. Recently, we published a study of how both child psychologists and early childhood educators understand issues of imposition and representation in research with young children (Jipson & Jipson, 2003), a question that has concerned us not only professionally, but also personally. Doing research together, we have continued to look at broader socio-cultural issues—at how the learning individual is linked to her own personal cultural, historical, and institutional contexts. In understanding our own research and teaching, we have learned to examine the links between classroom interactions and the broader socio-cultural system.

Always mother and daughter, in many ways we also continue to be each other's teachers. Sharing our experiences has allowed us to focus on how we have been constructed by academic discourse and cultural practices, by each other. We acknowledge, from our own experience, that pushing women into academically privileged language may deny many of their strengths and abilities, to a sometimes-crippling disjuncture. But we also have learned that we can sometimes "use" the discourse to our professional advantage. Personally, we have sometimes resisted but also supported each other in doing so. Rather than conforming to the strictures of such discourse, we also each try to enrich our own language with the particular, the contextual, the narrative, and the imagistic. Despite our reciprocal influence, each of us has developed her own discursive style—one that fits her particular discipline and geography—and yet we each also participate in the collective narrative of mother and daughter. After all, our understandings are constructed by the stories we choose to engage and what we hold in common far exceeds the difference. And often, when together, we find comfort in a discourse of silence.

NOTE

1. In the cited literature, "feminine style" most often assumes Euro-American ethnicity.

REFERENCES

Alcoff, L., (1989). *Feminist theory in practice and process.* Chicago: University of Chicago Press.

Anderson, K. & Leaper, C. (1998). Meta-analyses of gender effects on conversational interruption: Who, what, when, where, and how. *Sex Roles, 39,* 225–314.

Belenky, M. F., Clinchy, B. M., Goldberger, N. R., & Tarule, J. M. (1986). *Women's ways of knowing: The development of self, voice and mind.* New York: Basic Books.

De Lauretis, T. (1986). *Feminist studies/critical studies.* Bloomington, IN: Indiana University Press.

Gray, J. (1992). *Men are from Mars, women are from Venus.* New York: Harper: Collins.

Greene, M. (1978). *Landscapes of learning.* New York: Teachers College Press.

Jipson, J. L. & Jipson, J. A. (2003). How to know what kids already know. *Childhood Education, 79* (3), 167–169.

Leaper, C. (1994). Exploring the consequences of gender segregation on social relationships. In *Childhood gender segregation: Causes and consequences.* San Francisco: Jossey-Bass.

Marcia, J. E. (1966). Development and validation of ego identity status. *Journal of Personality and Social Psychology, 3, 551–558.*

Miller, C. & Swift, K. (1988). *The handbook of nonsexist writing* (2nd edition). New York: Harper & Row.

Rich, A. (1979). *On lies, secrets, and silence.* New York: Norton.

Rich, A. (2001). *Arts of the possible.* New York: Norton.

Ricoeur, P. (1992). *Oneself as another.* Chicago: University of Chicago.

Tannen, D. (1990). *You just don't understand: Women and men in conversation.* New York: William Morrow.

Erin and Martha

Chapter Seven

Two Gendered Journeys: Finding our Way(s)

Martha L. Whitaker & Erin L. (Whitaker) Schmidt

INTRODUCTION

Telling the Motherline—accumulating our stories—creates more than comradery and connection. Women's lives, positioned across cultures socially, culturally, politically, and economically as the less dominant half of an asymmetrical power relationship (Weaver-Hightower, 2003), can be sites of political understanding. The view from the margins of a social setting provides a form of clarity not available from the mainstream of society. But are women still living their lives on the margins? There are "feminists" today who are expending much time and energy asserting that the work of feminism in the United States is essentially finished. Political conservatives, they claim a classical liberal feminist perspective that discounts the constraining influences of gender socialization. Despite this dismissal of the power of subtle cultural influences to limit girls and women, they raise concerns about the institutionalized cultural oppression of little boys and the emasculation of men (Hoff-Sommers, 1994; 2001). They assert that women need to reclaim the power of their sexuality (Paglia, 1994), and suggest our culture is in a moral decline that can only be reversed if women return to rigid gender roles and embrace modesty and dependence as normative (Shalit, 1999). In June, 1998 (Bellafante), Time Magazine devoted its cover story to the telling question, "Is Feminism Dead?"

Complicating the conversation even further are claims that women really can't have it all (Belkin, 2003), and that a "revolution" of professional women opting out of the workforce is occurring. Young (2004) casts doubt on the depth of this social phenomenon suggesting it ". . . hardly amounts to a 'revolution.'

It's not even necessarily a steady trend." She points out that the number of married women with children under six who were in the workforce between 1998 and 2001 only dropped from 63.7 percent to 62.5 percent. Reminiscent of over a century of cyclical backlash aimed at negating women's progress, current reports must be examined carefully.

It is not an easy time to be a feminist. References to patriarchal domination are passed off as victimization mentality (Bartky, 1990). In spite and because of these contemporary social dynamics, we choose to name and examine the gendered nature of our journeys as they have unfolded within a social microcosm that openly embraces patriarchy as appropriate. Living in Utah as we do, the entirety of our mother/daughter relationship has been contextualized by an extensive and powerful Mormon community. Our developing understanding of patriarchy in general has been shaped by the dominance of this specific culture in local politics, work environments, schools, neighborhoods, and personal relationships. In each of these settings, decisions are made and expectations are colored by the official belief that gender roles are divinely inspired and influence not only our earthly choices but our options in the hereafter (Stack, 2001). Washed over by backlash (Faludi, 1991) and still struggling with problems that evade easy definition (Friedan, 1963), we hope that telling our mother/daughter story will deepen our collective understanding of current social circumstances and encourage daily choices that take into account the political nature of personal experiences. This ongoing process is education in the best sense of the term. The consciousness raising and demythologizing that have characterized the feminist experience are synonymous with genuine educative experience.

The story of any woman, any mother, any daughter, is not the story of every woman, every mother, every daughter. Each life is contextualized by ethnicity, economic conditions, sexual identity, religious beliefs, and more. Each woman's history is replete with social and political dynamics particular to her journey. This diversity is reason enough for us to tell our stories—to dismantle the false category "woman." Yet there is a reason for writing our lives that is grounded in commonality rather than difference. The thread that runs through women's lives across the globe and draws us together toward common goals is patriarchy (Eisler, 1987; Mies, 1986).

Institutionalized Gender Expectations

Of course, patriarchy has been a driving force within a wide variety of religious experiences. Today, fundamentalist religions still expect and promote the appropriateness of rigid gender roles. Mainstream and liberal churches struggle to change their exclusionary policies while continuing to reflect the subtle patriarchal messages that are firmly entrenched within the larger society. But the Mormon Church is unique in its ongoing commitment to the importance of patriarchal authority, centering its beliefs around traditional family structures and eternal marriage (Johnson, 1989; McConkie, 1966; Shipps, 2000).

Despite its official rejection by the denomination, polygamy continues to be practiced by many outside the official structures of the church and is still a subtext of contemporary doctrine. Here on earth, a man can be eternally "sealed" in a "temple marriage" to more than one woman but a woman can be sealed to only one man. The 19th century practice of polygamy is temporarily revoked but continues in heaven (McConkie, 1966; Stack, 2001). Additionally, Mormons teach that women's admission to the highest of the three levels of heaven is contingent upon being sealed in the temple to a worthy Mormon man. Should a couple achieve this status, they will be granted a world of their own where the spirit children that result from their heavenly sexual relationship will be sent to receive an earthly body for their journey toward their own eternal marriages (McConkie, 1966). Because spirit children from the Heavenly Father and Heavenly Mother of this world are awaiting bodies for their earthly pilgrimage, earthbound Mormon couples are encouraged to marry young and give birth to many children.

A second dynamic at work within the Mormon Church is exclusivity. Mormons self-identify as Christians but believe they are the only true church and intentionally remain separate from others, including other Christian churches, often excluding close relationships with anyone who is not Mormon or interested in becoming Mormon. The characteristics of a closed, "autonomous" culture have been documented by anthropologist John Ogbu (1992), and he refers to Mormons as one prototype of this protective dynamic. Autonomous minorities, Ogbu explains, intentionally insulate themselves from some of the effects of cultural difference by forming self-protective enclaves that sustain members emotionally, culturally, and even economically.

Finally, worthy Mormon young men can become members of the priesthood, an honor unavailable to women. Male members of the higher levels of the priesthood administer local churches according to personal revelation from their Heavenly Father, direction from the all-male General Authority, directives from the Council of Twelve, and the revelations of the current church president—"prophet, seer, and revelator"(Ludlow, 1992). Women (and men) in the church who publicly disagree with official doctrine or exclusive male authority risk excommunication and the accompanying eternal consequences (Beck, 2005; Johnson, 1989).

Minority Status Improves Perceptions: Sharing Our Views

It is not our intent to criticize our Mormon friends and neighbors but to state clearly the gendered nature of the doctrine of the church whose members form a sizable portion of our community. Outnumbered by our conservative Mormon neighbors, we have felt and observed the sting of isolation and judgment. In a strange twist of circumstances, we are part of a minority population in relationship to a group that does not usually have majority status. This circumstance has allowed us to struggle with our own unraveling of subtle forms of patriarchy within the context of this extreme form of male dominance.

All around us patriarchal reversal (Daly, 1973) is writ large. The rhetoric that pays homage to women, particularly mothers, contrasts starkly with the silencing of women's voices and the perpetuation of rigid gender expectations. This has enabled us to understand more fully the dynamics of patriarchy that shadow women's lives at home, at school and at work–locally, nationally, and internationally. Living within the Mormon community has shaped our commitment to interrogating the political nature of our lives and caused us to consider our obligation to speak and act against the limitations of patriarchy whenever possible. It has helped us to face and challenge romanticized notions of motherhood that interfere with the important work of developing new models of equitable and liberating relationships (Eisler & Loye, 1990; Eisler, 2000).

The four main sections of this chapter constitute our contribution to telling the Motherline. The gradual transition from a 1950s, white, middle-class, traditional view of gender roles to a more complex understanding of the importance of independence and personal liberation for women (and men) is characterized in Martha's Story. Our blended mother/daughter voices combine to create a Narrative of Our Life Together. Erin's Story discusses the challenges of working out the details of her adult life as a young female in a still patriarchal society within a subculture of intensified patriarchy. Finally, we will summarize our work together in the Conclusion with an eye toward the future and a shared vision of a culture that values genuine educative experiences that lead to liberating action in both the private and the public spheres.

Martha's Story: Living the Transition from a World of Tradition

I lived my part in the dramatic second wave of feminism, not at the forefront of the revolution, but as one of the many women for whom feminism was a gradual awakening that eventually amounted to a massive personal paradigm upheaval. Discovering that the unspoken rules that regulated my mothers' life choices were neither necessary nor appropriate for my life circumstances was a slow and disturbing experience. This awareness dawned on me as my dissatisfaction with traditional expectations within my marriage and the world of work (teaching elementary school) made me first discontented, then determined to unearth the source of my frustration. During those early years of my marriage I shifted from adjusting my decisions at all times to the unspoken expectations of my spouse (like most women of my generation, I had been carefully socialized to read his mind) to reconnecting with the person who was locked deep inside of me (Lennon, 1995). On a personal level, it was a spiritual experience. On an interpersonal level, I began associating with other women in new ways. We woke each other up.

In addition to informal conversations, I attended a consciousness-raising group at the Women's Center of a local university. Slowly my understanding gave way to action. I walked out of a work meeting where the silencing was obvious and unbearable. I changed my ideas about domestic responsibilities and worked to reconfigure some of our workload at home. Most significant was the daily practicing (and it required conscious practice) of the new skill of checking with myself before jumping to meet the expectations of others when making the simplest decisions about how I would spend my time. This was especially difficult with my spouse and it unsettled our relationship in un-comfortable ways.

A few stories are now being penned (e.g., Evans & Avis, 1999) about women who struggle within a relationship to change interactions, responsi-bilities, and decision-making in ways that create equity and opportunity for both partners. Women who choose such a path need the comfort and wisdom of their peers. I often thought about the decidedly non-Mormon composition of groups of women with whom I discussed such issues. I wondered how in-dependent women within the Mormon Church—and I knew they existed—managed to sustain themselves as they juggled the demands of life. And I felt a sadness about the limitations placed on the experiences of female com-radery within the Mormon Church. Homemaking, charity work, and church assignments allow friendships to flourish and reinforce each other's perspec-tives. But could these women speak to each other forthrightly? Could they disagree with authoritative views and work toward the goal of aligning their personal convictions with their public persona? I came to treasure beyond measure the friendship and support of women whose circumstances and goals were similar to mine. They have sustained me for 31 years.

This much we came to know: we are not our mothers. Neither are we every woman of our generation. Economically privileged, white, living within the traditional paradigm of marriage, our experiences have been textured by our circumstances. But the thread of patriarchy is woven tightly into the tapestry of our lives, as it is in the lives of U.S. women whose identities and chal-lenges contrast with ours, and the lives of women worldwide.

When Erin was born, I began a new chapter of my life. I thought quite a bit about the limitations of Mormon patriarchy and its relationship to my own patriarchy-related personal struggles. In a quintessential example of patriarchal reversal, we live in a community that flaunts the importance of children, yet fails to provide reasonable child care options, struggles with divorce and child abuse rates that exceed the national average, and burdens women with untold guilt if they work outside the home. As is typical throughout the U.S., Utah women who are employed (a greater percentage than the national average), usually work in family-unfriendly environments where maternity leave and schedule flexibility pale in comparison to the policies of other industrialized nations (Spain & Bianchi, 1996).

Economically privileged enough to arrange my life around our family's needs, when Erin was born, I downsized my life of eight years in the public sphere substantially. The rhetoric of motherhood, the lynchpin of patriarchy, enveloped my days. The newly developed independence was challenged by my own traditional upbringing and the seductive pull of the idealized mother (Ehrenreich & English, 1972). But, eventually, my decisions about work and additional schooling were a clearer reflection of the person I had become during the child-free years of my marriage. Graduate work provided a new vocabulary for my experiences and for my intuitively held beliefs and gave me new connections to others who were journeying along paths that paralleled mine.

I held on to my life in the world of schooling, honoring my years of teaching, and embraced the scholarship that supported my expanding feminist and critical theory perspective. My university teaching was mostly to young Mormon women and my dissertation began with the lives of six Mormon women who were mothers studying to be elementary teachers and ended with an analysis of their connection to a worldwide sexual division of labor. None of this set me up for being a welcome conversationalist in my private sphere endeavors and I walked a thoughtful and uncomfortable line, sometimes feeling alienated from people I loved whose relationships were important to me. My personal commitment to moving toward an authentic life sustained me and I struggled to change without losing those relationships. I had begun unsettling patriarchy in my own life. I committed to a daily approach to unsettling it in the lives of my children, other family members, my friends, and my students. There were times when it would have been easier to remain silent and I'm sure there were those who wished I would. A firm belief in the importance of commitment and a clear memory of my own arduous and prolonged journey out of the fog of patriarchy has kept me energized and determined.

As an adult I was sometimes excluded or judged by well-meaning Mormon acquaintances. An invisible wall discourages Mormon/non-Mormon relationships from becoming too close. Any negative response I might have was usually momentary and easy for me to understand. This isn't the case for children. They only know they feel left out. During their early years, our children's experiences with this subtle exclusion were limited to occasional neighborhood events. We sent them to parochial schools until they each decided during their middle school years that they were ready to move into the larger community. In middle school and high school, exclusion was an inevitable part of their experience but it was more readily understood at this age and balanced by the many energizing opportunities that accompany a move to a large school. Dating options were, of course, quite limited. As they moved toward adulthood, they were challenged by their minority status to think deeply about their personal convictions in ways that have shaped their views of gender, spirituality, and equity.

Throughout my prolonged and continuing awakening, I maintained my connection to my own religious heritage. My father was a Lutheran pastor who was also a civil rights activist. My mother was one of the small percentage of the women of her generation to earn a college degree. She taught school for three years before she married. Of course, once she married, she was no longer able to be employed as a teacher, despite a two-year wait for children. This interesting mix of tradition and social awareness prepared me for the unfolding personal journey that I have characterized as spiritual. I continue to find strength within a spiritual community and count myself fortunate to have been encouraged within that community to cherish intellect, to doubt with intensity, and to search independently for deeper understanding. These endeavors are understandably discouraged within the Mormon faith because of its hierarchical authority structure. But they are the essence of authentic educational experience—the central weapons in the fight against oppression of every kind.

Young women from my daughter's generation have been encouraged to connect with themselves, to understand their desires, to have the courage of their convictions, even in the face of obstacles. Many of their mothers have attempted to discard a formulaic approach to women's lives. But we have not been able to make major adjustments in our culture's deeply ingrained ideological and structural inequities. Working out the details of living a personally authentic and relationally rewarding life that includes a career, an equitable partnership, and children, is a challenge we have passed to the next generation. Before the conclusion of this chapter, Erin will discuss these challenges as she tells her story. What follows in the next section is a narrative of our mother/daughter experience. During the years this narrative represents, we were passing the feminist baton from my generation to hers. At the same time, we were participating in a shift from unsettling patriarchy to working out the details.

A NARRATIVE OF OUR LIFE TOGETHER

Early Years. I was 30 when Erin changed me. Among the flood of emotions and new experiences, I was most surprised by a keen awareness of her femaleness. I was instantly proud of her spunk; she complained about everything with gusto! Already struggling with my own understanding of gender and role expectations, I had a new reason to care deeply about women's lives. I diapered her with some fear and trepidation.

From my early childhood I remember mainly the simple childhood memories that are common to most children of a privileged background: playing with friends, spending time with parents (particularly my mother), games, vacations—snapshots of memory. My mother and I were very close; I loved playing and talking with her. It never occurred to me that her being home was different from what some children experienced. The other neighborhood children were Mormon and their mothers were home with them as well.

Unexpectedly, I felt sorry for Erin. I knew her choices would be conflicted. Her path would be uphill. Gender expectations permeated the baby gifts and the conversation. I prayed she would keep her spunk. A new awareness of the emotional, physical, and intellectual labor that follows the labor of giving birth continued to reinforce my concerns for her future. I was overwhelmed by motherhood. One day she might feel the same way. In a profound way I had given birth to a compatriot. I believed that life would make us strong allies in the end.

Unless it is particularly traumatic, children think that whatever their parents do is normal. So when my mother returned to school when I was seven, it never occurred to me that it was different from what other mothers were doing. I was in school at that point so her being gone didn't affect me very much. Even when she was at an evening class, my dad was home with me. Her new venture was probably more world changing for my brother, five years younger than I, than it was for me.

Middle Years. During Erin's first years in school her brother was born and I became restless. My part-time work and steady volunteerism was scheduled around everyone else's very important needs. My decision to return to school seemed small at the time but I was beginning to understand that enabling everyone else's lives at the expense of my own interests was not healthy for any of us. My non-Mormon friends may have struggled with similar issues but Mormon women I knew spoke of work outside the home as a troubling necessity—not a personally gratifying decision that would allow everyone the opportunity to grow and change. I needed a life apart, a personal life beyond the demanding work of mothering and domestic labor. It was a restlessness that changed us again.

By the time my mother started back to school, I was old enough to know that she loved what she was doing. I heard her talking about it with my dad frequently and excitedly. I still didn't think about her role differing from that of my friends' mothers. I loved my mother and was glad she was doing something that made her happy. However, in addition to her happiness, I was aware of the tension. As she progressed toward her degree there was occasional friction between my parents. I knew that the possibility of her looking for a career job at the culmination of her schooling would mean moving the family. No child wants to be uprooted, but in addition to concern about a possible move, I wanted my parents to be happy together.

What started as a few classes grew into a part-time job and full-time school with a serious goal. Life became a fragmented series of responsibilities and late night homework. I carried more than my share of the load at home. My partner was a willing supporter but we both lived out unspoken beliefs that it was all right for me to live on a steady diet of insufficient sleep with little time for "extras" like recreation and socializing. There were times when we both strained mightily under the weight of remaking our lives in a culture constructed around the breadwinner/housewife model.

One of the lessons that my parents worked very hard to instill in me was that I could be whatever I wanted when I "grew up." It was ingrained in me from a very early age that there were no limits to what I could do as long as I worked hard. When people asked what I wanted to be, I would reply without hesitation, "an astronaut, a ballerina, and a mommy." It is interesting to consider the origin of these three personas that I desired. I wanted to be a mommy, just like most other little girls, but I never questioned that at the same time I could have a demanding career like an astronaut. My desire to be a ballerina undoubtedly stemmed from society's portrayal of little girls as dainty princesses in pink. But no restrictions were put on my aspirations. I now realize that the experiences of other little girls I knew may have been different. Most young Mormon girls are taught that the most important thing they can contribute to the world is to bear children and be a good wife. While I wanted to be a "mommy," I was never under the impression that it would conflict with my other goals.

I was sustained by the joys of learning, new relationships at the university, the laughter and chaos of life with my elementary-school-aged children and a partner who was willing to rethink his gendered role expectations. But I struggled internally at work, at home, and in volunteer settings to do it all. My new life did contrast markedly with my mother's, but ideology dies hard. Working to rethink patriarchal recipes, I sensed my spouse was not nearly as content as my father had been. Many of the women around me, particularly my Mormon neighbors, seemed more tranquil, their lives less ambiguous. As women in these families found their way back into the world of work outside the home, it was assumed that their goals would be secondary to their husbands', their decisions constrained by a belief that they must always put family members first. I clung to the hope that living out my own dreams as well as supporting those of others would give my daughter permission to do the same and encourage my son to allow others that right. And I often worked a "second shift" (Hochschild, 1989) based on that hope.

Adolescence. In high school I was my own person, a nonconformist. I didn't wear much makeup or dress "like a girl," and I had very little interest in having a boyfriend. I was aware that those were the very three things that occupied the minds of many of the other girls I knew, and more than anything I was annoyed by the facade. I realize now that I had replaced one extreme with another. This isn't necessarily the best way to address a behavior or convention that you disagree with. I suppose that phase of my life was an important part in developing the person that I have become as an adult. Even now I continue to change and grow, but adolescence is a time for extremes—feeling your limits and finding yourself and your place in the world.

As Erin navigated the stormy seas of adolescence, I alternatively rode the waves of pride and concern. Now she was really becoming a woman. She was determined and her interests were expansive. Occasionally she complained about the other girls in her schools who seemed programmed to be acquiescent and to have little interest in intellectual matters. She dressed with no concern for the opinions of others and seemed to take no interest in boys or dating.

Many of my older friends comment that now, at age 23, I am more directed in my life than they were at my age. Perhaps my adolescent rebellion against conventional gender expectations enabled me to find myself sooner than others and be comfortable with the person I found myself to be. Rather than dating, shopping and spending an hour on my hair every morning, I was busy and involved in many other things. I played sports, kept my grades up, and was very involved in volunteering at my church. I had a career plan that involved graduate schooling and I was ambitious. My life was too full to spend time playing the game of catch-a-husband.

I had avoided giving Erin any messages about the importance of femininity. Would she be happy moving into a world where gender expectations were pervasive? In my own life, I had determined to keep all the balls in the air, even if it sometimes resulted in an oppressive workload. She seemed to be deciding to eliminate part of the workload of women's lives by ignoring social conventions. Inwardly I railed at a world that stacked the deck against women.

How quickly perspectives can change. The summer after I graduated from high school, I began dating someone. What began as a summer fling quickly escalated into a serious relationship. We dated all through college and, dur-

ing those years, I began to question for the first time my career plans and to think about family aspirations. Was it fair for me to put off plans of having a family for years while focusing on my schooling and career? Or, if I didn't, what would it mean for my children to be put into daycare? If my partner felt strongly that someone should stay home with the kids, how would he feel about that someone being him?

When she formed an increasingly close relationship with a young man, a whole new set of concerns emerged. Would she give up her educational goals? Would she shape her life around his? How would she manage in a world that said she couldn't have it all? For four years the questions hung in my heart as she seemed to move one direction, then another.

I never doubted that I was capable of any career, but began to wonder how family life would work along with it. I noticed that many of the other young women at the university had education as a goal but family, not career, plans; their college degrees would just be a "fall-back" if they needed it. I knew that I still wanted to have a career–something I loved to do, 'though I was still unclear about what it would be.

As she gradually regained her footing and moved toward ambitious goals, I felt a bittersweet relief. She seemed to be holding on to herself in a culture that agitated against her. Great news. Recipes for managing this are, however, nonexistent. While her Mormon colleagues and friends refer to a script that is not only clear but accepted as divinely inspired, she will write each act of her play from scratch. The tug of sadness I felt at her birth returned as I watched her carry on with a sleep-deprived determination all too common among women.

Adult Years. I steal a moment here and there to ponder the wonder of our mother/daughter life. Our journeys are separate, yet our gendered challenges have been shaped by our position in society, our whiteness, and centuries of misogynistic thought and practice. We share a particular understanding hard-won through female experience. But her world is waiting and it is different than mine.

In the year since I graduated from college, I have decided to apply for medical school. I knew all along that I wanted an ambitious career and have been fortunate to have a boyfriend (now husband) who is my biggest supporter, always encouraging me not to sell myself short. I have seen my parents work out two careers and a strong family life over the years. Maybe you can have it all? It takes more thought and planning than I ever expected.

As we write, I think back to the wash of emotions that accompanied Erin's birth. We *are* compatriots of sorts. Our journeys continue to unfold and I hope that our years of closeness have provided some of what she will need to stand against patriarchal constraints. As we view with some sadness the limitations that shape the lives of women within the more intensely patriarchal world of Mormonism, a renewed determination to live our lives as fully as circumstances permit shapes our choices.

Erin's Story: Working Out the Details

My mother often told me that when she graduated from high school there were three career choices available to her unless she really wanted to make waves and rock the boat. Her parents expected her to go to college, which eliminated secretarial work, leaving nursing and teaching as her perceived choices. Middle- and upper-class women of her generation decided to use their privileged position to rock the boat in many ways, fighting for civil rights, women's rights, and many other important causes. This generation of transition threw out the traditional "recipe" for life as a woman. As a result, there are infinitely more opportunities available for me and the other women of my generation in this new era. However, combining the ingredients of work and family to create a life not only palatable but satisfying is not a simple business (Bateson, 1989). This is especially true within the context of the strongly patriarchal Mormon culture where social conventions and politics remain conservative and career expectations continue to be heavily influenced by gender.

Entering the world of work is very different for me than it was for my mother. No one bats an eye when a little girl says she wants to be an investment banker, a professor, a doctor, or take on any other demanding professional position. It is, in fact, encouraged. Yet why are women still underrepresented in so many professional fields? The doors to opportunity are purportedly open; what prevents women from walking through them? The details. The Mormon Church provides an example of the way institutionalized gender expectations create an invisible barrier that constrains women's choices. Strongly supportive of education for women, Mormons generally don't encourage them to take advantage of their education by pursuing a challenging career. My own career goals, which have changed a number of times since childhood, have all been ambitious: astronaut, veterinarian, and doctor. Yet, when faced with my first serious relationship, I began questioning all of those goals, thinking that I could just get a job that would be less demanding and it would be easier on everyone involved. It would have been. But would it have been satisfying for me? If the daunting task of working out the details of a two-career relationship have made me reconsider my goals, how much harder would it be for a young Mormon woman to pursue a demanding career with the pressures of her whole social environs telling her to stay home, be a good wife and a mother to many children?

In earlier generations and in strongly patriarchal cultures today, the division of labor in heterosexual marriages is simple, and it is not questioned: husband as breadwinner, wife as homemaker. If a woman today decides to take on one of the many careers available to her, she faces the question of who will care for the domestic sphere. Often it falls to her anyway, influencing some women to take on a less demanding career so that working and taking care of the home and children don't quickly lead to burnout.

I have observed the push and pull of the work and home spheres first-hand in my parents as my mother moved from a position of homemaker to one of student and finally to having a demanding career. Over the years I knew there was tension between my parents as they struggled to define their changing roles. There were heated discussions at night and tense dinners. But because they were willing to face the conflicts and deal with the details rather than repress their dissatisfaction with new aspects of their relationship, they made it work. It could not have worked if my father hadn't been willing to take over some of the housekeeping responsibilities and cooking and other jobs traditionally performed by the woman, whether she works outside the home or not. And it would not have worked if my mother hadn't envisioned a new pattern for living and managed a difficult overload. My parents worked out the details of their lives in a new era and, as a result, still maintain a healthy relationship. Equal partners.

I certainly didn't want to become burned out from doing all the work, but I wanted to do something satisfying for myself. I am fortunate to be in a relationship with a man who is supportive of my goals and respects my intelligence. He is supportive in other ways besides verbal encouragement; we work towards an equitable division of labor, searching for a system that will lead to a satisfying life for each of us (Eisler & Eisler, 1990).

In a time of increased opportunity for women, each woman who wants to maintain a committed relationship and also have a career must work out the details of a new recipe that will make her own life satisfying. For me, the most important detail is having a supportive relationship with someone who is willing to be an equal partner. Men have to make the choice to be equal partners, which includes a willingness to take on responsibilities that would traditionally not have been theirs. But for each person in a relationship to be satisfied with their life's recipe, one partner cannot carry 75% of the burden. Equal partners. I fervently wish for an equal partner for my female Mormon friends but I often watch helplessly as their goals and desires are placed second to those of their husbands. Unfortunately it is difficult for men to give up their dominant role that is so entrenched in their religious beliefs and culture.

CONCLUSION

As the tension between patriarchal tradition and new gender models at home and in the workplace persist, we believe that the socialization of masculinity (and femininity) is changing. Just as there was a loud hew and cry over the feminization of schools and the emasculation of young men at the turn of the 19th century when women were demanding more equity and gaining an education and admittance to colleges in unprecedented numbers (Brown, 1990), today's backlash against the social progress of women is characterized by the work of similar alarmists. Amazingly, many of these activists today are women (Hoff-Sommers, 1994, 2001; Paglia, 1994; Shalit, 1999). But what may be called the emasculation of men is, in fact, the changing of male expectations and roles in conjunction with the changing female expectations and roles that are occurring as a result of feminist movements. Perhaps some men are learning that they can be happy in an equal relationship, that it may be more satisfying for everyone involved if they are not expecting to be catered to. If the masculinity that is taken away from little boys is that which held women and men in rigid gender roles for so long, then it is not a tragedy but a triumph. Such progress is essential if we are to eradicate the most deeply entrenched, openly expressed gender oppression in our society, homophobia.

The progress toward greater equity that we have experienced could not have occurred without legal changes that included women gaining the right to vote, laws against hiring discrimination and sexual harassment in the workplace, the requirement of equal pay for equal work, and increased equity in school opportunities. But social habits die hard. We struggle daily toward new patterns of living. In a culture like Mormonism that is so firmly entrenched in patriarchy, more would be required than a change in socialization for men to be willing to relinquish their patriarchal roles. A change in values and religious tenets as well as a willingness among women to push for equality would be needed. A new commitment to meaningful education—critical education that encourages genuine intellectual engagement, a willingness to doubt taken-for-granted assumptions, and an enthusiasm for searching independently for deeper understanding—would be required. A close examination of the way patriarchy is kept secure within the microcosm of the Mormon culture reminds us of the ongoing need for a multi-dimensional approach to gender liberation in the U.S. and worldwide.

Observing this strongly patriarchal cultural dynamic all around us has forced us to thoroughly evaluate our own convictions about feminism and patriarchy. There is a contrast between Mormon women's lives and ours, yet the thread of patriarchy that dominates the tapestry of our lives is still tightly woven into our daily experiences in subtle and sometimes unseen ways. We are reminded to examine our own lives carefully as we reference the traditional roles of the women in our community.

Although we feel strongly about the workings of our local culture and its relationship to women's experience, we began writing about our neighbors' lives with reluctance. Both of us have friends who are Mormon whom we love dearly. We knew we could never capture the complexities of their lives. We also knew, however, that we could not honestly tell our stories without including theirs. As we struggle along on our own journeys, we have been influenced substantially by the continual presence of patriarchal reversal—the shimmer of reverence cloaking oppressive social relations

We write because of our commitment to achieving what we can wherever patriarchy limits the lives of women and men. Most members of white, middle-class women in the U.S., whether Mormon or not, have their basic needs met. There are women both here and worldwide caught in our common web who are struggling with different and more severe incarnations of patriarchy: the social and psychological pain and death from eating disorders, domestic and sexual abuse, child prostitution, infanticide. Unless we understand the subtle connections that bind our lives to theirs, our stories might seem trivial. But as we acknowledge that the threads of patriarchy continue to operate in oppressive ways in the lives of women across continents and cultures, we are motivated to tell our own stories as women—to contribute to the writing of the Motherline.

REFERENCES

Bartky, S. L. (1990). *Femininity and domination.* New York: Routledge.

Beck, M. (2005). *Leaving the saints: How I lost Mormonism and found my faith.* New York: Crown Publishing Group.

Belkin, L. (2003, October 26). The opt-out revolution. *The New York Times Magazine.*

Bellafante, G. (1998, June 29). Is feminism dead? *Time Magazine, 151*(25).

Bateson, M.C. (1989). *Composing a life.* New York: The Atlantic Monthly Press.

Brown, V. B. (1990). The fear of feminization: Los Angeles high schools in the progressive era. *Feminist Studies, 16*(3), 493–518.

Daly, M. (1973). *Beyond God the Father.* Boston: Beacon Press.

Ehrenreich, B., & English, D. (1978). *For her own good: 150 years of expert advice for women.* New York: Doubleday.

Eisler, R. (1987). *The chalice and the blade.* New York: Harper and Row, Publishers.

Eisler, R. & Loye, D. (1990). *The partnership way.* New York: HarperCollins Publishers.

Eisler, R. (2000). *Tomorrow's children: A blueprint for partnership education for the 21st century.* Boulder, CO: Westview Press.

Evans, S. B., & Avis, J. P. (1999). *The women who broke all the rules: How the choices of a generation changed our lives.* Naperville, IL:Sourcebooks, Inc.

Faludi, S. (1991). *Backlash: The undeclared war against American women.* New York: Anchor Books.

Friedan, B. (1963). *The feminine mystique.* New York: Dell.

Hochschild, A. (1989). *The second shift.* New York: Avon Books.

Hoff-Sommers, C. H. (1994). *Who stole feminism?* New York: Simon and Schuster.

Hoff-Sommers, C. H. (2001). *The war against boys: How misguided feminism is harming our young boys.* New York: Simon and Schuster.

Johnson, S. (1989). *From housewife to heretic.* Albuquerque, NM: Wildfire Books.

Lennon, S. (1995). What is mine. In B. Findlen (Ed.), *Listen up (pp. 120–131).* Seattle, WA: Seal Press.

Ludlow, D. (Ed.). (1992). The encyclopedia of Mormonism. Farmington Hills, MI: The Gale Group.

McConkie, B. R. (1966). *Mormon Doctrine.* Salt lake City, UT: Bookcraft.

Mies, M. (1986). *Patriarchy and accumulation on a world scale: Women in the international division of labor.* London, UK: Zed Books, Ltd.

Ogbu, J. U. (1992). Understanding cultural diversity and learning. *Educational Researcher, 21*(8), 5–14.

Paglia, C. (1994). *Vamps and tramps.* New York: Vintage Books.

Shalit, W. (1999). *A return to modesty: Discovering the lost virtue.* New York: Simon and Schuster.

Shipps, J. (1987). *Mormonism: The story of a new religious tradition.* Champaign, IL: University of Illinois Press.

Spain, D. & Bianchi, S.M. (1996). *Balancing act: Motherhood, marriage, and employment among American women.* New York: Russell Sage Foundation.

Stack, P. F. (2001, July 8). Plural legacy reverberates in Utah today. *The Salt Lake Tribune,* pp. A1, A4.

Weaver-Hightower, M. (2003). The "boy-turn" in educational research on gender and education. *Review of Educational Research, 73*(4), 471–498.

Young, C. (2004, June 20). Opting out: The press discovers the mommy wars again. *Reason, 36*(2).

Chapter Eight

Mothers and Daughters Address Inequities: From Our Spheres of Influence

Caroline Sotello Turner,[1] Ruby Gabriella Harris, and Gabriella Sotello Garcia

Three generations of mothers and daughters as well as their work to address social inequities are profiled here.[2] We speak about our relationships and how our lives intertwine, one with the other, one affecting the other. Each of us has grown up observing educational and other social inequities affecting not only our lives but the lives of our families, our extended families, and many others in our society. Each of us, in her own way, has used her sphere of influence to work toward the betterment of opportunities for ourselves and others. We are speaking from our perspectives as individuals living at the same time, but growing up in different times. We have all used education as a way to address societal inequities.

Writing this chapter with my mother, Gabriella, and my daughter, Ruby, is a rare and wonderful gift. We have an obvious connection; working on this piece allows us not only to explore this connection but also to have the opportunity to voice our connection relative to the effect of education in our interwoven lives. Presently, each of us is working toward the support of our communities from our roles as a family elder (Garcia), as a community planning manager for a non-profit agency (Harris), and as a university professor (Turner).

GABRIELLA SOTELLO GARCIA

My Mother: Planting the Seeds

As a small girl, I remember going to the store with my mother, Gabriella, and holding on to her hand. As we approached the grocery checkout stand, I

Gabriella and Caroline

Caroline and Ruby

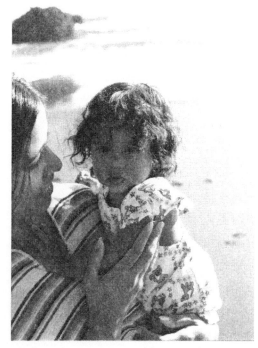

would ask her for a Little Golden Book on the shelf. My mother always said *yes* to this request and paid the twenty-five cents for the book. In this way and others I always knew that my family supported my love of books and learning, but it was not until much later that I fully understood the sacrifice made in order to pay twenty-five cents for a book instead of other much needed items. And this would not be the only or the largest financial sacrifice made by my family to support my love of learning. Later, when they sent me to college, my family gave up my potential income as a farm laborer or a grocery clerk for an endeavor unknown to anyone in my family. I know now what an act of faith and courage that was.

My Mother: Talking about Her Past

When my mother talks to me about her past, she describes a life, on one hand, of difficulty and loss but, on the other hand, full of pride and love for her family. My mom lost her parents, immigrants from Mexico, at a very early age. She was then placed, along with her siblings, with a foster family that punished the children if they spoke Spanish and beat them if they did not follow orders to the letter. In my view, the treatment she describes reflects a very abusive home environment. At twenty years of age, she married and had seven daughters and two sons. I have a female-enriched family. Fortunately my mother did not treat her children in the way she was raised. From my experience, for example, I remember coming home from school to my mom who fed me fresh tortillas and fresh-squeezed orange juice. To this day, she remains loving, nurturing, protective, and wholly supportive of whatever I do.

School Experience and Farm Labor Camp Living

Recently I sat with my mother to ask her about her experiences with school and life in the farm labor camps. She describes school as being hard and full of encounters with classmates and teachers who were mean to her. She says "I did not learn in school and I did not like school." She graduated from high school but said that she did not really study. However, she knew that education was a way to survive in the world and encouraged me to excel even though she did not have good experiences in school herself. When the time came for me to go to college, while she did not want me to leave home she told me that she was happy when I went because she was "afraid" of the life I might have if I did not go away.

I grew up and worked during the summer (my parents always made us go to school when classes began) picking tomatoes, cutting apricots, picking plums, topping garlic, etc. on farm labor camps in California. I remember my mom talking about her wish to live in a regular house in town with a telephone and air conditioning instead of living in the boss's corrugated steel shack in the middle of the fields. During growing season, when the sprinkling system was turned on, we had to live with the whirring sound day in and day out. However, I also remember playing basketball with my family and running around the acreage surrounding us.

My mom and I recalled the time when we had a chance to move to town and live in public housing, but my father felt he could control what we were all exposed to better in the countryside than in town and would not move. I remember being terribly disappointed along with my mother. At the time, his decision seemed unreasonable. After all, we would have an apartment subsidized by the government. Now, we both realize that he was trying to protect a growing family and he was also likely considering the cost of the drive from town to the fields where he worked.

My parents made every effort to provide adequate housing, clothing, food, and a protective environment for all of us, but it was a very challenging life fraught with many ways to run into trouble and get into trouble. Our household had very strict rules. I was not allowed to stay after school for any reason or to go out with classmates. Coming home and doing homework was stressed.

Parental Success

I remember several European American teachers and farm owners complimenting our family by telling us how clean and good we all looked when they saw us out. I believe they assumed that given our low socio-economic status (the low pay, lack of health care, and farm labor camp living conditions), that this was an accomplishment worthy of note. We were part of the no-collar labor class. I view my parents as a phenomenal success in promoting education to all of us. We all graduated from high school, quite an accomplishment for farm labor families then and, unfortunately, even now.

Faith in Education: Going to College

When I went to college, no one in my family knew what "college" was. I did not even know. Nonetheless, my father and mother thought that this would be a better alternative than staying at the camps. I know it was hard for my mother to let me go, but she hoped that education would provide me a way to live a better life. Though my parents' opportunities were limited, they valued education and made many sacrifices for me to pursue educational opportunities. Now, I wish I lived closer to my family, but at the time I was so excited to get away and do something different. My mother is a symbol of love and strength to me. Many barriers kept her from pursuing her own dreams, but she always supported mine.

My mom remembers going with me to buy a dress for my high school graduation. My relatives and extended family were very proud when I graduated and received several scholarships for college. She says that when I crossed the stage, "we were all yelling because we were so proud of you." She also remembers taking me to visit the University of California, Davis campus, where I was to be a freshman. My high school Dean of Girls (I had a lot of encouragement from her and my honors program counselor) knew of my mother's reservations to my leaving home and arranged to have two Cal Aggie alumni to take both of us for a campus visit. After the visit, my mother said that at least she knew where I was going.

In our large Chevrolet station wagon, I remember my whole family driving me to Davis, excited but also worried about my fate and wondering if I had enough clothes. We also carried a bicycle that my Uncle bought me when he found out that this was a good way to get around the campus. He also bought me some new clothing for school. One of my sisters, Monica, became car sick. Even though the campus was only a few hours away, this excursion took us the farthest we had ever been from home. It was a real adventure. As we passed the Cal Aggie Christian Association (CACA) house and Putah creek, my parents began to wonder[3] about the place to which they were entrusting their child.

Community Effort

I also remember my parents calling together some of the elders of our community. Knowing that I might need extra money, they all pledged to assist me if an emergency came up requiring extra funds that my family could not provide. My success was not only that of my family but that of my extended family as well. Sharing food and other resources across the community was one way many of us survived during times of difficulty. To my mother and her generation, I have many thanks to give for providing the support for many of my life accomplishments. Even when surrounded by inequities, they worked as individuals as well as community to overcome them. They planted the seeds in me to become a scholar advocating for educational access and equity. My mother has provided and continues to provide me with her unwavering support. As her first born, I have always felt a special bond with my mother. Even if I did things I was not supposed to do, even if I hurt or disappointed her, she was always there. Without her staunch belief in me, I would not be where I am now.

CAROLINE SOTELLO TURNER

Early Education: Positive Support and Negative Signals

I always remember doing well and the joy of learning in school. I attended a one-room elementary school in rural California. However, even though many of my teachers and counselors were very supportive and encouraged me along the way, I cannot help but think about the power unsupportive educators can have over vulnerable children. For example, when I graduated from elementary school, the principal told me that while I had done well there, in high school "you people get married and have lots of children" so he did not expect me to continue with my education. I remember saying to myself, *well, that is not what my parents say.* I had the strength of my family behind me but could only imagine the devastating effect of such words, from an educator we looked up to, on others.

The first day of high school, I received my class assignments in the college preparatory curriculum. I remember going to my first class. Even before I was able to take a seat, the teacher was telling me that I was in the wrong class and sent me back to the counselor for the correct class assignment. I went to the counselor and he walked me back to the class and told the teacher that I was properly placed. Grudgingly, I noticed, the teacher allowed me to take a seat. During the first class meetings, this teacher would challenge my understanding of the subject at every chance but I did my homework and was able to answer the questions to his satisfaction. I was the only child from a farm laborer family in this class and the only darker skinned student. However, to a certain extent, I got along with my classmates. In fact, I remember that some of them who rode the school bus with me would want to copy my homework.

But throughout high school I was a loner, not fitting in with either the college preparatory students or students in other classes. I felt awkward so did not try to bridge the communication gaps that existed between me and others. I found myself going to the library a lot during breaks and lunch time. There were a few other "outliers" who I joined there but we did not associate with each other in any other capacity. I did not know enough to be lonely as I had my family and also the world of books to keep me occupied. My biology and Spanish teachers would let me help them grade papers and assignments as well as set up lab experiments. I enjoyed these school activities but always had to be sure to catch the bus home so could not stay after school for any extracurricular activities.

Different Worlds: High School

When I was in high school, I began to realize that I lived in two different worlds. I was the only student in college prep classes who came from the fields. One evening at a community party, two boys my age got in a quarrel. One was Chicano, and a laborer, the other white, in college prep classes. They weren't in the same classes. Their families, friends and peers were separate groups. In all the school, as I remember, I was one of a very few who knew both these young men. My life was in both worlds. The quarrel led to a racist slur. The slur led to a knife drawn in anger. The stabbing led to death for one boy and prison for the other. I felt not one but both had died. Two families mourned, two communities separately suffered. They were worlds apart.

And because the communities—neither of which condoned the verbal or physical violence—had no habits or skills for healthy interaction with each other, there was no resolution in the school or the town that would act to prevent further violence. I asked myself, what can one do to remedy senseless loss due to racism? How can worlds apart be brought together in mutual understanding and respect?

Scholar-Advocate

I became a researcher focused on access and equity in higher education because I knew how important those issues were—and still are—to my home community. Though higher education has made strides in opening its doors to students, faculty, staff, and administrators of color, low rates of educational completion and achievement continue to exist for people from low-income communities of color.

Different Worlds: An Undergraduate

When I first arrived at college in the early 1960s, I was an alien in a world vastly different from the one in which I was raised: the food (there was so much of it, and we could go back for more); people who pretended to be friends, even if they did not like you (sometimes at home I'd had bruises and black eyes from people who didn't like me); even the music (a difference between reality and fantasy: I thought everyone at college would listen to only classical music). I also learned that while my family was highly respected in our community, in academe they were seen as failing to earn money and, therefore, perceived and treated as marginal.

During an early discussion in the dorms, a question was posed from one girl to another (there were no co-ed dorms then): "Why are people poor?" The response was that people were poor because they were lazy. All nodded their heads. To which I interjected, "but my father works all day, sun up to sun down, every day . . . he is not lazy and we are poor." Everyone looked at me but no one responded; they just walked away.

Where does such ignorance come from? Too many times, it is not unlearned in college. Chances to learn and understand do exist, but for real change to take place individuals must be open to the incorporation of new and unfamiliar ways of thinking. This change process forces those who are privileged by the current status quo to acknowledge the fact that a meritocracy, as they understand it, does not exist and that opportunities for talented students to go to college are far more prevalent for those in the middle and upper classes than for those in the lower classes. This was only one of a myriad of such encounters I was to have in academe.

Graduate Education

Conducting studies to examine the experiences of people of color in higher education, later in my college experience, I began to realize that the way people process everyday information leaves lots of room for misunderstanding and miscommunication. This disconnect is one major barrier that must be addressed if the many different groups in higher education are to reach some measure of mutual understanding and respect.

Graduate school expanded my understanding of issues confronting students of color on predominately White college campuses. As a doctoral student, I wanted to learn how Mexican American students experienced the transfer process from a two-year community college to a four-year college. Most of the students I spoke with came from farm-labor camps in the area. Their backgrounds were similar to mine, and they lived very close to where I grew up. They described individuals (mentors) who believed in them and helped them achieve their goals. This work helped me to realize that while mentors can be extremely helpful to individuals, the trajectory of a nontraditional student can be equally influenced by institutional structures, policies, and practices. To address educational inequities, research must address change at multiple levels.

Faculty Experience

When I obtained my first faculty position, for which I moved even farther away from my family and community, I taught a class for future teachers entitled "School and Society." I wanted the students not only to read about parent involvement and about the effects of tracking in schools but also to have conversations about schooling experiences with parents and children of color. Accompanied by a graduate student familiar with the communities of color in the area, I pursued this possibility. After some time, I established connections with families and was able to set up a dialogue between students and community people of color. This activity was, on the whole, well received by both students and families. However, senior faculty reminded me that taking the time to establish community connections and forums was not going to get me tenure. I realized then that the strong traditional norms of publication and tenure do not include establishing and nurturing community connections. My subsequent research examining experiences of faculty of color provides evidence about how undervalued such activities are in academe.

At this time, I became interested in the recruitment, retention, and development of faculty of color. The university administration was also very interested in supporting my work in this area. Not only was I able then to study this topic, but I was also able to develop a symposium bringing together scholars and practitioners interested in promoting racial and ethnic diversity in the professoriate.

Today, I find myself as a scholar-advocate, conducting research to illuminate issues of access and equity for racial/ethnic groups who are underrepresented as well as marginalized in higher education. Now, I combine research with service; my writing is for academic audiences and for practitioners as I try to do work to improve the quality of life for people of color in higher education organizations. As a direct result of this work, I serve racial/ethnic communities in higher education generally, professional organizations, and the university with which I am affiliated. My research has provided opportunities for me to address students as well as administration and faculty audiences who are interested in increasing racial and ethnic group participation in all levels of academe. I am frequently called to advise colleges and universities across the nation as they make efforts to promote racial and ethnic diversity on their campus communities. I give talks all over the country to provosts and other administrators interested in diversifying the faculty.

Graduate students and faculty of color, at times, come up to me, even at airports as I travel from one campus to another giving presentations, and say that my work provides validation of their experiences and support for them as they struggle to persist and grow in their doctoral and faculty work. Some make comments about my hectic schedule and express concern that I take care of myself as I am needed in the field.

Over the last decade, I have interviewed many women of color who are first generation undergraduate students, graduate students, faculty members, and college presidents. Many of these individuals feel that to succeed in academe requires them to leave themselves, who they are, at the door of graduate education and the tenure process. However, these women resist such stereotypes. By acknowledging who they are and how their identities affect their approaches to research as well as leadership a more viable work environment for all of us is created.

Sometimes I feel tired and want to quit working. Educational inequities continue. I begin to feel paralyzed and have times when I cannot pick up a pen or write on my computer. I begin to question myself, my work, and my overall effectiveness. But when I work with students and colleagues with similar goals, I gain much-needed energy, revitalization, and support for my work. As I write this, I am also thinking about my mother and her loving support, and I am thinking about my daughter and the conversations we have about our work. All of these interactions help to sustain my persistence. I realize the privilege of having opportunities to write about issues of great importance to me and my family.

Motherhood

During my time at the University of California at Davis, I married and had two children. While in graduate school at Stanford University, my children used to say that they heard the tapping of my fingers on the keyboard sometimes as they fell off to sleep and as they awoke. While I took Ruby and Nathan with me to university functions, and sometimes they went with me to classes and faculty meetings, my attention was divided, with a focus on completing school as well as raising them. I have wondered what my work meant to my children as they grew up. What was it like to grow up with a mother who was consumed by a challenging career as well as a mission to accomplish? What was gained and what was lost? How did they interpret our life together? How did that perception affect them as they were growing up? How did it affect my own thinking regarding the education of my children? I know that I always assumed that my children would attend college but felt conflicted that I spent much more time on my own academic work than helping my children with theirs.

In contrast to my mother's experience, however, sending my children to college was not alien to my experience. (As I write, I gain a deeper understanding and appreciation of my mother's experience, strength and accomplishments.) Like any parent, I did have to adjust to Ruby and Nathan's leaving and making their way in the world apart from me. In our case, my children's experiences in college helped them to better understand what it had been like for me to leave my family and community. For instance, my daughter, Ruby, wrote to me about an Ethnic Studies class she was taking in which the instructor spoke about first-generation college students. It was there that she understood more about my experience.

RUBY GABRIELLA HARRIS

Pre-College

I always knew I would go to college. It was the logical next step after high school. The idea of not continuing on to a four-year university never crossed my mind because I grew up in California college towns, first Davis and then Palo Alto. Many of my friends' parents were getting degrees along with my mom and all of this led me to believe that there was no other way but this natural educational progression.

I clearly remember living in Escondido Village (Stanford University's family housing) and loving the activity. How wonderful to have hours of play dates right outside of your back yard! My mom worked hard, but I remember being picked up every day right on time from my after-school program, eating together, doing homework, and sleeping while my mom stayed up late and woke early to study. As I am writing these thoughts, the realization comes over me that [I am having a similar experience as] like my mother did, I am working while my children are sleeping.

I also remember Mom's graduation day on the Stanford campus. The whole family came out to celebrate; everyone was dressed so nicely and there were many pictures. My mom was the first to achieve a doctoral degree in our family. I am not sure I understood that at the time, but I did understand that this was a big accomplishment and that everyone was proud of it.

California to Minnesota

We moved to Minnesota right after my 6th grade year. Starting junior high in a new environment was a difficult transition not without barriers. Upon arrival in Edina, a suburb of Minneapolis, I was shocked to find that people were making judgments of me before they talked to me. My mom had chosen to live in Edina for its excellence in education, which unfortunately often also means lack of people of color. In fact, I remember realizing that I was the only African-American and the only Latina in my junior high school when I entered. There were a few Asian students, so I had some company there.[4]

I found students who I could relate to, but was confronted with racist comments and was immediately placed in remedial classes. I complained to my mom that the kids in this class did nothing; they didn't take notes, they misbehaved, and spent the whole class acting out and getting into trouble. My mom went to the school and demanded that I be removed from these classes. I took a test and was then placed in all AP (advanced placement) courses. It saddens me deeply to think about it now. I am lucky to have a mother who knows about education, who can articulate her thoughts and fight for my rights. Without her type of advocacy, how many students are lost in this faulty system every day?

The fact that people would make assumptions about my abilities and my worth based on how I looked was a wake-up call for me. I had been taught that people were different and that's what makes us special, not that one

*group was superior to another. This experience is one of many that I encoun-
tered in my mono-cultural school that solidified my identification as a woman
of color as well as my drive to make a difference in the world.*

College

*I maintain this view on life to this day as I long for diversity and understand-
ing in all realms of society. It is in search of this understanding that I received
my bachelor's degree in Ethnic Studies and minored in City Planning. Ethnic
Studies provided the historical framework that I needed to work toward equity in our society. City Planning, on the other hand, gave me the tangible
tools that I would need to promote a greater quality of life in urban areas.*

*I became a mother during my junior year at Cal[5]. I became active with The
Student Parent Project, which was an incredible resource for studying moms
and dads like me and my husband. Through my experience as a student parent, I learned how to navigate complicated government and university
processes, as well as understanding the policies that stand in the way of low-
income families' ability to prosper. As a result, I have been fixated on how to
work within the system, while at the same time changing the system through
policy and advocacy.*

Who I Am Today

*Being born to activist educator parents has made me who I am today. My par-
ents are both first-generation college graduates who have dedicated their
professional careers to higher education and believe in social justice. I have
always been proud of my parents' continual fight for equity through education. Education and activism, in my view, are one in the same. They share
many elements, from the very practical—providing information that people
need to succeed, to the more intangible—instilling values and beliefs, and a
notion that things can be different.*

*The fact that my mother is a member of a large, immigrant, farm-worker
family, who has been able to overcome countless obstacles, connects me to my
past and many people who may not share my own personal experience, but
share in my heritage. It is easy, once you have experienced some level of pros-
perity, to turn your back on the community from which you came, but I believe
that each person has the duty to give something back.*

*My path into non-profit work was not easy or direct. In my effort to find
work after college, I immediately went looking for ways to make a difference
in people's lives through affordable housing. I remember interviewing at several affordable housing developers and noticing the lack of diversity in their*

staff. It is a very interesting dynamic that is prevalent in many non-profits: the people making decisions about what is best for a community are not, themselves, members of that community. I still wonder about this disconnect.

I wanted a job that would feed my soul, but I needed a job to help sustain my family, so after a few disappointments I went into the private sector—first, doing Human Resources work for a large retailer and second, being a researcher for a real estate consulting firm. Both experiences were important ones; they were challenging and exposed me to the corporate framework and many people who did not even pretend to be interested in equality or social justice. This only added more fuel to my fire for the movement and I soon found a position with my current employer, Mission Economic Development Agency (MEDA) in San Francisco's Mission District.

MEDA is a neighborhood-based nonprofit organization whose mission is to increase the Latino community's access to assets as well as their ability to remain in the Mission District. The Mission District has tremendous speculative pressures, which often result in displacement and leads to gentrification. MEDA works with both small businesses and residents in the neighborhood and Latinos throughout San Francisco to reach this goal. I feel connected to MEDA's mission and the people that I encounter every day through the experiences of my mother and grandmother, whose struggles can not be severed from my own life.

I began working at MEDA in 2000 to develop and launch our bilingual Homeownership Program. Over the years, this program has grown steadily and assists over 250 families a year toward their financial goals. The program helps people understand their own financial power and provides the information they need to make informed decisions on financial products that can benefit their families in the long-term. To date, the Homeownership Program has helped over 115 low-income households purchase property around the Bay Area, including San Francisco. Although this is a significant success, we don't view it as the only success. We are also happy that families are beginning to talk about their finances, that people understand credit, know about loan types, are saving an emergency fund, etc. Each of these intermediary steps gives families more security over time.

More recently, I have taken on additional responsibilities within the organization, including furthering our land use work. MEDA is a part of a coalition of community based nonprofits who are working to minimize displacement of residents and small businesses through zoning regulations. This work has been underway since the late 1990s and in the next two years will be coming to a close. The goal of the group is to ensure that land use reflects the desires of the people who currently live in the neighborhood. To this end, many community focus groups and surveys were conducted to understand the big issues, which include jobs, affordable housing, safety, and affordable products and services to name a few. Land use planning is a powerful and very controversial tool that communities can and should use to protect their communities.

Through my work at MEDA, I have been able to do the direct services such as helping families work the system toward their financial goals, while also looking at long-range policies that change the system to the benefit of people who are often the most profoundly impacted by change but are also the least heard in the policy-making process.

This work is extremely rewarding, while personally taxing. I often think it would be easier if I could take a break from advocacy work. It would be great to wake up each morning without the heavy weight of social justice, poverty, greed, and power. I often also think about switching jobs to take on a quiet, behind-the-scenes existence. Then it hits me—passion; passion for people, passion for my children's future, and passion to uphold the struggles of people who came before me. I can never fully leave advocacy work, although I imagine the nature of it will change.

Motherhood

I am a mother of two boys, Dion and Ryan. When I became a mother, I realized that the love that I have for them is the same as my grandmother's love for her daughter and my mother's love for me, and that this bond between mother and child has existed throughout time. How could I have missed this little detail when I was busy making my mom's life as difficult as possible when I was in high school? When I think about my kids and the future I wish for them, I begin crying. How can I shelter them while allowing them to grow? How can I raise them to be strong and sensitive men? How can I make sure that people see their potential, rather than automatically viewing them as another lost cause? I know that moms all over the world are thinking the same exact thing right now. Perhaps it is this perspective that causes me to feel for the moms that are losing their children's lives and/or their full potential on a daily basis to poor education, lack of health care, wars, gang activity, substance abuse, and any other of the myriad of social problems we are facing.

Having children, I believe, helps to connect each of us to our own legacies. There is something profound about giving birth and suddenly understanding the love that your own parents gave to you. I see this love through my grandma's frequent calls to check on me and my family as well as her inquiries into how my mom is doing. I also see this love through my mom's desire to spend time with us and grow closer to my boys. We are all interwoven through time and experiences, many the same and many very different. I consider myself fortunate because they have shared their experiences with me through oral history. The experiences of my mother and grandmother have helped me become who I am today. I hope to continue this tradition through my own children.

CAROLINE SOTELLO TURNER

This section adds more to my daughter Ruby's story. I use observations, e-mail messages, conversations, and MEDA brochures to provide information for the following observations.

Attending Daughter's Event

Ruby sent the following e-mail message to the family inviting all of us to attend a fundraising event celebrating the 30th anniversary of her agency, the Mission Economic Development Association (MEDA), described as "a community in search of economic justice." Her words to us say much about her commitment to increasing opportunities for others. She says: *As you know, I have been working with Mission Economic Development Agency (MEDA) for just about 5 years. We are a community-based non-profit organization in San Francisco's Mission District. Our work is focused on facilitating asset creation strategies in low income communities, including small business assistance, neighborhood planning, and homeownership. Our primary constituency is the Latino and Spanish-speaking community within San Francisco. The following is our Mission Statement, which lays the framework for all of our programs:*

> Mission Economic Development Agency is dedicated to economic justice with
> its efforts focused on the Latino community in the Mission District, and the
> businesses and institutions that serve them. Our mission is to maintain and
> strengthen the neighborhood's cultural integrity by facilitating asset building
> within the community combined with a community-based planning approach
> that looks towards the long-term health of the neighborhood in a manner that is
> culturally inclusive and able to sustain economic diversity.

I wanted to invite each of you to attend and/or support our organization, if you are able to. The work that I do is one of my passions (besides my boys!) and I believe that we are making considerable strides in the community and making a difference in many people's lives. I have attached the event invitation for

your review . . . let me know if you have any questions. The tickets are a bit
pricey and some of you are FAR away, I just wanted to be sure to include
everyone!

Can't attend? Well, you are in luck because I am also selling raffle tickets!

I chuckled at this last sentence. Ruby has a wonderful sense of timing and
humor. I am not sure that she recognizes that in herself, however. I attended
the celebratory event and met others who work with her. In addition to those
working within the MEDA organization, I also met MEDA clients, representatives from financial institutions, politicians, and representatives from foundations as well as others who help to support the work of the agency. One individual stated that her foundation supports Ruby as a leadership fellow,
recognizing her accomplishments and her capability for future contributions
as a leader in organizations that serve the community.

Ruby presented an award during this event acknowledging the accomplishments of new homeowners and their role in building a sustainable community in the San Francisco Mission District. A family was congratulated for
their persistence and successful efforts resulting in the purchase of their own
home. I am thankful to have had the opportunity to see Ruby among her peers
and to witness the acknowledgement she receives as a leader and a professional. I am very proud of her and her accomplishments.

CONCLUSION

Slices of our life stories and experiences are presented here. Our shared perspectives on the influence of education in our lives presents not a linear but
an interwoven and circular set of experiences. Embedded in our interrelationships is a continued reciprocity, a relationship of mutual dependence and
influence. This is a dynamic and emerging process that will continue to shape
our experience throughout our lifetimes.

While each of us enjoys the many roles we play in life, there are times
when we, collectively, have been challenged to meet all that is asked of us as
a wife, a grandmother, a mother, a daughter, a granddaughter, a sister, a
friend, a working professional, and a citizen of the world. It is in our understanding of as well as patience with one another that helps us each to embrace
these important life roles and to continue to do anti-racist and social justice
work to influence systems and institutions. Our stories, describe how, across
generations, we reinforce each others social justice agenda.

The experience of crafting this chapter together has helped us to understand more about ourselves in relation to one another. We see this experience
as one of those rare opportunities to give voice to our connections to people

who have given us life, who have nurtured our lives, and who have given us a meaning to exist. Each of us has influenced and continues to influence the life work and life chances of the other. In supporting one another, we learn about each other. In learning about one another, we also learn from each other. For example, our stories show that there are different contexts within which we can be an activist and an educator. Ruby makes an important point when she describes her work for a non-profit agency as that of being an educator. So often, we confine our discussion of education as happening only in places called schools or colleges. In addition, Gabriella's story underscores the importance of an individual who exerts an educational influence within a family context. This chapter reveals the interlocking paths we have taken to address educational and social inequities from our spheres of influence. Our paths differ not only from each other but also differ from the paths taken by others. However, our stories present some of the many important ways individuals can address critical issues in our society. We hope that what we have written here can inform not only our work but can also help to shape the perspectives of those generations following us.

NOTES

1. Because our professional and personal lives are so intertwined with our relationships with the men in our lives, we find it difficult to leave out the influences of these important people. However, as we are asked to write about ourselves as daughters in relationship to our mothers, our remarks illuminate these critically important interrelationships.

2. In this chapter, Caroline Sotello Turner presents her story and narratives derived from an interview with her mother, Gabriella Sotello Garcia, as well as e-mail correspondence received from her daughter, Ruby Gabriella Harris. Ruby Gabriella Harris also presents her story. Her narrative is placed in italics to make transitions from one voice to another clear to the reader.

3. To my family *CACA* and *Putah* have meanings typically not used as names for buildings and creeks.

4. My grandmother is Mexican, my mother is Latina and Filipina, and I am African American, Latina, and Filipina.

5. University of California, Berkeley.

Section III

TEACHING, LEARNING, AND LIVING SOCIAL JUSTICE ACTIVISM

Lily

Chapter Nine

Square Pegs in Hand-Crafted Holes: Developing Caring Teacher-Student Relations in U.S. Secondary Schools

Mary Louise Gomez, Elizabeth Gomez Sasse,
Anna-Ruth Allen, & Katherine Clinton

A MOTHER'S TALE: AN INTRODUCTION

As the parent of first, a preschooler enrolled in a university-based laboratory school and later an elementary school student enrolled in a small, private, non-sectarian "open classroom" type of setting, I sought caring teachers for my daughter. I defined caring as the building of nurturing relationships where teachers would support my child's talents and strengthen those areas where she required a boost, while introducing her to exciting new dimensions of the world. I found those kinds of teachers both at the preschool laboratory school that my daughter Elizabeth (or Lily as she has been known since she was a toddler) attended and at the Lake School[1] in my community. In both places, there were teachers who stayed with a group of students for two or three years and came to know them and their families well, teachers who valued the whole child, and saw the promise of a diverse group of young children whom they were fostering towards responsible and creative adulthood.

Later, when Lily entered a public high school with over 2,000 other students, I was bollixed: What would a caring secondary school teacher do and how would they demonstrate their care? I knew from personal as well as professional experiences as a teacher and teacher educator that secondary teachers would have many more students to teach per day, and the primary goal of many was to successfully teach their subject matter specialty. How would a secondary teacher with so many students meet the needs of teens whom they had never met, whose families and ethnic and cultural backgrounds they did not know, and of whose strengths, goals, and needs they were ignorant?

In the pages that follow, Lily and I explore what culturally relevant caring (Ladson-Billings, 1994) can look and feel like when teachers work with teenagers, and how two teachers in her freshman year at Belvedere High School enacted caring relations with their students. Conversely, we also explore what it did not look and feel like as she enrolled in a high-level math/science class later in the same school, and how she felt that the way that upper-class white boys often learn was privileged in the class. Together, we analyze what secondary school students might require of their teachers, and how these needs can be met. But, before we embark on telling and analyzing these stories, we offer an overview of the literature on care, particularly as this involves student and teacher relationships.

WHAT THE LITERATURE ON CARE TELLS US[2]

To date, there has been little discussion of care in secondary schools (White, 2003), as most attention to the development of an "ethic of care" in teaching has been focused on early childhood and elementary education (for example, Goldstein, 1998; Goldstein & Lake, 2000; Goldstein, 2002; Rogers & Webb, 1991; Swick & Brown, 1999). Researchers have developed a literature concerned with the central role of care as a means of supporting students of color and other marginalized in schools (for example, Ladson-Billings, 1994; Morris & Morris, 2002; Thompson, 1998; Wilder, 1999). Researchers also have investigated the characteristics of teachers that students interpret as caring (Ferreira & Bosworth, 2001; Hayes, Ryan, & Zsellerr, 1994; Valenzuela, 1999). Other authors have written about the relationship between caring and the roles of power and authority in classroom interactions (McLaughlin, 1991; Noblit, 1993).

Foundational work on the meanings of care and how it is enacted was conducted by two researchers, Nel Noddings (1984, 1986, 1992, 2001) and Carol Gilligan (1982). Their work primarily theorized care as a morality of responsiveness and connectedness to people (Gilligan, 1982), and discussed where, how, and by whom caring might be conducted (Noddings, 1984). Their notions of care primarily develop examples of women caring for others, and Noddings in particular extends notions of a caring mother to caring teachers. Gilligan and Noddings have been criticized on both counts—as attributing care as the responsibility and special capacity of women, and as a relation enacted that models the middle-class and white ideals of what mothering and, likewise, teaching might look and feel like.

Thompson (1998) is among those who have contested these apparent ideals of the middle-class, white parent. She argues that African American mothers have not experienced comparable luxuries to those of whites who can care for their children in a private, individual space, and expect that those in the public realm will mirror their actions. Rather, she says that African American women, and other women of color, have had to prepare their children for the racism of public institutions such as schools—and must stress independence, resilience, and strength of character as ideals of development for their offspring. Collins (1991) expresses similar sentiments, stating that African American mothers enact a complex notion of care, simultaneously pushing and pulling their offspring—launching them out into the community-at-large and safeguarding them from public view. Collins suggests there is a kinship between "Afrocentric and feminist values in the ethic of caring," and that race, gender, and caring are indeed intertwined. She emphasizes the role of "individual expressiveness, the appropriateness of emotions, and the capacity for empathy" (p. 216) that suffuses African American culture, highlighting how Afrocentric and feminist values are companionable, harmonious notions.

Valenzuela (1999) also raises the role of culture in providing a window for us to understand how care is conceived differently in various contexts and with diverse people. She offers an example from her study of Mexican American youth that shows how teachers' and students' views of care differed from one another. Teachers, who were for the most part white, believed that students did not care about school. Students believed that their teachers ought to first show them care, and then, youth would reciprocate with behaviors that showed their attention to teachers' and the institution's values. Valenzuela argues that non-recognition of such differences leads to student alienation and failure in school, as well as reinforcement of the teacher's original stance.

Tronto (1993) expands on extant notions of what care is and does. She sees care as a socially and culturally situated practice, "mark[ing] the intersections of gender, race, and class" (p. 168). Tronto views care as an activity to be conducted by all people for the well-being of the geographies in which we live, as well as our physical bodies, spirits, and minds. She sees care as an activity to be conducted by all for the well-being of all, and argues that such a notion involves personal, cultural, social, political, and institutional relations. She defines care as a "species activity that includes everything we do to maintain, continue, and repair our 'world' so that we can live in it as well as possible" (p. 103).

In this chapter, we acknowledge the foundational work on an ethic of care developed by Gilligan and Noddings. We also share the concerns expressed by Thompson, Collins, Valenzuela, Tronto, and others that early conceptions of care failed to account for the complex cultural, social, and institutional arrangements in which care is enacted and the varied ideals of the differing people who are expected to care for one another. We believe with Goldstein

and Lake (2000) that care includes: "the establishment of meaningful relationships, the ability to sustain connections, and the commitment to respond
to others with sensitivity and flexibility" (p. 862). Further, we see interpretations of care as culturally grounded and therefore, open to contestation and
misunderstanding by members of differing groups.

This brief review of the literature on caring and its relation to teaching lead
to some important questions for consideration, including: How do teachers
know when the ethic of care they are attempting to enact falls short? How can
teachers and students develop synchronous notions of what it means to care,
especially when these are enacted in large, complex, public spaces with many
youth to be cared for? What should the role of the institution—in this case,
the public secondary school—be in negotiating such differences?

LILY'S STORY

As a student in pre-school and primary school, my expectations of care from
my teachers were very different from what they are today. From kindergarten
through eighth grade, I attended a small private school that prided itself on
treating students as individuals and caring for their individual needs. The
teachers, for the most part, appreciated my creativity and single-mindedness,
and made compromises with me that allowed me to explore my own ways of
learning.

When I entered Belvedere, a large, public high school, I was apprehensive
about how teachers would treat me and what they expected of me. I had taken
algebra at Belvedere in eighth grade, as my elementary school had no algebra
or accelerated math program at that level. As a result, I felt that I had some
idea of how to behave in a public school setting, but I was still nervous. I only
knew five of the more than two thousand students at Belvedere, and those
who I knew were friends I had gone to school with for the prior nine years. I
was afraid of not fitting in, and of not achieving academically. I was afraid of
the violence, drugs, and judgmental attitudes of public school teachers that I
had heard rumors of in middle school.

MARY LOUISE'S TALE

I, too, worried quietly about the very dimensions of public school life that
Lily expresses here. As with far too many schools around the nation, Euro-
American students dominated the top-tier, accelerated courses aimed at
preparing students for college, and only in arts classes such as choir, dance,

or drawing were the talents of students of color recognized and appreciated. Whites dominated prom courts, homecoming kings and queens, and officers of most clubs and organizations. Likewise, the teaching and administrative staff members were nearly all white, while the student body enrolled 36% students of color according to the website for the school district. The hallways at Belvedere were crowded; often an undercurrent of racial and class tension erupted in noisy lunchroom fights, and the police were often called to break up these altercations. On the surface, the school ran like a well-oiled machine, but many youth of color were failing and dropping out.

However, Lily seemed confident and tremulously cheerful as she entered Belvedere. She at first stuck close to a particular Lake School friend, and continued the social relationships she had developed as a middle student. Gradually, she made new friends in her classes, and appeared happier and more confident. Despite her fears, she also was excelling in her classes.

LILY CONTINUES

I feel that two of my teachers in my freshman year recognized my distinctive situation and cared for me accordingly. These were my social studies teacher, Ms. Rose, and my freshman English teacher, Mr. Silver. By allowing for creativity, but still imposing a certain degree of rigidity in their curriculum, they seemed able to accomplish their goals, yet remain satisfied that I knew the material in the ways I could interpret and be playful with what they had taught me. Partly through my experiences with these teachers, I learned to adjust to high school and enjoy learning in a large, rather impersonal school. For instance, Mr. Silver would give out an essay assignment that would have four or five topics one could choose to write about, but at the bottom of the sheet it would say, "Feel free to ask me about your own ideas for a topic." I know he did not include this option especially for me, but it seemed to serve the needs of people who thought like I do, while also providing the structure that other students desired.

Ms. Rose also was adept at offering her students many different options for completing assignments, and offered extra credit for the fulfillment of varied projects. Also, she was willing to meet students before and after school and at other periods she had free, as was Mr. Silver. These extensions of what many teachers see as their personal time to correct papers or to rest during a busy day were important to me, as they said through these commitments that they cared about me as a student and were willing to take the extra time to hear about what I needed and was thinking about. I was lucky enough to have Mr. Silver again in my senior year for Advanced Writing, and I always will treasure how kind and thoughtful he was as a teacher and how he made room for all of us as learners in his classroom. I believe he took his cues from us as writers about what we needed and taught to those.

MARY LOUISE'S RESPONSE

I was delighted to find Lily so responsive to these two teachers in particular, and found their flexibility with assignments and their willingness to offer extra time to talk and mull over ideas with their students a refreshing interruption to what I had considered the (perhaps-imagined) faults of secondary teachers. As a parent, I found Ms. Rose and Mr. Silver to be very interested in how my daughter had developed as a learner, who we were as parents, and how we had raised such a curious child. In fact, Mr. Silver greeted us that first year in our parent-teacher conference with, "Wow! I am so glad to meet you. I am anxious to talk with you about how you have nurtured this child's mind." He didn't say our daughter was "so bright" or had done so well in his class, but he indicated his interest in how she had developed as a thinker. To us as parents, he was showing his awareness of Lily as a person who had things of interest to say, and who could contribute to discussions in which others also could participate. We took Mr. Silver's comments as a mark of his intense interest in Lily as a thinker and writer, and we were grateful.

As it turned out, I came to know Mr. Silver very well over the next few years. I came to know that he had been a police officer in our city before he had become a teacher here, and had seen many youth whose families were in crisis. He always spoke with humility and respect of teens whose families he had seen at their most difficult moments. I began to call on him when we, at the university, needed a particularly responsive teacher to work with diverse student populations in summer and other programs. I recommended him for teaching at a university-sponsored academy for youth of color, and he ably met the challenge.

When I think of Mr. Silver and Ms. Rose today, I smile. They meet the definitions of caring teachers as articulated by Goldstein and Lake (2000). Both seemed able to make connections with teens, to be flexible in their assignments, and to sustain connections with youth beyond one semester. Both recognized that youth met their expectations in varied ways. Both offered their time, a precious commodity, to those who needed it. Each was willing to speak with teens who required their affirmation and support. However, all of Lily's classes did not proceed with such seamless connections to her as a person. Below she tells about a harrowing experience with a teacher whose behavior left her in tears and frustration.

LILY'S NEXT STORY

By my junior year of high school, I had done quite well in math and science courses so I decided to take an accelerated science course that had an emphasis on math. I was again apprehensive, as I had heard from my female friends who had taken the class that the teacher who I would have, Mr. Davis, was not a "good teacher for girls." However, they were unclear as to what they meant by that. They only said the course didn't work for them. My male friends who had taken the class either loved Mr. Davis or saw no problem with the way he taught. His style of teaching was very much "hands on." He tended to give us a topic and materials, and we would have to design a lab without much prior knowledge of what we were to find. One complaint that students had was that Mr. Davis gave out worksheets and expected you to have them completed overnight, while he taught the lesson connected to the worksheets the next day. To the boys I talked with, this provided a challenge and a mental exercise that, if not welcome, was at least tolerable. The girls I knew often would struggle, and simply make up an equation so they would not be docked points when their worksheet was collected and checked for completion the next day.

This policy seemed unfair to me, as there was a correct answer we were looking for. I like to be creative and make up my own theories and opinions about a subject without knowing what others have theorized before. However, in this case, we were seeking one answer that had been "discovered" and replicated years earlier. I felt like I was being asked to reinvent Newton's laws.

Early on in the first semester of Mr. Davis's class, we were asked to complete a worksheet where two force diagrams were to be drawn and then dotted lines were to be drawn between the forces related to Newton's third law. I pondered the issue of where the dotted lines should go the night before while doing the worksheet, and, although I knew the definition of Newton's third law, I could not decide where the dotted lines should go—between forces in one diagram or between the two diagrams.

I am not one to ask for help, and as I said earlier, I am single-minded and would much rather find the answer to a question myself than ask anyone for help. However, after my group members expressed confusion over the same issue, I asked Mr. Davis to come to our table and tell us what the correct answer was. We were confused!

However, he only gave us the definition of Newton's third law when I asked for help. I replied, "I know [the law], but does the line go within the one or between the two?"

He repeated, "Newton's third law states . . ."

Increasingly frustrated and already humiliated that I had to ask the question in the first place, I said, "I know what the third law is; what I don't understand is where the lines goes." Mr. Davis repeated the definition again.

In exasperation, I said, "Mr. Davis, that is not what I am asking you!"

"Well, that's what I am telling you!" he said, apparently angry that I had questioned his teaching style.

I was so frustrated, I began to cry. As a matter of principle, I do not cry in public. I never cry in front of other people. However, Mr. Davis had pushed me to the edge, and I was so angry, I couldn't do anything but cry. Sitting with tears in my eyes before my silent group members, I vowed to myself that I would not listen to Mr. Davis for the rest of the year.

As counterproductive as not listening may be as a strategy for a student, it did make me feel better. I certainly did not ask any more questions. I would sit in class and stare silently ahead and write down the material on the board. When someone in my group questioned the answers I had on a worksheet, I replied, "You are probably right, I'm just stupid." I still achieved an A the first semester, but tension between Mr. Davis and me grew over the year. The number of days I came home in tears increased and my Mom called my grade-level principal to see what his advice was. Eventually he spoke to Mr. Davis, who said he was only trying to get me to learn, and that he did not understand why we were having so much trouble.

The reason we were having so much trouble was that Mr. Davis treated all of his students the same, regardless of differences in gender, personality, and circumstances. I felt that he was treating us all as if we were male students with a sense of humor like his and an innate understanding of the subject matter. The principle he seemed to teach by was "Treat others as if they are you."

I don't believe Mr. Davis is a bad man or that he had a malicious intent to hurt his students. But, I do believe he was misguided about what it means to care as a teacher. Treating students equally when all students are not the same only impedes learning and makes students feel they are playing second fiddle to the curriculum. Every person wants to be treated as an individual. Having been a square peg trying to fit into the round hole marked "student" by this teacher, I can say that I was not treated as an individual and that my education suffered for it.

MARY LOUISE'S RESPONSE

The year Lily spent in Mr. Davis's science class certainly was a frustrating one for her and for me as a parent, teacher, and teacher educator. I wanted my daughter to be respectful to her teachers, to do her very best in all of her classes, and to remain a curious and open-minded student. I recognized her dissatisfaction with the course and spoke both to Mr. Davis and Mr. Jellison, Lily's empathetic grade-level principal, about the course and the methods of teaching Mr. Davis was employing. I also wrote a letter to the school principal expressing my frustration—weeks later, his reply was that he had never had a complaint about Mr. Davis before. It seemed to me that both the teacher and school principal were saying implicitly that Lily was the problem, and she should "shape up." While I felt this was not the case, I was flummoxed by ways to interrupt this narrative line.

While my daughter is a resilient student with a supportive social network and few such encounters with teachers such as Mr. Davis, for many other young people such interactions with what they see as indifference may result in failure or may be one of a series of such encounters that result in dropping out of school all together. Before and after this difficult year, I have heard from many parents concerning similar instances where their child was, as Lily aptly describes, a square peg in a student container designed only for round ones.

DISCUSSION

What can we learn from Lily's stories of being a student in the context of the development of caring teachers? How might these stories be applied to the experiences of other students and teachers? Are there principles we might develop through which to see care and from which to analyze students' stories of classroom experiences when we hear and read them? How might we use these stories for the education of both in-service teachers and prospective teachers with whom we might work?

Lily's stories of her classroom experiences are emblematic of many of the stories young people tell. Hopeful, yet scared, they begin secondary school with vague notions of success. Sometimes they believe a new school setting will allow them to make a fresh start or achieve better grades than they had in middle school. Sometimes they believe new teachers will not know them and will see them with positive eyes. For the most part, they are optimistic. Sometimes these hopes and dreams are nurtured and supported by teachers who see the promise that lies within each of them.

Teachers like Ms. Rose and Mr. Silver seemed to genuinely enjoy young people as well as educating them about their content areas of expertise. They found ways to converse with teens and their parents about their lives. They made time for conversations with youth and offered extra help or clarification about assignments when they were needed. Like other secondary school teachers, they had a curriculum, which was fixed, and texts they were expected to cover; yet they also allowed for openings where students' interests, knowledge, and skills could be tapped. Further, they made students believe they counted. All students can benefit from such teachers, teachers who listen carefully to what students and their families are saying about what they need from us as teachers *beyond* the information we have to teach them. How did Mr. Davis differ from them and what can we learn from them and from Mr. Davis from which we could develop principles of caring practice?

Mr. Davis was personable and told jokes in his classes. He seemed also to enjoy young people, and spent hours after school preparing materials for his labs. He was knowledgeable about the subject matter he taught. Yet, what were missing were his efforts and interests in tailoring his curriculum to learning that failed to fit his model of teaching. What Mr. Davis could not or would not do was to handcraft the holes into which he expected students to fit. Rather, he single-mindedly set out to wedge the square pegs into round holes in which they did not fit. And he did not understand why this worked for some students—this seemed to be the white boys who dominated his course enrollment—and not for others. He had developed a model over the years about what his course content was and how best to teach it to the students he primarily enrolled—or thought he did.

We believe the following principles for caring teaching practice that can be developed from these stories include the following:

- Investigate who the students in your class are, and what they and their families seek from you. What do they expect and what do they need? Listen carefully.
- Offer your time and conversation to clarify and connect assignments to students' understandings.
- Work to include all students in your vision for classroom success. Offer alternate topics or assignments so that all students' talents and interests may be accommodated. Offer extra credit where possible to allow for poor test performance, an "off day," or a family emergency.
- Enjoy youth from many backgrounds and see yourself as a learner about their social, political, and cultural backgrounds.
- Envision yourself as a successful teacher for all youth, not for just a few or select students. Ask yourself: Whom do you serve and whom do you wish to serve?

Such questions can be seen as primarily involving caring teaching, but also can be seen as teaching for social justice and equity. The principles apply in either case. We suggest that teachers think hard about how their practices either support or deny access to all students in their classes, and remember Lily's words as they handcraft a place for the "square pegs."

NOTES

1. The names of all schools in which Lily enrolled and all of her teachers are pseudonyms.

2. University of Wisconsin-Madison colleagues, Anna-Ruth Allen and Katherine Clinton, collaborated with Mary Louise Gomez on a two-year research project on how prospective secondary teachers learn to care about their students, and also on the literature review for this chapter.

REFERENCES

Collins, P. H. (1991). *Black feminist thought: Knowledge, consciousness, and the politics of empowerment.* New York: Routledge.

Ferreira, M., & Bosworth, K. (2001). Defining caring teachers: Adolescents' perspectives. *Journal of Classroom Interaction, 36*(1), 24–30.

Gilligan, C. (1982). *In a different voice: Psychological theory and women's development.* Cambridge, MA: Harvard University Press.

Goldstein, L. S. (1998). More than gentle smiles and warm hugs: Applying the ethic of care to early childhood education. *Journal of Research in Childhood Education, 12*(2), 244–261.

Goldstein, L. S., & Lake, V. E. (2000). "Love, love, and more love for children": Exploring pre-service teachers' understandings of caring. *Teaching and Teacher Education, 16*, 861–872.

Goldstein, L. S. (2002). *Reclaiming caring in teaching and teacher education.* New York: Peter Lang.

Hayes, C. B., Ryan, A., & Zseller, E. B. (1994). The middle school child's perceptions of caring teachers. *American Journal of Education, 103*(1), 1–19.

Ladson-Billings, G. (1994). *The dreamkeepers.* San Francisco: Jossey-Bass.

McLaughlin, H. J. (1991). Reconciling care and control: Authority in classroom relationships. *Journal of Teaching Education, 42*(3), 182–195.

Morris, V. G., & Morris, C. L. (2002). Caring—The missing C in teacher education: Lessons learned from a segregated African American school. *Journal of Teacher Education, 53* (2), 120–122.

Noblit, G. W. (1993). Power and caring. *American Educational Research Journal, 30*(1), 23–38.

Noddings, N. (1984). *Caring: A feminine approach to ethics and moral education.* Berkeley, CA: University of California Press.

Noddings, N. (1986). Fidelity in teaching, teacher education, and research for teaching. *Harvard Educational Review, 56*(4), 496–510.

Noddings, N. (1992). *The challenge to care in schools: An alternative approach to education.* New York: Teachers College Press.

Noddings, N. (1997). Thinking about standards. *Phi Delta Kappan, 79*(3), 184–89.

Noddings, N. (2001). The caring teacher. In V. Richardson (Ed.), *Handbook of research on teaching* (4th ed.), pp. 99–105. Washington, D.C.: American Educational Research Association.

Rogers, D., & Webb, J. (1991.) The ethic of caring in teacher education. *Journal of Teacher Education, 42*(3), 173–181.

Swick, K. J., & Brown, M. H. (1999). The caring ethic in early childhood teacher education. *Journal of Instructional Psychology, 26*(2), 116–120.

Thompson, A. (1998). Not the color purple: Black feminist lessons for educational caring. *Harvard Educational Review, 68*(4), 522–554.

Tronto, J. (1993). *Moral boundaries: A political argument for an ethic of care.* New York: Routledge.

Valenzuela, A. (1999). *Subtractive schooling: U. S.-Mexican youth and the politics of caring.* Albany, NY: State University of New York Press.

White, B. (2003.) Caring and the teaching of English. *Research in the Teaching of English, 37*(3), 295–328.

Wilder, M. (1999). Culture, race, and schooling: Toward a non-color-blind ethic of care. *The Educational Forum, 63*, 556–562.

Chapter Ten

Who Could Be Against Social Justice? Reflections on our First Twenty Years Together in Activism

Blue Swadener & Beth Blue Swadener

I plugged a quarter into the phone at a small shopping center in Columbus, Georgia. My mom picked up on the second ring and I said quickly, "I wanted to call and let you know that I will probably get arrested tomorrow." There was a pause, followed by my mother's bewildered and proud voice saying, "Will you need any bail money?" I reassured her that I had worked it all out and was calling only to inform, not to request help.

It is difficult to imagine the journey to that point in my life. When I was very young and first forming a picture of my own life, I saw social justice work as an inevitable part of my future, but placed limits on the extent of my activism. I remember asking my mother "who could be against social justice?" How could anyone want something bad or unjust to happen to another human being? When my mother tried to explain that there are powerful interests and institutions that benefit from inequity, I was shocked to learn that arrest, abuse, and even assassination were used to silence voices for justice. At age four, I made a silent vow to myself that I would not be on the "front line." I would write letters or sit at a table but never put myself at risk or show up in the media.

Reflecting on that early decision now, I see not only the privilege of my position but also the influence of my mother's form of activism at the time. She was heavily involved with RESULTS and other ending-hunger projects that focused on education, letter writing, and petition gathering. Since that time, my mother and I have grown and influenced each other so that I could call her four years ago with the news of an impending arrest and expect support. We both felt pride that day when I defied the law against protesting on the military base that houses the infamous School of the Americas (SOA). My

Blue and Beth

decision resulted from witnessing the sentencing of peaceful protesters to six months in prison. This time, when I witnessed a large institution abusing those working for justice, my reaction was not self-protection, but the motivation to put my body on the line. I joined a small group designing a direct action that involved symbolically making the SOA (now called the Western Hemispheric Institute for Security Cooperation) into a crime scene. We did this to show that jailing a few resisters would not put an end to demands for justice for Latin American victims of graduates of the SOA.

People who know my mother and me often ask if I am an activist like her. The easy answer might be that, yes, I am an activist like my mother. But the rebelliousness in me, and the complexity of our relationship, has never resulted in a simple affirmation to this question. A more accurate answer might be that I am an activist like her just as much as she is an activist like me. There is no doubt that her values have influenced my life decisions. But, as with any healthy relationship, my values have also influenced her life decisions.

I remember Blue's call and my mixed emotions, mostly a warm glow of pride but also the unmistakable anxiety about how she might be treated during an arrest on a military base with a long history of protests. I also remember being struck by the creativity of the action they would carry out—essentially delivering a "ban and bar" to those trained at the SOA from Latin America and calling this training ground a "crime scene"! It had all the elements of a great direct action and my daughter was at the center.

Like many teachers and teacher educators who are deeply committed to social justice, anti-oppressive education, and inclusionary practices, I have brought these values to my roles as a mother—though not always as consistently or clearly as I may have intended. My research interests in many ways have mirrored the ages and stages that my daughter, Rachel Blue (hereafter referred to as Blue) has experienced. For example, I completed a dissertation on antibias and inclusionary practices in two child care centers while she was in preschool; conducted a three-year video ethnography of social problem-solving and peace curriculum in a Friends school, working with children in kindergarten through third grade while she was in primary school; and refocused my research on urban education issues in several Cleveland area school districts while Blue was a middle school and high student in the Akron public schools.

After Blue went to college and became a student activist, I served as a faculty adviser to several progressive student organizations and became more active in campus and community issues. My sense is that this is far from unusual. One way of framing this phenomenon might be to consider the degree of influence that children have on their parents and the reciprocal nature of mother-daughter relationships. Blue's influence on my research agenda and activism goes far beyond mirroring her developmental stages, however, and has more to do with her powerful questions, growing worldview, and constant challenge to my taken-for-granted assumptions about a range of issues.

These themes form some of the sub-texts of our separate narratives in this chapter. Through several anecdotes or "re-memberings," we unpack a number of critical incidents that relate to ways in which themes of social justice have been deeply woven into our lives during the past 25 years.

EARLY EXPERIENCES

Prior to Blue's birth in 1980, I can vividly remember balancing a clipboard on my ever-growing belly as I talked to people at the Madison Farmer's Market and the Student Union about various social issues, particularly world hunger and poverty. The first time her photo was in a newspaper was during a volunteer fair at the university where I was teaching—an infant sleeping through the event with a rape crisis escort service sign propped up against her baby carrier. From birth through her fifth year, Blue joined me nearly every Saturday morning for tabling at the Farmer's Market. I also brought her to countless meetings, "Ending Hunger Briefings," and other community events. While my memories of that time emphasize taking her everywhere possible, I know her memories of these years are quite different . . .

One of my mother's favorite stories to tell about me to activist friends of ours is about the days when she was working to end hunger. She had an information table at the local farmer's market for several years. As an infant and then a toddler, I was there with her every week. I don't remember this time together very well and could not tell you what pamphlets she had or about the content of her conversations. What I do remember, however, is how I began to think about what hunger meant. As a child I had an extremely active imagination. One day, a large black book arrived in the mail. It had big red letters that read "Ending Hunger," and I wondered what this meant. My mother tried to explain that many children do not get enough to eat. I could not imagine why anyone would not simply eat when they got hungry. Why did we need a big book to tell us this?

Later, my mother took me to a workshop she was giving about hunger. At one point, she led the group in guided imagery. She asked us all to close our eyes and imagine living in poverty. "First," she said, "open your refrigerator and remove its contents. The only items remaining are a bottle of ketchup, one carrot, and some beans." My imagination conjured up a clear picture of my refrigerator, my tin roof, the draft through the house, my large family and the smells of poverty as she described them. This experience was much more formative than the farmer's market.

When I was pregnant with Blue, I recall meeting Frances Moore Lappe', author of Diet for a Small Planet, *and telling her I had given up red meat after reading her book. She had come for an OXFAM-America benefit for refugees, and reading her books had a profound influence on me. In 2004, Blue and I met her again, when she came to speak at a Local to Global Justice Teach In we had helped organize. Anna Lappe' has joined her mother, Frances, in working on food sovereignty issues and they co-authored a book that affected both Blue and me deeply—*Hope's Edge *(Lappe' & Lappe', 2002).*

Blue was nine months old when I went back to work and she was in the loving care of Shadia, a family child care provider from Libya. Shadia and I functioned easily together sharing Blue's care and I served as a labor coach for the birth of Shadia's third child. I began a Ph.D. when Blue was not yet two years old and my research focused on multicultural education in early childhood. I carefully selected children's books and toys for Blue that reflected "antibias" messages and showed a range of cultures. Blue's first preschool experience was a very culturally and linguistically diverse parent cooperative nursery school.

When she had just turned five, I involved Blue in a press conference for the release of UNICEF's State of the World's Children *report. It was also time for her booster immunizations and we were looking for a good media "visual" for this annual event. The press conference was held in the Wisconsin Governor's Office. Fortunately we had a very progressive and understanding family doctor who agreed to administer her immunizations "on camera" and say a few words about the importance of universal immunization. We were in a cavernous conference room and I know that Blue remembers the big leather chairs, large dark room, and discomfort of some adults in talking to someone her age. While proclamations were read and cameras rolled, I was thinking about increasing the visibility of child and maternal health issues and the promise of local editorials while she was probably wondering what strange place I had taken her to this time.*

After a move to Pennsylvania, where I stepped onto the tenure track (at Pennsylvania State University), I remained socially engaged but not with the intensity that I had brought to a decade of community work and activism in Madison. I also began to travel more, including annual trips to Africa, and we experienced a change in "primary parent" on the home front. Daniel,

Blue's father, changed his work schedule to half time and was the "at home" parent after school and during my travels. His role as househusband and primary parent continued for many years. I did continue to involve Blue in occasional activities including CROP walks, fundraisers for UNICEF, and some meetings focused on peace education. I was also working extensively with students from Africa, particularly South Africa, so she was beginning to hear more about apartheid and the divestment campaign.

It was shortly after the move to Pennsylvania that I can recall Blue beginning to grasp the concept that most families had limited resources and that we could not get everything we wished for.

I remember vividly shopping for groceries with my mother one day when I was around six or seven years old. I asked if we could get a bag of candies. My mother's response was, "we don't have enough money for that." I asked her how much she had, ready to compare it with the price of my desired product. She opened her wallet and explained that we needed to spend the money inside on other necessities. Being a lover of math, I quickly added it up and realized that she did not, in fact, have the money to buy extra candy. This honesty and openness had a profound effect on my conception of resources and need. I was often repulsed by the antics of children my age to demand unneeded items.

FINDING AN ALLY VOICE

With a move to Ohio and a more urban setting, I felt reconnected to my earlier activism and scholarship on anti-racist, multicultural education. We moved to a more racially diverse neighborhood in Akron and Blue spent the next 12 years growing up in a working class neighborhood. Working with several schools in the greater Cleveland area, colleagues at Kent State and I founded an Institute for Education that is Multicultural. I also connected quickly and deeply with a new faculty member in counselor education who was to become a dear friend and great influence on my work—Mary Smith Arnold. We began to co-facilitate an "unlearning oppression" workshop that she had been part of developing while working with the Iowa City Women Against Racism group. Blue participated in several of our workshops while she was in middle school and high school and I know that some of her thinking and social justice action has been influenced by these principles—particularly about what it means to be an ally and to interrupt oppression. For many years, I have included stories about Blue's interruption of various forms of oppression in the workshop.

Mary and I were also among the co-founders of a women's group called "In the Company of Our Sisters," that focused on interrupting oppression in daily life and had a diverse membership from the community and university. Blue was the youngest member and the oldest was a retired faculty colleague with a strong union organizing background, who became very close to Blue. Thus, Blue had the opportunity to experience a feminist consciousness-raising environment and truly found a strong voice during these years. Her influence on the group was palpable, as she helped us confront our ageism.

I grew up interacting with academics in an informal way. My mother hosted many parties that her colleagues attended. In this way, I saw professors and instructors primarily as people with hobbies and humor and families. This no doubt influenced my later interactions with teachers. Throughout college, I have continued to view my professors as people, approachable and not above making mistakes. My later challenges to institutional authority are not unrelated to this early dismantling of hierarchy.

This is not to imply that challenging authority is easy for me. However, I view authority as it relates to respect. If a person earns my respect and admiration, I consider them a strong authority in my life, someone to look to for guidance. In high school, I had a history teacher whom I respected very much. He had high expectations for his students, which I longed to fulfill. One day in class, he lost my confidence and, with my mother's support, I challenged his authority.

He was defining different marital structures, including polygamy and polyandry. One of the students inquired, "what if a man has multiple husbands?" Laughter followed the question and my teacher responded, "Well, I don't know of any word for that except disgusting." More laughter followed. My face turned red, and my eyes teared up as I searched the room for any other revolted faces. There were none. I came home crying and my mother consoled me and then asked what I wanted to do. I wasn't sure, so I decided to consult Anne, a woman from "In the Company of my Sisters," who was a counselor. With the help of both Anne and my mother, I wrote a letter to my teacher. I provided information about the suicide rate for lesbian/gay/bisexual/transgendered youth and requested the same respect I had for him be returned with an acknowledgement of his hurtful mistake. He gave no apology, but I also never heard him make another homophobic comment.

KENYA

When I was thirteen, my family went to live in Kenya for nearly a year. I was starting high school, had never traveled outside the United States, and had no idea what to expect. The transition, to the say the least, was a challenge. I will never forget the first day we walked to the store and a small child dressed in rags grabbed onto my arm, looked into my eyes and pleaded, "mommy?" The image of that child is burned into my memory — it was the first time I had looked into the eyes of poverty. I have friends who speak of the need for hearts to be broken in order to understand the need to care for others and work for a better chance at life. Though my heart has broken many other times since that day in Kenya, it has yet to be broken more deeply.

Thinking about our year in Kenya and what such a move may have meant to a 13-year-old, I am struck again about how both differently and similarly we construct life events. I tend to frame our year in Kenya as my "Fulbright research year," or "the year I volunteered with street children and single mothers while doing research on changing childrearing." I rarely frame it as a year that our whole family faced challenges together and individually, or the year I uprooted my daughter from friends and "the familiar" at a critical time. Reflecting on her experiences there, I think the stark contrasts between children of great privilege (those attending the international school where she was enrolled) and those with whom I did extensive volunteer work (children living or working on the street near our apartment) had a profound impact on Blue's growing consciousness regarding poverty, power and privilege. Her fourteenth birthday party, for example, included friends from both these groups. We also faced water shortages most of the year and shared a car with another Fulbright researcher. In other words, we all learned lessons of water conservation and alternative transportation, and began to question some taken-for-granted assumptions that living in the U.S. had promoted.

MOVING TOWARD DIRECT ACTION AND MOBILIZATION

By the late 1990s, the anti-corporate globalization movement had grown to an international coalition of groups focusing on a range of issues from environmental and labor to human rights and food sovereignty. The World Trade Organization (WTO) protests of 1999 in Seattle and many similar mass protests since that time have put these issues in the public view in an array of creative new ways. At Kent State during this time, Blue had become a student activist and was a founder of CHANGE (Coalition for a Humane and New Global Economy), a group that ran a successful anti-sweatshop campaign. While I had been focusing primarily on social policy, electoral politics, and union leadership issues at that time, my research on impacts of World Bank and other global policies on children and families in Kenya contributed to my growing concern about so-called "free" trade policies and their devastating impacts.

Thus, I joined with Blue and other students in some of the organizing activities on campus and attempted to involve our faculty union in these events. During fall semester 2000, a bus tour of student activists (Call to Action) visited our campus and their direct action training was the first major event that Blue and I worked on together. One of the workshops focused on guerilla theater and I joined students in a die-in in front of the Student Center. I also donned a pig mask, tie, and jacket, and stood on a chair in the cafeteria in a role-play about the influence of big business on elections.

By now Blue had been involved in several mass protests, had been with puppet-makers who were arrested in Philadelphia during the Republican National Convention, and participated in SOA protests several times. I was just beginning to recapture some of my much earlier phase of activism—marching for civil rights and against the Viet Nam war. Although I have yet to participate in a large-scale direct action or mass protest, I am deeply proud of Blue's willingness to put herself on the line for issues in which she believes. Her courage and example has challenged me to consider forms of activism I likely would not have otherwise.

There is no doubt that our forms of activism have influenced each other. A growing creativity and spontaneity in the streets have been some of the most enjoyable developments in recent social justice work. Because I believe that joy is what makes life worth living and justice worth fighting for, I often approach social justice work in playful ways. Puppetry is one of my favorite outlets. I have worked on most of the puppets used for local protests. I was also working on puppets in Philadelphia in a warehouse later raided by police under false pretenses. Ah, the power of the puppet! Once, at a large local anti-war demonstration my mother and I had helped organize, I saw my mother out in the street with a giant puppet. Young anarchists and an angry looking line of police officers on horseback surrounded her. At the same time, I was busy working on logistics and making sure that everyone had enough water to drink in the heat.

Shortly after moving to Arizona, both Blue and I were among the founding members of several organizations and coalitions that formed soon after 9-11-01, including the Arizona Alliance for Peaceful Justice, Women in Black (against war and violence), and Local to Global Justice. As members of Local to Global Justice, we have helped organize several large anti-war protests and have worked on an annual Teach In, which drew a diverse group of over 500 activists this year. Thus, we often find ourselves at the same table—organizing

*events—and, away from the table, debriefing meetings and various dynamics
in the activist community.*

*Although we have worked together on a number of community mobilization
efforts, I have tended to be far more focused on electoral politics and citizen
lobbying. Moving to a "Clean Elections" state (i.e., with public financing of
campaigns for state office), it has been particularly satisfying to work on the
successful campaigns of two women currently in the state legislature. While I
put in countless hours going door to door for clean elections' signatures and
$5.00 donations for progressive candidates, Blue has preferred direct actions
and community-based volunteer work. Though critical of the hegemonies of
the current system, I still work within it in terms of much of my advocacy,
while my daughter is more actively working toward a different system alto-
gether. A good example of these contrasts would be how we spent our Sun-
days over a period of months in 2004. While I went door to door, campaign-
ing for a young progressive candidate for state legislature, Blue was cooking
and serving healthy vegan meals to homeless people.*

SOCIAL JUSTICE AND CAREER PATHS

*As we've worked on this chapter I have wondered how my own
motherline—connecting to a socially engaged mother who died when I was
barely ten years old—relates to my relationship with Blue. I am struck that
issues of social justice are pervasive in my work and life. Whether facilitating unlearning oppression workshops in my classes, or conducting research
projects that foreground issues of social inclusion, decolonization, and children's voice, my research and teacher professional development work has
focused for most of my career on these issues. As do many teacher educators who are also mothers, I have proudly shared about Blue's activism in
many venues and context, whether she was asking powerful questions as a
young person or participating in direct action in more recent years. I frequently draw from our work together in my teaching, faculty leadership
roles, and research. Blue has also helped me in my efforts to interrogate my
own research and life practices, as part of a sustained effort to "decolo-
nize" my work at home and abroad.*

My mother's work and values have impacted my life choices greatly. Growing up immersed in learning environments, I find school stimulating and enjoyable. There was a time that I considered becoming a teacher myself. Although life is unpredictable, I currently have no plans to teach or complete a
Ph.D. Instead, I hold a B.S. in Justice Studies and am pursuing a career in

medicine, motivated by a love of learning and a need to make a direct, physical difference in people's lives.

CLOSING REFLECTIONS

As we've worked on this essay, we have both come to better appreciate the depth of our mutual influence and love. Our shared passion for social justice and willingness to engage—often in contrasting ways—with struggles for equity have brought us closer together, while also presenting challenges and complexities in our relationship.

We have added to each other's available discourses and often have served as one of the "voices" of each other's conscience or as ethical compass. For example, consumption issues, including factory farming, the labor practices of Coca Cola and other multinational corporations, and the need to conserve limited resources, are largely guided by Blue's commitments and life choices. This has had an impact on Beth's consumption patterns and lifestyle. When encountering oppression, Blue draws in large part on her mother's strategies for interrupting it. When facing challenging situations we both often consider what the other might do and sometimes literally hear the words she might say in that situation.

We have also made connections between our relationship and those of countless other mothers and daughters, including those who are fighting for social justice in far more demanding circumstances. For Beth, standing with Women In Black evokes images of a "universal maternal"—not a romanticized mothering, but the universal experience of losing a child or having a family threatened by violence. For Blue, selling goods for Zapatista women's collectives is directly involved with helping families survive—not only in terms of finding markets for fair trade, but serving as a vehicle for raising awareness about the struggles of indigenous people in Mexico. Beth has worked for a number of years with a mothers' self help group in Kenya, which she helped found while working with street children there.

As we look toward the future we know that we will continue to have a profound influence on each other while growing in our separate identities. Blue will no doubt be influenced by Beth's mothering practices when she has children, yet it will not be a simple repetition of patterns. Blue plans to raise children in community, outside of a nuclear family structure and the institution of marriage. In contrast, Beth has a strong marriage and raised an independent, feminist daughter within a nuclear family. We both anticipate new challenges, opportunities and hope in the future, when Blue becomes a mother, and Beth a grandmother—complicating the Motherline in wonderful new ways.

REFERENCES

Lappe', F. M. (1971). *Diet for a small planet.* New York: Random House.
Lappe', F. M. & Lappe', A. (2002). *Hope's edge: The next diet for a small planet.* New York: Jeremy P. Tarcher/Putnam.

Chapter Eleven

Ferocious Tenderness: Negotiating Mothering and Activism with Courage and Hopefulness or The Nazis are Marching and My Daughter Wants to Protest

Mara Sapon-Shevin

INTRODUCTION

I struggle even to begin this narrative. Do I say, "I am a mother and an activist" or "I am an activist and a mother"? "Activist mother" sounds breezy and glib; "motherly activist" sounds matronly—worse! With some embarrassment, I acknowledge that both of these titles are somewhat true. I was/am the "activist mother" dragging my children to protests and demonstrations, loading the diaper bag with snacks in case the speeches were boring. And this "motherly activist" does indeed pass out cookies to the younger activists and encourage them to "button up" as we stand on frigid street corners. Must I, even in my opening sentences, prioritize, rank order, or sequence two of my life's most powerful identities? I decide, for lack of a better reason, to begin with my activism because it pre-dates my parenting, not because it is separate from or more important than being a mother.

I *am* a long-time activist, standing on corners with placards, demonstrating in Washington, in front of our local federal building, at busy intersections, being interviewed on television and radio, writing editorials. I live a public life as an activist, often coming into work and hearing, "I saw you on T.V. last night." Many times I cannot accurately discern the speaker's unspoken second sentence. Might it be: "Wow, I'm impressed to see you standing up for your beliefs that way" or "It's so embarrassing to have one of our colleagues making a spectacle of herself"? Sometimes, I ask (trying to seem casual), "Oh, what did I say?" hoping that the answer to that question will guide the rest of the discussion.

157

Mara

I am *also* the mother of two daughters, Dalia and Leora, whom I love deeply and unconditionally. In proposing this chapter, my daughter Dalia named my mothering stance "ferocious tenderness," a generous and appreciative expression of my passionate zeal and energy in supporting them and keeping them safe, happy, and connected to me and what they love.

While these are two powerful ways in which I define myself, spend my time and energy, struggle and grow, I have other identities as well. I am also a social justice teacher educator who tries to expand my students' understanding and commitment to changing the world. I teach courses about diversity, cooperative learning, community building, and non-violence. I do anti-racism work with students and with faculty, and I also use music and movement to teach social justice principles. There are few separations between my "personal life" and my "professional life": my involvement in a group called "Women Transcending Boundaries," formed after September 11th, 2001; my leadership in the Syracuse Community Choir for Peace and Justice; my work with children and adults on "Peace Movement" through dance and music—all of this is "of a piece" in my life.

In this chapter, I attempt to explore the following questions: How do these roles connect? What are the ways in which my mothering has been informed by my activism? How has my activism been shaped by my experiences as a mother? Am I a better activist or a *different* activist because I am a mother? Have my political understandings and commitments strengthened my parenting? How have my activism and my mothering changed my work as a teacher educator? What have been the points of convergence, struggle, and confusion in these varied roles?

I begin my story conscious of its one-sidedness and partial nature. My daughters have chosen not to write this account with me, and so I am both "free" to say what I want, and hyper-aware of the limitations and biases of my storytelling. I can imagine their voices saying, "Oh, come on, not really" or challenging my perceptions, but I am left alone to hold myself to a standard of honesty and self-revelatory disclosure. I want, of course, to sound like a "good mother," although Lerner (1998) helps us to see the bankruptcy of that phrase. I also want to present myself as a committed peace and justice activist, in it "for the long haul." But most of all, I want to interrogate the struggles involved in each of these roles and, more importantly, in their combination.

Writing this chapter is a daunting task, but not that different from the struggles about which I write; there are ironic parallels between writing a balanced narrative and struggling to live a balanced life of parenting and political action. Just as I feel I can neither give up being a mother nor an activist, I feel compelled to muddle through my stories, trusting that the reader will feel, if not compassion, at least sympathy for this tension and negotiation.

My children have been at many political protests in their lives, beginning when they were far too young to voice their agreement or dissent with the action or my decision to have them there with me. Many images and memories spring to mind as I begin to write:

Dalia at age two in a stroller at the anti-Apartheid march in Cleveland in front of the South African Embassy.

Leora at eight weeks being carried by her father in a Snuggli at a vigil to mourn the Sabra and Shatilla massacre in Lebanon. This moment was captured as a half-page photo in the Cleveland Plain Dealer, my activism and my parenting public for all to see.

Dalia and Leora marching with a large contingent from Grand Forks, North Dakota to the local air force base to protest the addition of B-1 bombers to the weaponry there.

Leora at age nine, standing on a street corner in 40 below zero weather in North Dakota, dressed in a one-piece snowsuit, protesting the U.S. invasion of Iraq in 1991.

> *Dalia standing at a busy intersection with me, passing out leaflets as a member of "Women in Black," protesting the occupation of the West Bank and Gaza in Israel/Palestine. When a passenger screamed at her, she came to me and asked, "Mama, do you know what I'm doing?" "Of course I do," I responded, "why?" "Because," said Dalia, "that man just screamed at me, 'Does your mother know what you're doing?' so I thought I'd ask you."*
>
> *Marches to Washington, D.C., for gay rights, for women's rights, for peace and justice, for Central America, against different wars and invasions; long bus rides, lots of chanting and singing, tired feet, sunburned faces, a huge collection of political T-shirts.*

I also have memories of my daughters trying to make sense of their (and my) political involvement. Once, on a family vacation to Washington, D.C., Dalia couldn't understand why we were there if there was no protest. When I told her we were there as tourists, she refused to look at the Vietnam War Memorial because it was too upsetting and she spit at the White House fence, making me worry about our safety.

Leora's earliest memories of her activism include standing on frozen street corners being yelled at by the drivers of passing cars; later, when she imitated those who had yelled at her, her nine-year-old version came out as "Get a job! Move to Russia! Get eaten by a snowdrift!" (an interesting compilation of things she thought she had heard).

Usually, it felt wonderful to have my children be a part of my political life, my commitments to public protest and demonstration. It was a shared experience, time together, a way for me to teach them what I believed and to help them take their own small steps towards civic engagement and an understanding of the politics and power of protest. There were also moments of both pride and embarrassment, such as the time my daughters explained to the departmental secretary that they couldn't buy the candy being sold as a fundraiser for her child's school because "That's Nestlé's candy, and they kill babies."

But there have also been events that have challenged my comfort and my confidence in this combination of activist mothering. In the summer of 1993, the Nazi Party announced that they would hold a march and rally in Auburn, New York (a town near Syracuse where I live). The march was scheduled for Yom Kippur (the most sacred of Jewish holidays), and the route was to be from the Auburn Town Hall to Harriet Tubman Square (a landmark to the famous African American abolitionist who once lived in Auburn). For weeks, a small group of us met to decide on an appropriate response to this demonstration of hatred and prejudice. There were many who favored doing nothing, arguing that silence and lack of attention was the correct response. Leaders in the Jewish community and the Black community were among those counseling the wisdom of ignoring the Nazi's behavior. Although this logic, like the old phrase, "What if they gave a war and nobody came?" was appealing, it became clear that the considerable advance media coverage would result in a well-attended event, if only by onlookers. The group decided, after many meetings, to assemble as a "visible presence" wearing black t-shirts adorned with symbols of those exterminated during the holocaust: yellow stars, green triangles, pink triangles, and so on, and holding signs that said, simply, "No!." Another group of people appointed themselves as "peacekeepers" and committed to positioning themselves between the Nazis and the protesters, maintaining the peace and keeping things from becoming violent.

The period of planning for the march was a tense time for me. As a Jewish woman, I was very distressed by the images and the anticipation of a confrontation with Nazis and swastikas. I felt particularly vulnerable and frightened. But my feelings were even more intense because Dalia, then 14, decided that she wanted to be part of the demonstration.

As a mother/activist, I was so proud that I had raised a daughter who was willing to take a stand, who went to 30 hours of meetings as well as to a ten-hour nonviolence training over two weekends. Before the march, I asked her, "Dalia, why do you want to do this?" She told me that she thought it was important to take a stand against people who represented hatred and prejudice. She said, "History has shown us that ignoring that kind of thing just doesn't work to make it go away." "But aren't you scared?" I pressed. "Yes, of course," she responded, "but what's that got to do with it?"

But—and—still—as a mother/activist, I was terrified by the possible ramifications of allowing my precious child to participate in an event during which she might be seriously hurt. Was that responsible parenting? Was I somehow abdicating my parental duties in the name of activism? Should I forbid her to go? Should I stay home myself rather than risk my child's safety? I wrestled with this question through many sleepless nights, images of swastikas and bloodied heads haunting my dreaming and my waking. I was somewhat reassured by the other activists who made personal commitments to look after Dalia during the march and go to jail with her if she was rounded up separately from us and taken to a different holding facility. But other friends challenged my parenting, telling me, "I'd never let my child go into harm's way like that." "Aren't you scared?" they asked, assuming that my affirmative answer would mean that I would veto Dalia's participation.

Meanwhile, my younger daughter, Leora, was not slated to go to the protest. We had decided that she would spend the day attending synagogue with Robin, a friend of the family. This decision also made me worried and guilty. The Jewish High Holy Days are typically a time of deep reflection and contemplation, a time for family togetherness, elaborate meals and celebratory interactions. I was sending my daughter off to do those things with some-one else, while I went to Auburn to lead chanting and singing in the face of the marching Nazis. What kind of priorities were those?

In the end, the march itself turned out to be singularly anti-climactic. The Nazis were few in number and left after a brief confrontation during which a small group of protesters (not our group) pelted them with nuts and bolts. But I learned important lessons from both my daughters. From Dalia, I learned yet another lesson in what courage looks like. Her steadfast commitment to this action, her deep understanding of the importance of taking a stand, and her refusal to be silenced were both mirrors of my own feelings and a purer, more distilled version as well.

From Leora, I learned another important lesson. Because Leora, at 11, wor-ried a lot about the people she loved, we had not shared every details with her. Riding in the car two days before the march, I said to Leora, "I just want to tell you what's happening on Saturday: Papa, Dalia and I are going to Auburn to march and you are going to spend the day with Robin." Leora immediately began to cry. "Why are you crying?" I asked. "Because I'm scared," she re-sponded. "What are you scared of? I persisted. "I'm scared you'll get hurt," she replied.

I reassured Leora as well as I could that we were committed to nonvio-lence, that we would take every precaution and that we would leave if the march became violent or frightening. Leora began to cry again. "Now what?" I asked. She looked at me plaintively. "Why are they doing this?" I took a deep breath. My experience (as a parent and early childhood educator) has al-ways been that when children ask a question, they want a real answer. They don't want research or statistics, or an article to read; they want an immedi-ate, understandable answer. Perhaps, this has always been the truest test of my own understanding of political issues: Can I explain them to my/a child? "Well," I ventured, "I think that the Nazis are confused people who think that only White people should live, and that anyone who is Black or Jewish or gay or lesbian or disabled or an immigrant shouldn't be allowed to live." She looked at me, paused for a moment, and then, shaking her head, offered, "Picky, aren't they!"

Leora's characterization of race hatred and a politics of violence and ex-clusion as "picky" is both laughable and completely on target. Knowing that my child saw the ridiculousness of such a practice of exclusion and hateful categorization, I was pleased by her deep understanding and values, even as I felt distressed that I was making my daughter anxious and worried.

Because this particular story had a "happy ending"—no one was hurt or injured, and positive lessons about activism, voice, the power of numbers and the importance of taking a stand were visible—it is easy to think that my mothering has always been enhanced by my activism. It would be satisfying to tell only stories about the ways in which my children's involvement in my politics enhanced their lives and deepened their commitments to social justice.

OUR BARBIES, OURSELVES

But, in fairness, in retrospect, I believe there have been times and ways in which my strongly held beliefs and commitments have made my daughters' lives more difficult and more challenging as well. My tendency towards dogmatism was colored by political righteousness, making it a daunting force. I acknowledge that, perhaps, my fierce insistence on specific political stances sometimes interfered with my ability to be a responsive, relaxed mother. Take, for example, the Barbie episode.

As a strong feminist, my constructions of what it means to be a woman center on power, voice, visibility, and equality. I wanted my daughters to be smart, powerful, self-confident and committed to making a difference. I never bought them little make-up kits, dress-up high heels, or purses. I was pleased when Dalia requested an F-clamp for her workbench on her seventh birthday and when she eschewed dresses and things pink. I thought this meant that I was doing a great job as a feminist mother. My visions of liberated womanhood definitely did not include having my daughters play with Barbie Dolls. Dalia didn't have any Barbies, and, conveniently, she never asked for any. But, at her fourth birthday party, one of her friends gave her a Barbie Doll with several outfits. I hadn't thought to write "No Barbies" on the invitations as some of my friends now write "No war toys" on their son's party invitations. It seemed impossibly impolite to snatch the present out of her hand, but I was pleased that she seemed fairly disinterested.

Two weeks after her birthday, I entered her bedroom and found her on the floor with her Barbie doll. "What are you doing?" I asked (Mother asking a stupid question). "I'm dressing and undressing my Barbie," she answered. Then, because I have been singularly unable to maintain a respectful silence around Barbies, I said, "Well that looks pretty boring." She looked up at me, her blue eyes steely and clear, and responded, "Mama, not being sexist doesn't mean I can't play with girls' toys; not being sexist means I can play with anything I want to." I quietly shut the bedroom door and left.

Although this story is very funny, it continues to give me pause. What is the line between integrity and principled behavior—and rigid dogmatism? My daughters have continually forced me to interrogate that difference. Clearly Dalia understood better than I did what it means to resist sex-role stereotyping! Did my fierce insistence on what is now derisively labeled "political correctness" keep them from a fuller range of experiences? Did I make my daughters outsiders to mainstream culture by my insistence on constant vigilance and attentiveness to principles? I wonder now whether my activism, my beliefs, my politics made me unable to "lighten up" when this might have been appropriate. More directly, did I learn something from this experience so that I reacted differently to my second daughter's interest in owning and playing with Barbies?

I would like to say "Of course," but this isn't exactly the case. I did a little better when Leora spent endless hours playing Barbies with her friend Erica. I did, however, try to convince her to let Barbie have a "profession," but found out that even owning "Doctor Barbie—a doctor by day, a glamorous date by night" didn't insure the discourse I hoped for. I was a bit reassured to enter the girls' room one day to find them playing "Pirate Barbie" and pushing various Barbie and Ken dolls off the top bunk—making them "walk the plank." Still, I was uncomfortable. Only now, in my fifties, have I come to realize that I can be proud of my kayaking muscles and also enjoy the luxury of a pedicure, a lesson learned too late for my daughters' comfort.

And then there was Halloween. I have always been uncomfortable with this particular holiday: The focus on scaring people, the seeming greediness of children demanding candy, and the connections between Halloween and the Pogroms of Eastern Europe have made me less than an eager participant. For some years, I was able to convince my daughters that this holiday wasn't for us, and that while they could pass out the candy, they didn't have to go out trick-or-treating themselves. When we moved to Syracuse, however (they were nine and 12), Halloween was everywhere and so I relented and allowed them to go trick-or-treating for the first time.

The girls went out on their candy haul in the neighborhood and then went to a friend's house to sort and trade. They returned home and again, spread out their candy on the floor for me to see. Leora, who at nine was trying to figure out how to "be political" like her parents and older sister, announced proudly, "I traded all my Nestle's candy!" Dalia, not apparently trying to one-up her sister said, "You traded? I just gave away all my Nestle's candy. I didn't think I should profit in any way from Nestles." Leora was crestfallen; her look bespoke the feelings that she would never get it right in this political family.

At the time, I was proud of my daughter's insights about boycotts, the power of the purse and personal politics. Now I wonder: Couldn't I have just let them eat the damn chocolate? But lest I present an image of children's lives ruined by their mother's activist stances, there are also many ways in which I know that my children understand and demonstrate their own deeply held politics: Leora recently returned from six months in Chile studying the relationship between the arts and activism, and the role of resistance in the Chilean struggle for independence; Dalia is a writer and artist whose understanding of community building is manifested in all that she does and in her keen ability to connect to everyone. Although they were impatient with my insistence on cooperative games and not competitive ones, Dalia now shares those same cooperative games with the children with whom she works. And Leora is considering becoming a bilingual teacher, demonstrating deep perceptiveness about the ways in which language and education can change people's lives.

One could argue that they learned their activism, their self-confidence and their power both because of me and in spite of me. Only now do they share some of their stories of their own resistance to my dogmatism: they did find places to experiment with "being girly" and to play with Babies out of my sight. They each have a strong sense of personal agency, and they reassure me that they aren't sorry I was off leading marches and picketing. Dalia said, "Mama, you made cookies *and* went to protests. You showed us that women could do lots of things." They have both spoken to me of their appreciation of my modeling of a woman whose life was larger than her own family, whose commitments went beyond traditional boundaries and assumptions. I am pretty sure that my activism didn't ruin their lives, but still, there were those Barbies . . .

UNDERSTANDING SOCIAL JUSTICE AS A MOTHER

The second half of the equation, how my activism has been strengthened or deepened by the experience of mothering, is less muddy for me. I am confident that becoming a parent, feeling that deep "mother-love" has significantly changed the ways in which I understand and commit to my social justice work. Although I always held an "anti-war" position, giving birth and mothering two babies made the sanctity of human life salient in dramatic ways. After I gave birth to Dalia, I had no words to explain what that love felt like. I was overwhelmed by feelings that were unlike any I had ever had before. Giving birth to a second daughter both strengthened those feelings and made it clear that one could, indeed, feel that loving and passionate about more than one person.

But birth isn't the only experience that connected me to the sacredness of life. When Dalia was 15, she nearly died after getting a poisonous insect bite while we were traveling in Australia. She spent two weeks in a coma on full-life support with the prediction of very low odds for survival; it was a time of devastation and terror. But, through incredible medical care, a huge network of love and support, and her own tenaciousness, she survived. This experience radically re-set my priorities: loud music, outrageous clothing, purple hair, messy rooms, piercings, tattoos and other features of adolescence that others rail against now seem largely irrelevant to me. I became deeply centered in the belief that breathing and life are essential . . . and that everything else is negotiable. And I had a terrifying glimmer of what it might mean to lose a child.

How did the general experience of mothering and the specific experience of Dalia's near death (and survival) affect my activism? This consciousness of mother love made me look at war differently. Suddenly, the killing was much more personal. Of course I had been opposed to war before, of course I realized that killing was devastation, of course I understood that parents grieved. But suddenly, those mothers holding their dying babies in their arms were like me, their babies like mine. Because I had almost lost Dalia, I could not imagine willfully making another mother suffer what to me would have been an unspeakable tragedy.

Even more distressing to me has been the rhetoric about the Middle East: "Those people just don't value human life the way we do." "The Palestinian mothers want their children to be suicide bombers." "They're just not like us; we can't understand their world view." The audacity, the blatant racism and hypocrisy of that language now strikes me as even more reprehensible than before. When people say, "They just don't value human life the way we do?" I ask, "And you know that how?" I tell them that I have to assume that that mother in Iraq holding her dead baby feels the same way about her baby as I do about mine. After the bombing of Afghanistan began (shortly after the World Trade Centers fell), I wrote a song expressing this feeling. The chorus of the song says, "It's hard to believe that their hearts aren't breaking. It's hard to believe that their tears don't flow. I may not be clear on the smallest of details, but a mother's love I know." One of the verses asks: "And now I see mothers in Afghanistan, holding the dying babies we have slain. And all I have left is the simplest of questions: Will their grieving heal our pain?"

Being devoted to my own children has made me even more committed to the world's children. I am less and less able to separate my desires to keep my own children safe from a vow to make the world safe for all children. As I love my daughters with "ferocious tenderness," my circle of love and caring grows to include the whole world.

WE CAN ONLY TEACH OURSELVES

Although we may try to separate our identities and utter statements such as "Speaking here as an educator," or "As a mother, I feel . . .," the truth is that we are always the same person, even as we choose to name or privilege a particular role. Although my courses and my keynotes have many different names, essentially, as someone pointed out to me, I tend to "teach myself."

With this in mind, I now answer my own questions. Yes, being a mother has made me a different activist, and, I would argue, a better one. My commitment to life, to peace, and to social justice is grounded not only in a set of principles and beliefs, but in the very real bodies and lives of my daughters. There is nothing abstract about my activism. I relate much more directly with the struggles of people all over the world through my understanding of families, love, and unwavering connection. The faces of the mothers as they survey their dead children and families are my face, their tears are my own, their broken hearts pound irregularly in my own chest. This is not to say that people who aren't parents can't be incredibly wonderful, powerful and persuasive activists; simply that I know that my activism *feels* different to me because I am a mother.

As to how my activism has impacted my parenting, this is something that I continue to reflect upon. It would be glib to assume that any issues my daughters have had, have now, or will have are a result of my politics and focused personality, or the combination of the two. I do know that my daughters have never doubted either my love for them or my fierce commitment to making the world right. But if I had it to do over again, I would probably be just as determined and dogged in my insistence on equality, peace, human rights, and social justice . . . and less rattled by Barbie and Ken and my daughters' desires to collect vast quantities of chocolate.

Most clear to me, however, is that I bring all of my identities to my teaching and that my commitment to social justice informs all that I do in the classroom relative to classroom community, curriculum, and pedagogy. My social justice work has taught me that we can only grow and change when we have a solid base of community from which to examine our differences and our conflicts. This understanding informs my teaching and is manifest in the amount of time and space I devote to community-building activities, class ground rules, and constant vigilance relative to voice, power, and visibility. My students hear endlessly that "time spent building community is never wasted time." Political work in the wider world has taught me the critical nature of not only *what* work we do, but how we do the work and how we interact with one another while doing it.

My curriculum—of anti-racism, diversity, inclusive classroom practices, cooperation, and conflict resolution—is closely related to my political work. I seek to help students learn about people whose voices have been silenced, the contested nature of knowledge and truth, and the importance of coalition building and solidarity in the face of oppression and marginalization. At a concrete level, that may include how to teach about Christopher Columbus in more inclusive ways, what to do when a child calls another a "faggot," or how to bring parents' voices into the classroom.

My focus on pedagogical processes that are constructivist—building on the knowledge and experiences of the participants, and on ways of interacting that promote collaboration and cooperation rather than competition and individualization—are all part of a broader political understanding about change processes and human potential. I know from my political work that we need every voice, that silence in the face of oppression is collusion, and that there is strength in numbers. Small group work, cooperative games, singing, dancing and movement, discussion and sharing all are used to model alternative visions of how the world can work, without hierarchy and segregation.

In everything I do, I strive to make the world a kinder, safer, more peaceful and inclusive place. Whether as a mother, a social justice activist or an educator, I tend to privilege process, connection, closeness, and community. These roles converge, overlap, merge and re-emerge whenever I offer a cookie to a protester, annoy my students or colleagues by insisting that we "check-in" at the beginning of a meeting, or embrace my daughters with the knowledge that their lives are—all lives are—precious.

Editors' Biographical Sketches

Leigh O'Brien is an associate professor in the College of Education and Human Services at Montclair State University (New Jersey), where she teaches early childhood/special education courses. Her research interests include teacher preparation for a democratic society, the role of narrative in education, women and education, and inclusive pedagogy. A recent recipient of a Fulbright scholarship to study early childhood policies and practices in Stockholm, Sweden, her publications include numerous journal articles and book reviews, as well as two book chapters; this is her first book. Before going into post-secondary education, Leigh spent seven years as a preschool teacher and administrator. She has a 12-year-old daughter and builds on what she has learned as a mother to add to her evolving understanding of what she thinks should happen in education settings.

Beth Blue Swadener is professor of Early Childhood Education and Policy Studies at Arizona State University. Her research focuses on social policy, anti-oppressive education, dual-language programs in preschool and kindergarten, and child and family issues in Africa. She has published seven books and numerous articles and chapters. Beth is active in several peace, social justice, and child advocacy projects, including co-founding the Jirani Project, which works with Kenyan orphans and vulnerable children.

About the Contributors

Marianne (Mimi) Nieman Bloch is a professor in the Department of Curriculum and Instruction at the University of Wisconsin-Madison with a specialization in cross-cultural and historical constructions of childhood, and early education and child care policy. She has been a member of the Reconceptualizing Early Childhood Education group since its first conference in 1991. Among other publications, she has edited Bloch, Beoku-Betts, and Tabachnick, *Women and Education in Sub-Saharan Africa: Power, Opportunities, and Constraints* (Lynn Reinner Press), and Bloch, Holmqvist, Moqvist, and Popkewitz (2003), *Governing children, families and education: Restructuring the welfare state* (Palgrave Press). She is the very proud mother of Emilie Sondel and Benjamin Bloch!

Emilie Bloch Sondel graduated from the University of California at Santa Cruz, and then completed her Master's in Counseling Psychology at Lewis and Clark College in Portland, Oregon in June, 2005. While at UCSC, she studied abroad in Ghana, and focused her work on cross-cultural human development. In Portland, she worked at the Wellness Project, a free mental health agency focusing on therapy and support for un-insured individuals and families. She is now living in Madison, Wisconsin, and is a teacher for the Dane County Transition School, an alternative charter high school, as well as a Child and Family Therapist for the Rainbow Project in Madison.

Mary Louise Gomez is professor of Literacy Studies and Teacher Education at the University of Wisconsin at Madison where she teaches graduate courses on narrative as a research tool, and the role race plays in our understandings of ourselves and the world. She studies how prospective and practicing teachers learn to teach diverse populations of youth. Recent work includes publications in *Teaching & Teacher Education, Anthropology & Education Quarterly*, and *English Education*.

Elizabeth "Lily" Gomez Sasse is a sophomore at Carleton College where she is studying biology, and plans on a career in medicine. *Anna-Ruth Allen* began as an assistant professor of Literacy Studies at the University of Rochester in fall 2005, and is the mother of toddler Simon. *Katherine Clinton* is completing her dissertation in Literacy Studies at the University of Wisconsin at Madison.

Janice Jipson is a professor of Interdisciplinary Studies at National Louis University and is the mother of co-author Jennifer Jipson. Jan's publications include *Repositioning Feminism and Education: Perspectives on Education for Social Change* (1995) with Petra Munro, Susan Victor, Karen Froude Jones, and Gretchen Freed Rowland; *Daredevil Research: Re-creating Analytic Practice* with Nicholas Paley (1997); *Intersections: Feminisms/Early Childhoods* (1998) with Mary Hauser; *Questions of You and the Struggle of Collaborative Life*, with Nicholas Paley (2000); and *Resistance and Representation: Rethinking Early Childhood Education*, with Richard Johnson (2001). She is currently doing research on Elizabeth Peabody and the American kindergarten.

Jennifer Jipson is a professor of Child Development at California Polytechnic University at San Luis Obispo. After receiving her Ph.D. in Developmental Psychology from the University of California at Santa Cruz in 2000, she went on to complete a two-year postdoctoral training program at the University of Michigan. Her published work includes articles and book chapters on children's science learning in out-of-school contexts, language development, and early childhood education.

Suzanne Lamorey received her Ph.D. in Special Education (with an Early Childhood emphasis) from the University of Oregon in 1992. She is an associate professor in the Child and Family Development Program at the University of North Carolina at Charlotte. Her teaching and research interests include the development/evaluation of non-traditional early childhood personnel preparation program models in addition to on-going analyses of the critical elements of home visiting and in-home childcare.

Ann Monroe-Baillargeon, Ph.D., is an assistant professor of Inclusive Education at the University of Rochester-Warner Graduate School of Education, and teaches courses that prepare teachers to teach *all* students effectively. She holds New York State certifications as a special education teacher, teacher of grades K–12, and for both school and district administration. Ann has taught in education departments at Syracuse University and Nazareth College of Rochester, and internationally in West Africa, South Africa, Bangladesh, and Bangkok. She currently serves as liaison to the New York Higher Education Support Center for Systems Change Midwest region, a collaborative consortium of faculty in inclusive education from colleges and universities throughout the Midwest region of New York State.

Ann's research investigates the lives of teachers in inclusive classrooms, collaborative teaching practices, and the creation of a universal design for learning through instructional technology as an effective means for teaching all students. She has published in venues including the *Teacher Education Yearbook* and the *International Visual Literacy Association Book of Selected Readings,* and has served as the Principal Investigator for several government and national foundation-funded research projects.

Ann's older daughter *Emma* is a freshman at the University of Pittsburgh studying bio-engineering and *Martha,* her younger daughter, is in her senior year of High School at Nazareth Academy. Martha plans to begin college in the fall of 2006 studying International Relations and Anthropology.

Sue Novinger is an associate professor in the department of Education and Human Development at SUNY-Brockport, where she coordinates the early childhood certification program, and teaches courses in early childhood education, literacy, and teacher inquiry. Her current research projects include examination of pre-service teachers' construction of teaching identities, and the politics of early literacy teaching and assessment practices under the No Child Left Behind Act. Her recent scholarship includes young children's mathematical discourse and symbolization, the possibilities of mathematical discourse for education for democracy, and engaging teachers in critical examination of how the past is constructed and presented.

Sue was a preschool and kindergarten teacher, as well as the director of a university laboratory school prior to joining the faculty at SUNY-Brockport. She is the mother of two sons, Jason and Matt, and grandmother of Hannah, Leah, Kirsten, Alex, Trevor, and Eli.

Mara Sapon-Shevin is Professor of Education in the Teaching and Leadership Division of the School of Education at Syracuse University. She teaches in the University's Inclusive Elementary and Special Education Teacher Education Program that prepares teachers for inclusive, heterogeneous classrooms. She is active in working with schools to promote the full inclusion of all students and the creation of cooperative school communities. She frequently consults with districts that are attempting to more towards more inclusive schools, providing workshops and support for teachers and administrators, and has also served as an expert witness in several due process hearings related to students with disabilities. The author of over 140 books, book chapters, and articles, Mara writes extensively about the fields of cooperative learning, full inclusion, and teaching for diversity.

Caroline Sotello Turner is a Professor in the Division of Educational Leadership and Policy Studies and Higher Education Program Coordinator at Arizona State University. In addition to her publications, she is often invited to speak at national and international venues on topics related to the recruitment, retention, and development of students, faculty, and administrators of color in academe.

Ruby Gabriella Harris, who has a B.A. in Ethnic Studies and City Planning from the University of California at Berkeley, is the Community Planning Manager at Mission Economic Development Association (MEDA) in San Francisco. She manages MEDA's Homebuyer Education, Commercial Corridor Revitalization and Planning departments, where she works to connect merchants and residents to appropriate resources that result in increased community stability, asset accrual, and long-term policy changes. Ruby volunteers as a research and policy analyst as a member of the Students of African Descent Caucus at her son's elementary school.

Gabriella Sotello Garcia recently celebrated her 80th birthday and, as a family elder, provides continued support and guidance for her family. In addition to her seven daughters and one son, she has nineteen grandchildren and twelve great grandchildren. Two more great grandchildren are on the way. She lives in Campbell, California.

Blue Swadener has a B.S. in Justice Studies from Arizona State University. She is a grassroots organizer, working on issues including peace, fair trade, human rights, and the environment. She is a compassionate spirit and had her first child, Liam Merle Russ, in November of 2005.

Martha Whitaker is an associate professor in the Department of Elementary Education at Utah State University. She teaches courses in the foundations of education and qualitative research. Her research interests include gender equity, feminist theory, and curriculum theory. She participates actively in local, state, and national efforts to forward the cause of equitable educational policy and practice. Her adult children, Erin and Scott, continue to help her learn and grow.

Erin (Whitaker) Schmidt lives in Southern California with her husband, David. She is an M.D. / Ph.D. student at Loma Linda University. When she graduates, she will specialize in academic medicine or medical research. She is an avid birder, and cares deeply about the environment. In her spare time she likes to return to Utah with her husband to spend time with family and friends.